GOVERNMENTS
——— IN THE ———
MUSLIM WORLD

GOVERNMENTS
—— IN THE ——
MUSLIM WORLD

THE SEARCH FOR PEACE, JUSTICE, AND FIFTY MILLION NEW JOBS

CHARLES F. BINGMAN

iUniverse, Inc.
Bloomington

GOVERNMENTS IN THE MUSLIM WORLD
The Search for Peace, Justice, and Fifty Million New Jobs

iUniverse books may be ordered through booksellers or by contacting:

iUniverse
1663 Liberty Drive
Bloomington, IN 47403
www.iuniverse.com
1-800-Authors (1-800-288-4677)

ISBN: 978-1-4759-9409-4 (sc)
ISBN: 978-1-4759-9410-0 (ebk)

Library of Congress Control Number: 2013910220

Printed in the United States of America

iUniverse rev. date: 06/18/2013

CONTENTS

CHAPTER I

BACKGROUND AND DEMOGRAPHICS

Introduction

The two most important things for the people of the Muslim world are their religion and their governments. This book will not attempt to deal with religion; it is aimed at assessing the nature and performance of Muslim governments. There has never been a time in recent history when it has been more important to understand what these governments are like and what they can and cannot do. We are finding that they are extraordinarily varied, complex, and often puzzling and incomprehensible even to Muslims themselves. Why do countries rich in oil money have some of the highest rates of poverty in the world? Why are there more than thirty armed conflicts involving Muslims killing other Muslims and non-Muslims alike? Why is it that Muslim countries, with an old and honored tradition of education and human care are now among the worst in the world in providing their citizens with adequate education and health care? Why is so much given to the military and so little to social services?

In general, Muslim societies are finding it difficult to move beyond their simpler past into the realities of the modern world. These governments, and the society they represent they tend to have a number of common characteristics.

All Muslim governments without exception are highly centrist and power driven and they are directed by a small elitist group of insiders: some combination of a perceived strong leader, the military, and increasingly the intelligence apparatus, acting as internal spies and enforcers. Far less significant are those agencies dealing with social services, public infrastructure, economic development or even religious affairs. Statist psychology centers around the insatiable yearning for power and its implacable retention in dictatorial patterns supported staunchly by the elites of the military, the intelligence organizations, state ownership and control of major sectors of the economy and a patronage system often relying on family or tribal bonds.

The leadership then tries to draw on three sources of support—first, the merchants and business people who want stability but often hope to profit from regime money; second, the poorest in society who have the greatest needs and may be swayed by government subsidies; and third, unemployed youths whose energy can be channeled into ways supportive of the regime. This system does not resist corruption—it utilizes it as lubrication in elaborate systems of payoffs, rewards and preferment.

Similarly, a serious failure stems from leadership policies that deliberately stir up and exacerbate any disparities between segments of the population, whether it is ethnic or religious or clan, or geography: plus rich vs. poor, young vs. old, urban vs. rural, or native vs. foreign. The one conflict that is peculiar to the Muslim world is SUNNI VS. SHIA. This has been a deep and abiding conflict between religious beliefs, sustained for almost 1400 years. This zealous urge for conflict is further extrapolated in sub sets of each of the two great streams of the Muslim world.

There is a further concern that once these centrist rulers achieve power, their grip is so strong that they have proved to be almost impossible to dislodge. The tenacity of leadership is amazing. Hosni Mubarak was president of Egypt for 28 years. In Tunisia, Zine al Abidine Ben Ali has been in office for 22 years. Ali Abdullah Saleh has been president of Yemen for more than thirty years. Jordan is still run by the Hashemite family, father and son, after fifty nine years; Morocco by the Alouite family since 1956; Saudi Arabia by the al-Sauds for more than seventy years. In Kuwait, the ancient al Sabah dynasty shared power with the British from

1899 to independence in 1961, and is still in power. Muammar Qaddafi ruled Libya for forty years. Syria has been ruled by the al Assad family since 1970 (forty two years), and the Sudan has been under the control of its Arab regime since 1956 (56 years). The government theocracy now running Iran came to power in 1979 (33 years and counting).

A very fundamental flaw in the governments and societies of the region is their inertia against change, but this inertia is overwhelmed by the great tide of change that represents reality in the world, whether wanted or not. Change is always a threat to some interests and a great boon to others, and the tides running in a given country are a fascinating blend of these pluses and minuses. There seems to be a decline in public acceptance of two philosophies: one, that Islam has strayed from the True Path and can advance only if they return to that path; and two, that everything bad can be blamed on Western colonialism and the perversions of western thought. Increasingly the compelling concept in the Muslim world is change, and the recognition that, in fact, the world has always been changing, usually for the better, and the ultraconservative leadership is increasingly perceived to be seriously and stubbornly resisting reality. If Muslims want to change their world, they are now more likely to recognize that they must bring it about themselves.

But as modern societies and governments become more complex and interrelated, they tend to be better able to resist total upset, and to limit change to a reluctant rebalancing of forces within society, and this seems to be the case in much of the Muslim world. Such rebalancing is incremental, and it is often accepted by reformers as the best they can achieve, and in the last analysis, better than the destructive consequences of insurrection or revolution. Governments when making concessions will retreat as little and as slowly as possible. Those who seek change have a very hard time creating any real organized leverage on a powerful regime. Many opposition groups are unskilled and poor at building coalitions and often, they end up fighting themselves. The average age in Egypt is 24; in Algeria, 26; in Morocco, 26. On the other hand, the numbers of people 60 and older is less than 7 percent. [5] Modernist Islamists tend to base themselves in mosques; communists favor labor unions; state socialists utilize government ministries; and intellectuals and students thrive in universities.

Government regimes in turn are very skilled at retaining power by building up all possible conflicts between elements of society—religious, ethnic, political, regional, clans and tribes, economic levels, rural vs. urban, rich vs. poor, youth vs. the elders, and anything else they can think of. Regimes have learned to use their intelligence agencies for internal people-watching and information control. And finally, the police and the military are always available to prevent any pressures for change from getting out of hand. Some of the strongest institutions in truly open countries like the courts or legislatures are, in Muslim countries weak and subordinated, easily dominated by the centrist elite. It is also bitterly true that, for large numbers of the power elite, patronage and corruption are far more attractive and rewarding than efforts to provide "good government".

Muslim Agonies

In the Muslim world, there is a pervasive sense of unrest, of a loss of past glory, and of the inevitability of conflict. There is huge and universal dislike and even hatred by Muslims for their self-selected leadership who are seen as vicious, tyrannical, and grossly incompetent, but somehow can't be got rid of.

Islam is locked in self-denial. There seems to be a profound sense of greatness lost, and much of this feeling is misdirected. Muslims tend to feel that the world took unfair advantage of them in the form of European penetrations and colonial dominance, and yet Muslims tend not to mention their own thousand year long history of often brutal invasion and conquest. Muslim, mostly Arab invasions came in three great waves over more than a thousand years of history. (1) The first wave occurred under the direction of the Umayyad Caliphate, beginning shortly after the death of

4

the Prophet Muhammad in 632 and lasting until the middle of the eighth century. In a remarkable period of less than 150 years, Muslim forces invaded and conquered huge areas of what are now the modern states of Syria, Palestine, Iraq, Egypt, Iran, the Maghreb, Transoxonia, the Arabian peninsula including Yemen and Oman, Lebanon, Libya, Tunisia and Morocco and even into parts of Spain and Portugal. In addition, conquests included Afghanistan, Uzbekistan, Turkmenistan, Byzantium, Azerbaijan, Crete and Sicily. The second great wave was the penetration of the Indian peninsula and conquest of the Sind valley and other parts of India.

The third wave of invasions and conquests occurred under the attacks of the Ottoman Empire beginning in the thirteenth century and running for more than 300 years. Conquests included Hungary, Romania, Bulgaria, Greece, parts of Russia, Armenia, Croatia, Serbia, Macedonia, Kurdish lands and again the North African coast. Further incursions into Europe were only prevented by defeat of Muslim forces in central Spain and the successful resistance at the siege of Vienna in 1683 (after an earlier salvation in 1529).

These waves of invasion were aimed at permanent conquest and occupation. They were in large part motivated by religion and sought the Muslim conquest of "the infidel", and their conversion to the Muslim faith, by force if felt to be necessary. When Muslims yearn for the old "glory days" they all too often mean these periods of great conquest when they were the "terror of the world".

Muslims have every right to see themselves as victims, but cannot assign blame only to the outside world, and excuse themselves or their rulers. Greatness must be earned, and the meaning of greatness has a strong moral dimension. Where now is Islam great? Where are its great men? Will there ever be numerous great Muslim women? Is Islam's only claim to fame its ability to nurture conflict and create terror? There is hatred of the West because it supported bad regimes, but it is the Muslim population itself, country by country, that has been the main support of their own tyrannies. Who are the fat cats and corrupt officials who form these tyrannical elites? Whose sons become soldiers and police men and intelligence agents? Who offers the bribes, and who accepts them? Most Muslim legislative bodies are captive and inert, and the media is under the control of governments and they too strengthen tyrants, and help to justify centrist control.

In most Muslim governments, the track record of the politicians is a disaster. They seem only to know how to engage in sterile internal and external conflicts and feuds, and do not seem to understand the need for, and the skills of negotiation and compromise. As discussed below, more than thirty-four countries in the Muslim world is caught up in armed conflict. These Muslim leaders have never forgiven the creation of Israel by Western powers. Even worse, they have never forgiven each other for the schism that eternally exists between Sunni and Shia, which began with the death of the Prophet Muhammad in 632 and which has poisoned the Muslim world for fourteen hundred years. Most Muslim regimes have endless yearnings for power, yet keep their people powerless.

Even in religion, Muslims are experiencing significant conflict. Islam is usually interpreted to mean a religion of peace and it prohibits the killing of innocents, and of suicide, and it calls for universal peace. But many Imams invent their own form of Islam and especially in the Shia community they are usually obeyed. Just as people distrust their political leadership, they are increasingly coming to believe they must beware of their own religious leadership. Radical religious elements are at war with the very idea of governments, or even individual nations. Instead, they envision the image of the umma—a united all-encompassing international community of Muslim believers that would be guided (and controlled) by one set of religious beliefs as centrally defined by religious leaders and thus cannot be questioned. Yet in the name of Islam, they sponsor terrorists who slaughter innocent civilians, and induce young men and women to blow themselves up.

But in fact, it seems that the general Muslim population rejects both the current set of political leaders and the more fundamentalist religious leadership. They are beginning to believe that there is a middle ground. They are sick and tired of both incompetent tyrants and Jihadist/Fundamentalist extremism and violence. Muslims reject and feel betrayed by their own governments, and see them as corrupt and incompetent. But they morph this into hatred of the West because in the past, it has supported these regimes. The fact is that these regimes really are bad and lack legitimacy. But most of them are skilled at fobbing off blame, often onto the U. S. There is a culture of victimhood—"Not our fault! Somebody else is to blame!" There is an almost universal avoidance of responsibility and accountability, especially for the failure to deliver public services. The people wish for the emergence of <u>moderate</u> Islam, and they begin to see the beginnings of a shift from fighting to more legitimate and acceptable political competition, as followed by the revamped PLO, or the Muslim Brotherhood in Egypt or the Muslim parties in Morocco. Similarly, it is felt that, when confronted with Islamic movements that seek to impose strict Sharia law, most people will draw back from such strict interpretations in favor of the far more moderate interpretations of general usage. Almost all movements that seek to impose strict Sharia law and only Sharia law are seen as rejecting democracy, minority tolerance, "equality", women's rights, self determination, independence of thought (from religious leadership), secular laws, multiple political parties and much more. Yet these are the very things that public opinion polls in the Muslim world show that the people yearn to achieve. **(2)**

But there is real concern that dictatorships or a fundamentalist government would not hesitate to use official terrorism to keep the population under control. And yet, the heart of Sharia law as moderately defined, is almost always positive and constructive, and its adoption would seldom present any serious problems even in tandem with a broader base of secular law. Here again, care must be taken in recognizing that many of the worst Islamic fundamentalists argue loudly for the adoption of "Sharia Law", but it is a narrow interpretation of their own making simply to garner populist support.

So if the general population feels tyrannized by their political leadership and distrustful of the motivations of much of the religious leadership, where do they turn? The United States and

Europe and others tend to think—and hope—that eventually the Muslim world will turn to representative democracy and that then two things will happen. First, countries will replace their dictators with duly elected governments which of course will be wise and efficient. Second, Muslims will abandon governments tightly controlled from the top because they have failed. It will then be recognized that more effective market based economies will replace them and will generate enough new wealth that the wiser and nobler governments of the future will deploy this wealth to meet the people's real needs.

There is a far greater likelihood that, for a substantial period of time, Muslim governments will experience a different pattern—one in which the tendency for top down centrist regimes will persist, but where the actions of these regimes can be mitigated by new pressures and perhaps new motives. Who really challenges Muslim state power? Mostly other Muslims: the political opposition, religious moderates, students and intellectuals, women's movements, anti-terrorist groups. Of the sixteen largest Muslim governments, thirteen are, or have been, centrist dictatorships, and most have built structures not for program effectiveness but for power retention. Muslim governments not only tend to avoid responsibility, but they show little interest or skill in resolving problems or settling differences The power base includes not only the military, but increasingly a growing intelligence apparatus, capable of dealing with domestic opposition and the increasing importance of social networking capabilities. In addition, the bureaucracy is usually loyal and favored and arrogantly corrupt. The new pressures will probably come from both Islamic and secular sources, in some forms of political cooperation. Islamic forces probably feel that they can't displace powerful entrenched regimes, but they can be more effective by finding ways to penetrate the power system and moderate it in a few critical ways. Secular interests will undoubtedly press those arguments that center around the rapidly changing real world within which Muslim people must ultimately live. Little of this is really about religion, even where regimes constantly cloak themselves in Quranic righteousness. This is not "Islam vs. the West"; it is "Islam vs. Itself." In essence, moderate Islamic movements want to push themselves into some middle ground where they can portray themselves as a viable alternative to incompetent tyrants and excessive zealots.

It now seems to be recognized that Muslim governments are badly served when they cater excessively to the zealots of religious fundamentalism, and they had better avoid having their politics and political parties defined as this overly zealous fringe. At the same time, when confronted by Jihadist extremism, most governments fight back and many have won or are winning.

Who must do this redefinition? Certainly not the U. S. or the West, but Muslims themselves, country by country. Muslim governments have fought against radicals—in Chechnya, in the Palestinian Authority, in Egypt, in Indonesia, in Algeria, Saudi Arabia, Somalia, Yemen and in Afghanistan, and elsewhere. Yet there is the fear that the "Arab Spring", which is really in opposition to tyrants, will open the flood gates for armed Islamic disruption, leaving these countries in a state of turmoil for years. Said another way, moderate Muslim politics and governance would be more widely developed but for the inhibiting fear of fundamentalism. Such fears have already surfaced in Libya and Egypt. Muslims increasingly see fundamentalism not as religious but as power struggles that can destroy but cannot create. The real hope seems to be in the reinforcement of moderate, liberal, secular and responsible elements of Muslim society—country by country, bottom up and at the people level first and then at the political level.

Thus, the outside world should restrain itself from automatically deciding that, for the Muslim world, representative democracy defined in Western concepts are the only legitimate solution, nor can it be assumed that if moderate Islamists emerge they will define themselves in Western terms. It is unfortunate that the terms "democracy" and "secular" have been stigmatized as the policies of aggressive American/European regimes. A whole series of recent public opinion polls and a growing number of analyses are showing that the concepts that really do motivate the Muslim community

9

are especially fairness, peace, justice and economic development meaning more jobs and better pay.

Other positive concepts of great influence in the Muslim community are such things as "good government", or anti-corruption, or law based society, or rights of minorities or women's rights. Muslims are not against government—only bad government. Most would appear willing to accept an active government if it deals with the critical bottom up needs and does not get mired in poisonous political/military conflicts and power struggles. The most extreme Muslim fundamentalist views reject the very idea of governments because they believe all things must be decided and implemented in accordance with their own limited interpretation of the holy documents. Yet few really believe their alternative: an all encompassing single international Muslim community of believers that would be guided (and controlled) by one set of religious beliefs that are centrally defined and cannot be questioned or defied. Increasingly, the Muslim world must accept the reality of its own diversity and redefine itself toward moderation, greater justice for all, more wealth and wealth distribution, and rejection of tyrants of whatever persuasion.

The future of the Muslim world does not lie with the West; it lies almost entirely within the Muslim world itself. Initially, one can expect to see the results of the Arab Spring mainly by a broader range of interests and organizations entering the power base itself, usually over the resistance of the old establishment. Even in "Muslim countries" not all citizens are Muslim, nor are all Muslims the same. How can a Muslim citizen and family lead a devout Muslim life while still getting all of the advantages of a modern society and economy? State Socialism failed this test; most current dictatorships are failing this test. Increasingly there is the hope for something new.

Hopefully, there will be a gradual emergence of a more people oriented agenda—better elementary and secondary education, real health care widely available and affordable, rational measures to expand and enrich the economy in each country while avoiding the old patterns of the thieving rich and the rest of the population in poverty. Bottom up facilities such as food distribution centers, "store front" health clinics, vocational training centers, better sanitation, youth programs, and genuine anti-corruption attacks are relatively cheap and can be developed rapidly. There is a lot of potential help from the international community through government assistance, non-government organizations, and private sector investment. In fact, the U. S. and European nations could start up a new idea: a "war on social neglect" the equal of the current "war on terror."

Muslim Governments

Governments are defined as Muslim where a majority of the population is Muslim, and the government is stated or de facto Muslim. The following countries are generally considered to have Muslim governments:

1. Indonesia: 213 million people
2. Pakistan: 162 million

* Note: India has an estimated 134 million Muslims

3. Bangladesh: 130 million
4. Egypt: 71 million
5. Turkey: 69 million
6. Iran: 67 million

Note: Nigeria has an estimated 55 million Muslims

7. Morocco: 32 million

Note: Algeria has an estimated 32 million Muslims

8. Afghanistan: 30 million
9. Saudi Arabia: 26 million
10. Sudan: 26 million
11. Iraq: 25 million

12. Yemen: 21 million

Note: China has an estimated 20 million Muslims.

13. Syria: 16 million
14. Tunisia: 10 million
15. United Arab Emirates: 8 million
16. Libya: 6 million
17. Jordan: 5 million
18. Lebanon: 4 million
19. Kuwait: 4 million
20. Oman: 2 million
21. Qatar: 2 million

Thus, about 879 million people live in these Muslim countries. In addition, another 154 million live in India and China, and in combination, this is about seventy-three percent of the world Muslim population. Several countries are considered to be committed to religious fundamentalism; that is, the extremely conservative and reactionary range of Islamic religious observance. These countries are Iran, Iraq, Afghanistan, Sudan, and Syria—and they have 138 million people, or just twelve percent of all Muslims. But most Muslim countries are essentially "middle of the road": Indonesia, Bangladesh, Pakistan, Egypt, Turkey, Nigeria, Ethiopia, Morocco, Saudi Arabia, Uzbekistan, Tanzania, Mali, Niger, Senegal, Yemen, Tunisia, Jordan. Even Libya is now seen as trying to abandon its past fundamentalist policies. These countries contain 914+ million people, or 85 percent of the population of people under Muslim governments. Some countries have large Muslim populations, but they are not close to being a national majority. Examples are India (134 million Muslims), Russia (21 million), China (19 million), and Tanzania (13 million). These countries contain 228 million, or 19 percent of the world Muslim population. Many countries have already faced serious challenges from extremist fundamentalist elements of the Muslim community and beaten them back or neutralized them: Pakistan, Afghanistan, Algeria, Egypt, Somalia, Jordan, Libya, Philippines, Russia, Tajikistan, Turkey.

The population of these countries totals 879 million or about 65 percent of the world total of one billion three hundred and thirty million Muslims. Almost all Muslim countries have some blend of Sharia, secular and older common law, but only four have a primary system of Sharia Law: Afghanistan, Iran, Saudi Arabia and Sudan. In addition, Nigeria has twelve northern states that have adopted Sharia Law, with an estimated population of about sixteen million. The influential League of Arab States, led by Saudi Arabia, includes Algeria, Bahrain, Comoros, Djibouti, Egypt, Iraq, Jordan, Kuwait, Lebanon, Libya, Mauritania, Morocco, Oman, Saudi Arabia, Somalia, Sudan, Syria, Tunisia, United Arab Emirates, and Yemen. (See Attachment A).

And of course, many more Muslims live in other countries of the world. All of these countries have mixed populations. Even when the Muslim population is in the high nineties as a percentage of the total population, there are divisions within the Muslim world: Sunni and Shia, urban and rural, rich and poor, young and old, religious or secular. Most of these countries have long histories where people (as opposed to rulers) have proved perfectly able to live peacefully with one another. This then is the first critical point to be made about Muslim governments—the leadership is more aggressive and less balanced and willing to compromise than the general population.

There are wide differences in the relative wealth of these states, and they are generally ranked as follows: **(3)**

Low Income ($735 equivalent per year or less): Afghanistan, Bangladesh, Indonesia, Pakistan, Sudan, Yemen

Low-Middle Income ($736-$2935 per year): Egypt, Iran, Jordan, Morocco, Syria, Tunisia, Turkey

Upper-Middle Income ($2936-$9075 per year): Lebanon, Libya, Saudi Arabia

High Income (> $9076 per year): Bahrain, Kuwait, Qatar, U. A. E.

Of the low income countries, four: Afghanistan, Pakistan, Sudan and Yemen—are in terrible trouble, and they are destined to sink even lower on the economic scale. And they will probably be joined by Low/Middle income Syria. Only Indonesia in the lower income countries seems to be on the economic upswing.

To a disturbing degree, the Muslim world seems to be ridden with corruption. Transparency International measures corruption in most nations, and it ranks Muslim nations as follows:

TRANSPARENCY INTERNATIONAL RANKINGS OF GOVERNMENT CORRUPTION 2011

<u>COUNTRY</u>	<u>RANK/SCORE</u>
(Canada)	8/8.7
(United States)	24/7.1
Qatar	22/7.2
United Arab Republics	28/6.8
Brunei	44/5.2
Bahrain	46/5.1
Oman	50/4.8
Kuwait	54/4.6
Jordan	56/4.5
Saudi Arabia	57/4.4
Turkey	61/4.2
Tunisia	73/3.8
(China: 25 million Muslims)	75/3.6
Morocco	80/3.4
(India: 134 million Muslims)	95/3.1
Indonesia	100/3.0
Egypt	112/2.9
(Algeria: 32 million Muslims)	112/2.9
Bangladesh	120/2.7
Iran	120/2.7
Syria	129/2.6
Lebanon	134/2.5

Pakistan	134/2.5
(Nigeria: 55 million Muslims)	143/2.4
Yemen	164/2.1
Libya	168/2.0
Iraq	175/1.8
Sudan	177/1.6
Afghanistan	180/1.5
Somalia	182/1.0

This rating system is not perfect, but it is based on both statistics (shaky), and numerous surveys, studies by independent institutions, and knowledgeable expert assessment, and the ratings are generally accepted. They measure primarily the corruption in the public sector involving the bribery of officials, contract fixing, kickbacks, theft, embezzlement and also the relative effectiveness of anti-corruption programs and law enforcement. Muslim countries, aside from the oil wealthy are generally rated very corrupt, and there are close links between corruption, poverty, and high levels of national conflict.

Conflicts Involving Muslims

Afghanistan

The Soviet invasion created an enormous extremist reaction. Islamic "freedom fighters" rose to the aid of the Afghan government. When the Soviets withdrew, the surprising rise to power of the Taliban led to the American/western invasion and restoration of a more moderate government. Now, the government has a vested interest in acting against fundamentalists but they remain powerful and aggressive, and the government is dangerously bumbling and authoritarian.

Afghanistan became the first great target of international Islamist movements. By 2001, between 20-25 percent of the Taliban's combat strength came from non-Afghans who flocked to the country to take part in the jihad. The Taliban however was bankrupt as a government, and in that sense, the Taliban movement had little impact on other Islamist movements elsewhere. "The Taliban showed itself to be incompetent—it could not even feed its people, and relied almost entirely on international charity. The Taliban regime amounted to mounting repression, intolerance and self-defeating harassment even of foreign aid organizations, along with its deepening drought and famine." [4]

But the defeat of the Soviets seemed to signal the ultimate triumph of the power of armed and zealous Islam—if the Soviets could be defeated, why not the US? The victory was a Sunni one—and one that seemed to dim the luster of the Shiite triumph in Iran. But the ascendancy of the Taliban was also a first test for which the Islamists were absolutely not prepared—how to run a government. The radicals wanted the Taliban to "show the world" how an Islamic state could succeed. Yet it simply added to the record of failure of fundamentalist regimes such as those in Sudan, Iraq and for many, Iran. Afghanistan revealed once again that the real conflict in the Muslim world is S. Arabia vs. Iran—highly conservative Sunni Wahibism as practiced in Saudi Arabia vs. a Shia religious fundamentalism in Iran—a war of extremists.

Algeria

The country suffered through a virtual civil war for ten years against Islamic extremists backed by al-Qaeda. The government has virtually "annihilated" the opposition. Algeria was one of the first real tests of al-Qaeda as a movement, and it was a failure.

But in 1992, an Islamic political party won the election, but the army denied them power. This created the Islamic Salvation Army, the militant wing of the party. The government is now trying to implement an agreement to disband the ISA. The President Abdelaziz Bouteflika, has little freedom of action. He had no political party of his own, and he owed his job to the military and intelligence chiefs. The legislature and a number of scattered political parties are manipulated by the military, and apart from rubber stamping the budget, it has little to do. The President controls the state media. Reform initiatives—reform of the press, reform of the judiciary, improving education, reforming the economy, stamping out corruption—all languish. Investors shy away.

Bahrain

Muslim Bahrain suffers from the usual problems of the region: an inadequate economy, high unemployment, lack of adequate social services, a corrupt and inefficient government. This in turn has generated a new wave of civil protest. The government is compounding the problem by unleashing its brutal, heavy handed security police who go after any form of protest even if peaceful. The punishment of peaceful activists is now producing a surge of additional resistance to the regime.

Bosnia

Islamic extremists tried to preempt the freedom fight in Bosnia to create a fundamentalist state, but failed to make more than temporary penetration of the government or the military. It proved to be true that most people, even those who purported to act on religious grounds, were not religious at all in the sense that they were driven by religious beliefs. Iran intervened in Bosnia in a serious way, supplying money, weapons, training and religious "education". But after thirteen years, there is still no serious indication that a majority of Muslim Bosnians or Kosovo Albanians are disposed to embrace Islamist movements. Nationalism is a far more compelling motivator, meaning "the religion of Albanians is Albania." Saudi Arabia targeted Albania, and more than 200 mosques were funded by Saudi money and influence, but ethnic bonds proved stronger than religious coherence. Muslimness emerged as a shared environment, cultural practices, a shared sentiment, and common experience and not reliance on Muslim theology. Opponents of Islamist extremism included not only non-Muslims, but secular Muslims and Muslims who argued the need for a multi-ethnic and religious state. In many cases, the nations in the area see themselves as European, and seek to identify with European culture rather than stifling Middle East theologies. This tide runs despite the enduring resistance of the more radical Islamic mullahs, and the interventions of Iran. Here also were the usual patterns: the failures of governments in both economic and democratic terms; the persistence of ugly corruption, and the self-inflicted wounds of the Milosovic regime on its neighbors. The same tides were running in Kosovo. Long before Milosevic, they sought independence, but the tide was nationalistic and not religious, and the Kosovo Liberation Army was confusingly half fascist and half Marxist—and never Islamic.

Chechnya

Chechnya declared its independence in 1991, but is still retained by force as part of the Russian Federation. This is a rogue state in which Islamic extremists mix with Chechen independence freedom fighters, and a bunch of corrupt criminals running drugs and other criminal activities in Russia, Europe, Central Asia, and even the U. S. It is unquestioned that the Chechens have a long history of anti-Russian and anti-Soviet activity, marked especially by rebellions in the 19th century. Chechnya is also mainly Sufi—which is esthetic, moralistic, unorthodox, and mystical. In 1944, Stalin exiled more than 400,000 Chechens to Kazakhstan, and they were not permitted to return until the 50's. After independence, a new constitution was drafted that was mostly about representative democracy and secular legal principles. Islamic law and principles were recognized, but the constitution had no reference to Islam, and instead religious liberty was emphasized.

But the Chechen conflict with Russia became one of the great targets and rallying points for the international Islamic movement, and drew Islamist fighters from across the Middle East. New Islamist religious and political leaders wrested a lot of power from the older more moderate Muslim leaders, and began the

"Islamization" of the country, culminating in the declaration of an Islamic State in 1997. But it became obvious that Islamic slogans and the new laws could not provide a stable government, and government failures discredited the regime. But armed conflict between the Chechen separatists and the Russian forces continues to this day.

Egypt

Egypt has been the long term home of Muslim movements from "Islamic socialism" to moderate Muslim development, to Arab nationalism, to Islamic extremism. Egypt has beaten back extremists, and now represents a middle ground, and has little internal trouble with extremists. The Egyptian public lost interest in utopian solutions based on obsolete doctrine. The views of the devout middle class began to emerge as the country got beyond conflict and negotiated a form of "cease fire" with the radicals. The retreat from State Socialism and the adoption of new policies of privatizing and modernizing the economy led to the emergence of a new class of entrepreneurs. In the Arab Spring of 2011, the Muslim Brotherhood (MB) played a great role, but not a terrorist one. In the subsequent elections of 2012, they won almost 50 percent of the vote, largely exactly because they had abandoned their more extremist positions and took on a moderate appearance. They have since won an election and formed a government. But there is now a growing concern with lawlessness and Muslim terrorist gangs in the Sinai Peninsula. Egypt is likely to become a crucial case of a Muslim government in conflict with Muslim extremists.

Eritrea

The government has been in long term armed conflict with Ethiopia and is now linked with the extremist Islamist terrorist groups in Somalia which are being fought by Ethiopia; thus, the country continues to be the implacable enemy of Ethiopia.

Ethiopia

There have been internal conflicts involving Christians versus Muslims, but the recent history has been war with Eritrea, and more recently, interventions against Islamist revolutionaries and terrorists in Somalia.

India

There has been fifty-five years of irreconcilable conflict with Muslim Pakistan; they have fought three wars and continue in heavy conflict over Kashmir. In addition, there is serious conflict with Islamic fundamentalist groups in Northeast India. Even after the creation of Pakistan and Bangladesh, India still has a population of about 134 million Muslims—almost as many as Egypt and Turkey combined, and the third largest population of Muslims of any country in the world.

Indonesia

Several years ago, a bomb in a tourist nightclub in Bali was exploded—one of a series of terrorist attacks in the country. This attack was attributed to an al-Qaeda associate group, but in the last elections 2004, no Muslim party garnered any significant voter support. This is extremely important since Indonesia has the largest Muslim population of any country in the world at about 215 million people. Indonesia has largely avoided the intractable conflicts that infect Arab countries, and is enjoying a resurgence of reform, mostly in the direction of improving democracy and public wellbeing. This, along with better and more serious police and anti-terrorist activity has greatly reduced the terrorist activity.

Iran

The revolutionary regime came to power by combining the frustrations of unemployed youth and the hopes of the devout middle class, along with the rationalizations of the religious elite. But an important cause of the revolution was the fear of the Shahs government which was considered too secular, and too oppressive. Yet the current regime is probably worse. Its sins include authoritarian and tyrannical shadow leadership typified by the Council of Guardians, who control events without having to be elected or to carry direct responsibility for governance. This hidden leadership inflicts upon the country a narrow, religiously based doctrine that is rigid, uncompromising, inappropriate to real problems, and obsolete.

The government sector is excessive, unproductive, and intensely bureaucratic. Most of the people in the country are discriminated against in some way (women, minorities, the "unfaithful", private businessmen, etc.). Corruption is seen as far worse than in the Shahs time, especially in terms of rewards for the regimes friends and punishments for its opponents, and many of the most important enterprises in the country have been seized by the Revolutionary Guard. The economy is faltering, in part because of sanctions imposed by the UN and other countries, but even beyond these sanctions, economic policies are perverted and repressive, resources are misallocated, there are few successful attempts to diversify the economy, and private businesses are harassed or suffer from corruption. There is no sense of accountability or consultation on the part of the hidden elites of the government including the religious leadership.

Iraq

The post war country is the victim of serious and continuing conflict between the Shia based government and the Sunni population, including remnants of the Quaddifi regime. There are also conflicts between the Sunni population and the Kurds in the

21

north of the country. Unfortunately, the new Shia government is seen as largely ineffective and corrupt.

Israel

There has been unremitting conflict between Israel and its Muslim neighbors ever since Israel was created. Muslim citizens in Israel are treated as second class citizens, with reduced legal rights. The newest threat in a series extending over the last 60 years, is the specter of an Iran, with a nuclear weapon, threatening publically to destroy Israel, aided by a burgeoning Hamas in Gaza.

Jordan

There are dangerous internal tensions within the country, in part because almost half of the population of the country is expatriate Palestinians, many with loyalties outside of Jordan.

Kuwait

This Muslim country was the victim of invasion by Muslim Iraq in 1990, and rescue by the U. S. and other countries has cost billions.

Lebanon

There are long standing conflicts in the country between Muslims and Christians, Hezbollah vs. the government, and Syria which has, for 30 years, meddled in the internal affairs of Lebanon.

Libya

Muammar Gaddafi headed a so-called Socialist state, but it was really a dictatorship in which Gaddafi announced his own version of Islam. Libya had long been a sponsor and supporter and trainer of extremist terrorist Islamic groups, but this support has been largely withdrawn in recent years because of world-wide outrage. Gaddafi tried to pursue a more moderate set of policies, but it was too late. Libya is now struggling to work out a new government and define its role, but it now appears that Islamist extremists are a growing threat which the government is not capable of handling.

Malaysia

Malaysia achieved its independence from Great Britain in 1957. Britain had imported large numbers of Indians to work in the rubber plantations, and it had encouraged the investment of Chinese merchants in trade, banking and manufacturing. As a result, Malaysia possessed a population that was half native, one third Chinese and about 15 percent Indian, and has ever since, taxed the ability of the government to maintain an equitable multiethnic society. It seems unfortunately true that the mass of young Malays had little or no access to the benefits of their own country, and the Chinese and the local elite controlled almost all wealth and power. This then became the heart of the campaign mounted by the militant Islamist movement offering the usual vision of an idealized Muslim society. But the main Islamist group—the Muslim Youth Movement of Malaysia—was not the only tide of Muslim activism. The Malaysian Islamic Party was a more moderate middle-of-the road party that elected representatives to Parliament, and entered into coalitions with the government. The local version of the Muslim Brotherhood has also become more active. But there are also many fanatical sects, and even bands of armed extremists to contend with. Thus, within this one country, there were at least four major interpretations of the meaning of Islam, and of the Holy Texts.

The government decided that it must set about the definition of an acceptable form of Islam that mitigated the influence of the extremists and put the majority of Muslims in a favorable relationship with the government. One of the basic strategies employed was to expand the teaching of a conservative (Wahhabi) but modulated form of Islam in state schools. This not only served as a counter balance to the even more radical teachings in certain mosques, but it provided legitimate employment for young people at all levels in the education system. Similarly, the elite group of Islamist students were incorporated into country's governments at all levels, and began to move into positions of power and influence.

What has emerged is a pattern similar to that in Egypt: as long as Islamist organizations confined themselves to preaching and the moral values of individual religious practice, or a responsible participation in the political process, the government gave them a lot of room to function, because such religious leadership was seen as an effective counter to the more extremist views, and it was far more popular with the devout middle class of Malaysians. It was also much more accommodating to other important necessities for the country—modern technology, the expansion of the economy, the presence of foreign money and industrial operations, and a greater tolerance for non-Islamic people and ideas. Thus, Malaysia may be seen as a prototype of a new and mostly moderate Muslim state.

Mali

A revolt led by the Islamic fundamentalist group Ansar Eddine has allied itself with a Taureg National Movement for the Liberation of Azawad and they have driven the Mali army out of the eastern half of the country and declared the creation of the new nation of Azawad. The Muslims are patterned on the al-Qaeda in Islamic Magreb, and it is said to be the closest any al-Qaeda group has ever come to forming a government. But a shaky deal has been negotiated, with the government because the Tauregs themselves essentially want their own secular state modeled on Egypt, while their Islamist allies want a full Sharia state, narrowly defined.

Mauritania

This is a Muslim country that has occupied Western Sahara against the wishes of the local Muslim population.

Nigeria

There are constant conflicts between the Muslims and the Christians and Animists in the south—over the imposition of Sharia law and over the corrupt use of oil revenue which enriches the powerful and leaves millions of abject poor. The twelve northern states of the country, having as many as 15 million Muslims, have adopted a fairly comprehensive system of Sharia Law.

Pakistan

The government has tried to have it both ways: it wants to sponsor Islamic extremists to gain credit in the more conservative wing of the Muslim world, but it wants to be seen as "democratic" to gain U. S. support and aid. Pakistan supported Islamic extremists in the take-over of Afghanistan. When Afghanistan fell, many of the extremists moved to Peshawar in NW Pakistan and have been a constant threat to the Pakistani regime itself. In addition, Pakistan sponsored Islamic extremists in terrorist acts against Indian Kashmir, and India. The country now suffers greatly from the depredations of the very Islamist terrorists it earlier sponsored. Meanwhile, the government founders and the economy deteriorates.

Palestinian Authority

There is now a constant clash within the Palestinian movement between the Fatah and Hamas, which is more violent and fundamentalist. This is however not a fundamentalist issue, but it is over the future of a Palestinian state. But the fundamentalists constantly try to penetrate various elements of the movement. Both Fatah and Hamas are in constant conflict with Israel, and this is mostly about power or the lack of it. Hamas is supported and largely dominated by Iran.

Philippines

Extremist Islamists infiltrated an independence movement in the south. After attempts to negotiate, the government finally launched a major assault against the insurrection and has largely contained and decimated it. But somehow, it keeps resurging. Only very recently has there been the possibility of some negotiated peace agreement, but this has failed many times before during the almost 20 years of conflict.

Russian Federation

While it had been suspected that there might be mass uprisings among non-Russian peoples in the Soviet Union at the time of its collapse, there was in fact remarkably little such unrest, and no Muslim group played any role at all in that collapse. The great diversity of Muslim populations precluded any centralized manipulation. Most Russian Muslims are Sunni Hanafi moderates. Shiites are strong in some places such as Azerbaijan. Muslims have been remote from the wilder versions of Islam in the Middle East, and are more "Turkic" or European in character, and they have no serious interest in Wahhabism or radicalism. By the 1970s, it was estimated that only about 25 percent of Muslims were actively religious.

Saudi Arabia

For 40 years, S. Arabia has tried to be the leader (relying heavily on oil money) of the pan-Arabic movement in the world, and it advanced the conservative, almost puritanical precepts of Wahhibist orthodoxy. Its greatest opposition has been Iran, which is even more fiercely fundamentalist. In S. Arabia itself, a fundamentalist movement supported by Iran has been contained and all but eliminated. But Iranian Shiites tried to take over the Great Mosque in Mecca in 1987, which led to rioting. After that, most Saudis seemed to rally behind the government in quashing fundamentalist meddling. Yet a third force in the Muslim world, characterized as "the Arab Spring" has emerged, and it has involved authoritarian regimes like Egypt, Iraq, Libya and Syria where the "unity" of the Muslim faith has often been used as a cover story to mask heavy centrist tyranny based on nationalist justifications. The Saudi regime has outlasted all but Iran, and in recent months, has seen a troubling resurgence of very ironic fundamentalist attacks which have labeled the Saudi government as "too liberal"!

Somalia

Somalia has been in the grip of an al-Qaeda linked Islamist militia called the Shabab for more than 20 years and it has effectively destroyed the government, killed or injured or displaced huge numbers of the population, all but terminated most public services, and has left roads and other public infrastructure in a shambles. The African Union and troops from neighboring Ethiopia have been involved in reinforcing the inadequate protections of the Somali military. But recently, prospects have turned for the better. A new president is seen as honest and trusted, and he has begun to put some things back together. He heads a new Peace and Development Party which has links with more moderate Islamic elements associated with the Muslim Brotherhood.

Sudan

The tragedy of Sudan is that it has suffered from twenty years of useless and avoidable conflict between the Islamists, Communists, and the southern Christians/animist population. Sudan is now a rogue state that actively supports some version of Islamic fundamentalism. It is the only place in which a Sunni Islamist movement has actually gained control of a legitimate state (later joined by Afghanistan).

The leader of the conservative Islamic movement was the scholar Hassan al-Turabi, who created the Islamic Charter Front (NIF), and ultimately Turabi led a revolt which took control of the government. This began a purge of Sudanese society, the banning of all political parties, purges of the judiciary, and a step-up of the war in the South. Yet, even Turabi admitted that the government did not have any concrete policies for Sudan, despite his mostly intellectual assertions in support of the formulation of his political party.

Between 1983 and 1999, some 1.2 million people died in Sudan as a result of the civil war, and famine, much of the tragedy was laid at the doorstep of the NIF. Thus, the NIF once again demonstrated that an Islamist-inspired regime could not create a government based on consensus, could not stop a hysterical civil war, damaged rather that helped the economy, and became more vicious and oppressive than its ugly predecessors. Inflation ran out of control, public services disappeared or deteriorated, every force in Sudan was against them, the international community was appalled, and even the Muslim Brotherhood split away, not wanting to be tied to the debacle. The corruption of the government was amazing, even by African standards. Economic policy seemed to consist mainly of extreme predatory techniques diverting assets to party loyalists, and harassing and blackmailing traditional merchant entrepreneurs. Sudan was kept afloat mainly by its small but valuable oil industry, supported mainly by murky contracts with foreign investors. In 1999, President Bashir declared a state of emergency, and Turabi, who was then in the legislature, tried to pass legislation to curb the power of the President—and landed in house arrest where he remains today.

Sudan, post-Turabi, has shifted to a more moderate strategy. The government approved legislation to establish a democratic state and move Islamic law from a mandate to one of a "duty of the community". Eventually, a peace agreement was created with the Southern forces, and a new program of privatization seemed to stabilize the economy and begin to persuade foreign sources to invest in the Sudanese economy. But all of this was BEFORE DARFUR. Darfur signaled once again that the essential regime is still vicious, relying on force to rule. The failure to carry out the intent of the peace agreement culminated in the successful campaign in the south to break away from the vicious regime and form the new country of South Sudan. The two countries continue in conflict with each other, largely over the allocation of wealth from oil fields that lie on the border area between them.

Since the early 1990s, Sudan has undergone a serious shift in policy toward economic liberalization and resource allocation largely driven by greater oil income, and it has experienced considerable success. But agriculture remains the backbone of the economy providing 31% of GDP. It is a large share of export revenue and it still is the main source of livelihood for 80% of the people.

Syria

The key to recent Syrian history is Hafez al-Assad, an Alawite (a subset of Shia Islam) who came to power in 1970. Alawites have a basic religious philosophy which is "polytheistic" and not the rigid monotheism of the majority of Muslims. Apart from Assad himself, it has been said that the only men who exercise power in Syria are the heads of military intelligence and the secret services, all of them Alawites.

Syria joined with Egypt to form a new joint Arab state in 1958, but this lasted only three years. During this period, the Baath Party was formed and began to grow. The Baath Party, centered around the military and led by al-Assad was essentially both socialist and populist, and had little understanding of economics. As a result, the economy stagnated during the 70s and 80s, oil development was bungled, corruption was rampant, and most economic expansion took place in the informal economy. It was not until the 90s that al-Assad changed his thinking toward a more market based economy, but typically, change was slow, uncertain, and badly managed.

In international matters, his regime has been an unmitigated disaster. He helped to lose the war against Israel in the Six Day War of 1967; he blundered again by sending tanks to help the PLO in Jordan where they got decimated. He entered the civil war in 1976, but only made it worse. Syria lost so much of its credibility that most of the world turned against it. Egypt was able to use these blunderings to restore its leadership role in the Islamic community. And his long standing alliance with Iran has offended most of the world, and especially the Arab world.

Hassan al-Assad died in 2000, and was successfully succeeded by his son Bashar al-Assad. But the long term continuing force behind the Syrian government continues to be the *mukhabarat*—the secret police. Constant attacks and pressure from the Muslim Brotherhood (under the rhetoric of Sunni vs. Alawite) precipitated a full scale war in 1982 in which as many as 25,000 people were said to have died. Thus, Syria has been an obsolete tyranny, marked by endless, pointless leadership for more than 40 years. It is little wonder that the Syrian people have finally been forced to arm themselves against their own government, but the country has now been plunged into a totally destructive civil war which threatens to destroy the country.

Tajikistan, Kyrgystan, Uzbekistan

Tajikistan, Kyrgystan, and Uzbekistan have all been subjected to mounting pressures of Islamic extremists, backed by Iran and, until recently, Afghanistan. The change of regime in Afghanistan has eased the pressure, along with more Iranian moderation. All three countries have fought off serious insurgencies, but all remain essentially nationalist dictatorships—in part justified by the stated need to ward off Islamic threats. Tajikistan came under pressure from spillovers from the Afghan conflict, and Communist Party leadership failed to respond and lost most of its credibility.

Tajikistan declared its independence in 1991, and a more or less united front of nationalist, anti-Russian movements began to form, including the Islamic Revival Party—but it became essentially pointed toward nationalist, pro-Western and secular policies, and found it could form alliances with many other groups. Insurrections against the Soviet regime continued through 1992, and actually captured Dushanbe, but were driven back mostly by aid from Russian and Uzbek soldiers "invited" into the country. A peace treaty was finally concluded in 1997. Since the end of the fighting, there has been little enthusiasm for the creation of an Islamic state. The main Muslim group (IRP) is very moderate and inclusive. There is a more radical wing of Islamic action, but "it is not yet clear that those who want a greater Islamic presence in Tajik society are prepared to leave the IRP for a more shadowy and underground organization." While the economy is bad and corruption is rampant, there is little belief that the radicals offer any better solutions.

Thailand

Ethnic Muslims in the south of Buddhist Thailand are using a terror campaign to scare off Buddhist and Christian residents and claim the province of Yala as an Islamic state. This is part of a decades long insurgency fed by poverty, drug-running, lack of political recognition, and discrimination. The objective seems to be not independence, but semi-autonomy.

Tunisia

This is a moderate government that has successfully suppressed fundamentalist Islamic opponents, and the fundamentalist party has been outlawed.

Turkey

Turkey has been a staunchly secular state since 1924. A shock was experienced when an Islamic (but not fundamentalist) party won elections in 1996, and an Islamic Prime Minister was appointed. But he lasted less than a year, when the army pushed him out in favor of a PM who returned the country to the secular position. Yet another moderate Islamic party has won recent elections, has proved to be moderate and competent, and is highly popular.

Yemen

The whole country has been inflamed by extremist Muslim terrorist groups, backed by al Qaeda. Parts of the country have been taken over by these groups, and the government troops are struggling to take them back.

Throughout the region, nation building and the implacable quest for power has been far more prevalent motivations than religious zeal. What has been new is the build-up of an intellectual and educated class who prefer to be more pragmatic than their more conservative elders. Muslim religious and political organizations have remained localized along national lines, and resist any attempts toward a Pan-Asian or Pan Islam movement. In the present day, there is a continued resistance to unification, and in fact a deterioration of such efforts. There are also region-wide concerns about ethic conflict, and the addition of extreme religious conflicts is greatly feared. And there remains—forever—the irreconcilable and horribly destructive conflict within the Muslim world between the Sunni and the Shia. Thus, Islam is emerging as a cultural and social force and a religious force, but centrist governments stoutly resist the emergence of any type of political Islam as part of the basic structures of society.

Government Program Failings

With one or two possible exceptions, governments are held in contempt by most people in their countries. They are seen as corrupt, incompetent, indifferent, and misguided. What people want most is not so much "democracy" but an end to UNFAIRNESS. They hate the insolence of office, and not having a voice. Almost all of these governments show serious weaknesses in their ability to face up to problems. They don't seem to know how to negotiate or compromise or to mitigate conflict. In fact, there are endless examples of cases where the government itself has been the instigator or perpetuator of conflict. Mostly, they "preside" rather than lead or manage. City governments are weak, and under severe pressure. The whole of the Muslim world is moving toward increasing urbanization, and Muslim cities are not up to the task of dealing with swelling populations and greater unmet needs. In many cases, there is little government provision of even vital social services, many of which are really supplied by an unplanned tangle of private organizations, mosques and other religious organizations, civic associations and trusts, and foreign non-government organizations (NGOs).

Many Muslim regimes joined the world trend toward State Socialism which became so predominant in governments after WW II, and like so many other countries in Europe and Asia, State Socialism proved largely unsuccessful in both economic and social terms. In the Muslim world, movement toward more market based economies was hampered by old religious concepts, corruption and inefficient government. In world terms, Muslim countries tend to be in the lower levels of country comparisons. In a number of areas, Muslim countries are not necessarily bad, but may simply be late in coping, or slow to evolve. There was continued experimentation with the apparatus of government: parliaments, independent judiciaries, constitutions, managerial effectiveness and so forth, but the reality seems to be that tyranny still trumps all. Government systems seem unable to curb dictatorial power. Most governments are crude, unskilled and usually vastly corrupt. Most just preside;

they don't really manage and are big on grand pronouncements and short on actual accomplishment.

Perceptions about the Arab world are increasingly grim. The Middle East is largely an Arab world and it is seen as stagnant and obsolete politically, and has failed with respect to the needs of youth or for general social welfare. Arrogant Arab aggression is now seen increasingly as obsolete, along with restrictive religious practices. Arabism has strong elements of longing for lost glory, the urge for new glory, a sense of oppression and fatalism, and a lot of guilt about "failure". But there is increasing disenchantment by other countries in dealing with governments that are so bad and discredited, and many of these foreign governments have jumped to support the Arab Spring. So now what?

In the Muslim world, the great believers in change are the people, but the great resisters to change tend to be the holders of power. Almost all regimes resist change because they see it as a potential loss of their own power. The more centrist and elitist a government, such as those that control the Muslim world, the greater will be their fear of loss. And in the Muslim world there is the special fear, even among advocates of change, that things will get out of hand and produce disaster—e. g. a government that is far worse rather than better, or one seized by some dreaded fundamentalist group such as the Taliban.

Governments have seriously mishandled economic development. Foreign direct investment (FDI) is limited because investors do not trust the political leadership, or the environment for business. They see too much corruption, and too many bad laws. Economies are seen as old fashioned—not bad, but not keeping pace with the modern world. There continues to be heavy government ownership of economic elements but far too many of the State Owned Enterprises (SOE) proved inefficient and ended up operating at a deficit. The governments tend to extract too much money out of the economy, and too much of it is wasted. Many countries continued to pursue import substitution policies long after it became clear that, beyond a certain point, they did not work. Banking systems tend to be state dominated and are forced into perverse lending policies. Private enterprise is heavily taxed and regulated and is secondary to state enterprises which are heavily subsidized. There is a growing trend where the public is rejecting religious, or religiously justified extremism. This is not just a rejection of Islamism as a justification for terrorism. It is also a rejection of the idea of theocratic governance a la Iran.

Perhaps one half of Muslim governments have been unwilling to accept responsibility for providing adequate social services, continuing to rely on older self reliance, or provision by religious charities, including private religious trust organizations. In competition for scarce public funds, economic development and the military always beat out social services. But there has been increasing guilt about these failures, including lack of public infrastructure. Periods of state socialism were failures on this score.

There is widespread disaffection about the power of elections. Who runs? Hand chosen candidates for the corrupt regime; inexperienced and intimidated opposition; religious militants; earnest innocents. The long term suppression of alternative political organizations has been highly damaging. Yet, the events of the Arab Spring were still pointed toward the hope that some real elections would finally make it possible to remove bad governments peacefully. But in the Muslim world, "out" parties seldom succeed.

There seems to be increasing public rejection or questioning of the false justifications offered by terrorist organizations, and the recognition that they stand for nothing and deliver nothing but pain. It must be recognized that most Muslim countries have suffered from severe and protracted conflict, from terrorist attacks, from insurgencies, to outright civil war. Most countries have suffered from extremist attacks or have been forced to suppress them—often harshly. But this is an endless loser circle: government oppression breeds or justifies these attacks; the attacks are so vicious and menacing that the government must respond; the response is so harsh that it breeds further attacks.

Without debating the nature of these conflicts, it is certain that they have caused serious disruptions and destruction of assets and the provision of civil services, including medical facilities; and many educated professionals who have movable skills have been driven away. On the other side, few Muslim governments are entitled to claim that they have met the social services needs of their citizens. In fact, most of them would be considered to have failed. While civil servants continue to try and teach school or run hospitals or put out fires, the political leaders seem far too preoccupied with fighting each other, and nobody really runs many of these countries. These policy failures also lead to huge misallocations of funds; too much money for war and too little for social services.

There is an unwillingness to speak frankly about the most serious schism in the Muslim world—that between Sunni and Shia, because admission makes both forces seem wrong. There are few admissions about its corrosive consequences, and certainly no admissions about the fact that nobody has any idea of what to do about it—or even whether. Both publically and privately, hug energy and vigor seems to be in the pursuit of Sunni/Shia conflict. Nearly all Arab leaders express a sense of unity with other Arabs, and yet historically Arabs have been among the most persistent antagonists among themselves of any segment of humanity in the world. The Arab world is also broken up into hundreds of quarrelling sects and schisms, based on religion, religious aberrations, geography, history, culture and the competition for political power. The idea of a broader Pan-Arabism has been around for a long time, but has never really taken hold, in no small part because Arab nations have so often been ruled by egotistical tyrants. This Arab agony seldom reaches Muslims in the Far East: Indonesia (230 million), Pakistan (162 million), India (134 million), Bangladesh (130 million) and China (20 million) in total have just about half of the Muslims in the world.

Corruption is universally hated and condemned, but the truth is that it works so well and is so profitable that it seems almost universal. It is a set of recognized skills with well known successful techniques. In addition, it is not just the actions of an individual, but it is usually a refined management system, a conspiracy designed to reward all and protect and conceal all. Most developing countries with weak economies have almost ubiquitous deployment of corrupt practices among the rich and powerful, but they also develop a huge cottage industry of small scale corruption.

But of course, Muslim countries are not alone. China has never seriously tried to curb corruption among the elite but they have prosecuted many local government officials. It is still estimated that 1.3 million party members (one third of total of official workers) are guilty of some form of graft. The Party secretary for Shanghai was dismissed for misappropriating $700 million from the Social Security Fund and using the money for personal investments. The head of the drug approval agency was executed for sanctioning counterfeit drugs. The chairman of the China Construction Bank was sent to jail for 15 years for pocketing $ 500,000 in bribes for construction contracts. In December, 2009, an official national audit summary found that Chinese officials had embezzled or misused some $ 35 billion of government funds. It is no surprise that even oil rich and resource rich states are at the bottom of the Transparency International corruption rankings, and people find themselves facing restive populations, poverty, disease, and violence.

According to a United Nations report, **(6)** in order for the MENA countries to achieve really adequate economies over the next few years, they will somehow need to create 50 million new jobs. Whether the 50 million job estimate is accurate or not (and other estimates are higher), the basic problem is critical. Are MENA nations capable of expanding and enriching their economies enough to generate such a huge increase in employment? If so, how? If not, why not?

These nations do have some significant strengths. Obviously the greatest of these is the widespread availability of oil, and to a lesser extent, natural gas, and other valuable mineral resources. Oil wealth in turn has created rich states like the UAE, Saudi Arabia, Qatar, Kuwait and others that have become big sources of investment money in the region. And these resources have increasingly attracted great interest from China and India which have insatiable needs for energy and industrial mineral sources. Thus, investment money is available if governments and the Muslim private sector in the region know how to use it. MENA countries have a population of about 415 million, and there is easy access to other large populations in the rest of Africa.

But—balanced against these advantages is a daunting array of problems, beginning with a record of serious failure of economic and social leadership. Many of the countries in the region adopted some form of State Socialism, which has proved seriously dysfunctional. State ownership of productive resources, especially oil, energy, minerals, manufacturing and banking produced general patterns of inefficiency, low productivity, distorted policies, distorted prices, low adoption of new technology, failure to provide for adequate maintenance and repair, and lack of effective human resources development. The talent base of these countries simply fails to utilize the current and potential contributions of women, and even where young people are able to get a higher education, these economies are notorious for their inability to provide real jobs for their youths—hence the call for fifty million new jobs.

Another telling failure of leadership in Muslim countries has been the lack of adequate social services—in primary and higher education, health care and health insurance, old age and retirement protection, assistance for the poor, and an overwhelming neglect of the region's fragile environments. Often, public infrastructure, especially in cities overwhelmed by skyrocketing populations, is pitifully inadequate. These conditions make it very hard to attract foreign investors or really talented people, and it has produced a badly divided social structure of a small, powerful and wealthy elite, lording it over the general population that is poor, undereducated, with little future and little hope.

Much of the physical world is very challenging. There are unfriendly climates, severe water shortages, semi-arid deserts and choking wind storms, and in most cases, conditions are getting worse rather than better. Deserts are expanding, water resources are shrinking, pollution is universal, and none of these problems are being dealt with.

But perhaps the greatest impediment to the development of this whole MENA region is its record of unending armed conflict—wars, insurgencies, vicious terrorism, and constant clashes and disruptions at the level of clans or sects, or villages or regions. In a sense, the reasons for these conflicts are secondary since all produce deaths, wounds and injuries, massive people displacements, destruction of property, and the interruption or termination of social services such as schools or hospitals. There have been untold losses of personal property and an unbelievable wastage of money, lives and both public and private services, along with the poisoning of all elements of human relationships. In this world, the only people who can prosper are the crooks, the thugs, the power hungry and the super greedy.

And finally, it is tragic that indeed, the greatest of skills in the region are the skills of the corrupt. No nation escapes this curse. <u>Corruption is not a characteristic of the political/economic system</u>—**it is the system.** Even where governments try to provide social services or build public works or let valuable contracts, or stimulate elements of their economies, these efforts are all too often beggared and crippled by thieves and crooks and cheats who divert scarce money and make it disappear.

In a sense then, economic development in the Muslim world faces such great and intractable impediments that rapid and sustained economic development often seems like mission impossible. Muslim economies, for economic, social, and religious reasons, are obsolete and mired in the past. Even bright, sensible efforts at development are really seen as puny compared to the magnitude of the problems. Fifty million new jobs? Not very likely unless, somehow, the leadership is radically changed, away from the tyrants and the war makers and thugs and the thieves, toward new leadership that really wants to practice cooperation, manage the country and put the efforts and funds of the government to work "bottom up" on the real life needs of their countries.

Islamist-Extremist Movements

Almost all of the time, Islamist-extremist movements are primarily about power and not about religion, even when religious elements are involved and manipulated. Islamist leadership is usually more extreme than the general Muslim population, and they drive out the more moderate leaders, both religious and secular. Where Islamist regimes have gained power, they have proved no better than the regimes they replace (e. g. Iran, Sudan, Afghanistan, Pakistan, Algeria, Iraq, Libya). Failure to perform well by solving economic problems or providing adequate public services swiftly deteriorates public support—the inevitable failure of the "vision of perfection".

There is no "caliph" or Muslim pope in Islam. There is an amazingly complex, swirling mass of groups and movements, and extremists come from a variety of sources. They are the radical theological leaders who press the view that all Muslims must accept fundamentalist interpretation of the Holy Documents, and failure to do so is intolerable apostasy. A surprising number are in the new Islamic intellectual class—religious intellectuals, academics and preachers; an emerging educated middle class such as doctors, lawyers, engineers and others who have been strong supporters of a vision of a perfect Islamic world; urban street youth who are frustrated by lack of serious employment and rage against tyranny and will buy into extremist solutions; and finally, the self-serving elite—always authoritarian, usually tyrannical, not really religious, but looking for levers to achieve power. Radical Islamist movements are made stronger and more radical by oppression by the regime. They find it easy and profitable to attack incumbent regimes for their undoubted incompetence and corruption.

Regimes react to these extremist groups in a number of ways. Some can be co-opted by being taken over and made to support the holders of power. In some cases, the devout middle class can become disillusioned and simply strive for a better relationship with the current establishment, however unsavory. Or movements can be attacked by the regime and made so risky they are defeated or wither away. Public disillusionment from the bottom up may cause the rejection of violent extremist groups and the shrinkage of their sources of people and money. Or it may finally dawn on everybody that it is better in the end to cooperate than to fight. But what has seldom emerged is moderate middle of the road leaders who can form a durable alliance with the devout middle class.

If there is one common element that seems to appeal to most Muslims it is the application, in some form, of Sharia law, yet most Muslims seem to have little real understanding of the content of Sharia law beyond the personal parts, and they tend to realize only after the fact that its "interpretation" of broader issues by some Imams can be dysfunctional and oppressive, and that the stringent and constraining application of Sharia almost always produces public dismay and disillusionment—especially for women. The most purist and fundamentalist Islamic views insist that the Quran cannot be interpreted—but it is done all the time, even by the purists. Some Imams insist that individuals are not allowed to interpret the holy documents, but must obey the interpretations furnished by the religious leaders, yet the Quran is intended to be a guide for the individual devout Muslim, and most are urged to study it and find their own truths. Similarly, Sharia law is meant to be interpreted as a full blown body of laws, and its content and meaning is constantly being reinterpreted. The main question is by whom. Among Shia Muslims, each Imam can become the interpreter for his congregation. Among the Sunni, who are 85% of the worlds Muslims, the old order gave the authority for interpretation to the clergy. In the modern world, that authority has passed to official governments, with religious leaders as advisors.

Public Corruption

In every Muslim government, better ways to attack corruption are vitally needed. This is another trap into which governments all over the world have fallen. Corruption is so easy and so profitable that it has become almost the standard of the world, and it is now all too often seen as normal, inevitable and acceptable. Every government in the Muslim world suffers from rampant corruption, most of it involving government programs and officials, but it leads to enormous loss of scarce public assets and funds, and universal distrust of, and contempt for government organizations and leaders—terrible prices for any government to pay. The rankings of countries by the Global Integrity Report (2008) ranks integrity in seventeen Muslim countries as "weak" and an additional twelve as "very weak", and only one—Indonesia—as "strong". (7)

This corruption problem extends down to governments in states or provinces and in cities. What are the most serious arenas of corruption? Legislation, construction, land use, big development projects, customs, taxes, permits and licenses, foreign aid, and government inspections. Religion per se has little influence on corruption, and many religious institutions themselves are corrupt. The developed world believes in top down activity; the corruptors believe in bottom up activity. For example, the OECD has a "Convention Against Illicit Payments", and the UN has a "Convention Against Corruption" and both, while descending from on high, are widely and safely ignored, with the exception of some tracking of corrupt bank accounts. Accusations of corruption are now a routine commonplace element of almost every election in developing countries—and unfortunately, they are often right. Corruption is so serious that is has become one of the key ways of attacking ruling regimes. Somehow, campaigns against corruption never quite seem to work.

Governments need to recognize that corruption is far more than the old fashioned sins of bribery and theft. It has become far more sophisticated, attacking the workings of government in much more sophisticated ways, and it is practiced not only by thugs and crooks, but by very bright and able people who are clever, organized and innovative. For example, the capacity for profitable corruption may start with the laws that design public programs at the very beginning, and far more attention must be paid by the methods by which program designs can be kept honest. For example, programs must avoid the capacity for political pandering. They must be kept limited and focused on the serious real targets. There is a tendency for politicians and government officials to allow programs to expand into low value marginal clientele, or to those who are capable of taking advantage of weaknesses. There is also a tendency to allow program benefits to grow more generous, often beyond real need. Often, it is not the real poor or needy who get the aid, but the richer or better connected or the more venal.

The most difficult problem comes where the decision rests with a political official who is not controlled by the mechanisms applied to the career staff. Many ministers or agency heads have broad and unchecked authority under agency enabling statutes. They may make arbitrary decisions based entirely on their own judgment, and on political factors not considered in the staff technical evaluation. Factors such as the geographical location of bidding companies, or contributions to political campaigns, or the desire to reward the allies of the regime are not uncommon. Few career officials will have either the authority or the courage to challenge such political distortions.

In almost every country, human linkages are often more important than the formal structure of agencies. This is especially true in governments where the official structure is weak and ill conceived, or in governments that are authoritarian rather than democratic or merit based. Thus, the appointment of key leadership to government posts is always carefully controlled to favor the hand of the regime leadership. The most favored basis for appointment to important government posts is political loyalty, but other criteria may include shared interests or common goals, including "causes" such as environmentalism or the alleviation of poverty. Many countries allocate top positions in the government based on the strength or popularity of specific groups. In some governments with many political parties, this allocation may mean the assignment of positions to each of the parties in the controlling coalition. In developing countries, there is a tendency to allocate based on the divisions in the country such as race, religion, tribalism, clans or even villages or important families. The power to appoint thus becomes the source of many kinds of pathology.

In corrupt governments, appointments designed to perpetuate and extend networks of corrupt officials into the arenas where corruption is most profitable. The acid test for appointments is merely loyalty to the leadership, and not merit or skill. Loyalty is most likely to be to an individual and not the institutions of government. Ability may not be totally ignored; many appointments, even in pathological regimes are from "the brightest and the best", but still the criterion is "the best from among the loyalists".

The narrower the range of selection of top people the more it is visibly seen as unfair since it deliberately ignores large segments of the population and is seen as "in your face" prejudice. The loyalist group, whatever its competence, is seen as the ultimate special interest grip on power. The whole government is seen as a special interest bloc, and the consequence of this special interest cronyism extends itself into skewing or manipulating the values of public programs. The most recent high visibility situation of this kind was that of Saddam Hussein who not only gave important posts to his sons but put much of the government into the hands of people from the village where he grew up. In most cases this control extends itself into penetration of the whole national economy.

Another example now coming home to roost is in Syria where President al-Assad deliberately gives senior posts in government to his Alawite sect members. Such tainted appointments can be expected to be carried down below the crucial top positions. Unless the number and location of authorized positions is tightly controlled, the agency can be filled with numerous, largely meaningless jobs such as special assistants or assistant deputies or deputy assistants which are payoff jobs for loyalist hacks. Elaborate corrupt networks are buried in the more formal structure of the agency. At each level, the boss is expected to develop whatever corrupt practices are possible, with the illicit profits shared upward to the agency head. Such a perverse structure is self-concealing and self-protective, and it presents a formidable resistance to any efforts for reform.

Few programs should be created which subsidize organizations that can and should provide for themselves. There really should be no gravy train programs that subsidize profit making organizations. This applies equally to private commercial businesses, to state owned enterprises, and to non-profit organizations which can adequately finance themselves from contributions and sales.

Where possible, governments should design programs that employ loan guarantees rather than actual loans or outright grants of money out of the state budget. And guarantees should not be paid where fraud or corruption is involved; repayments of government loans should be strictly enforced. Similarly, programs should be designed and laws written to insist on fixed price contracting, which is cheaper then cost plus contracts and easier to keep honest. Incentive contracts are even better.

Administration of government programs is even more subject to gaming and cheating. Many developing countries that suffer from underpowered economies and high unemployment fall into the trap of using the government itself and government state owned enterprises and contractors as employers of last resort. This is always politically popular, but it results in redundant employment (workers with no real jobs) which is unproductive and extremely expensive. In some cases such as the old Soviet Union, it was shown that up to 40% of workers in many industries were redundant. Under such a policy, both politicians and government officials find themselves actively defending this disaster, and once hired, these workers are almost impossible to remove. State owned enterprises and companies are at a serious disadvantage in any economic competitive situation because of the money wasted on redundant employment. It also seems true that such redundant workers get little or no training, few advancements and few wage increases, ending up as drivers or "tea ladies". And they suffer from serious resentment by the "real" employees of the organization.

Once programs are created, there are literally hundreds of ways in which their operations can be corrupted, and most Muslim governments lack the skill or the will to deal with all of these vulnerabilities. To begin with, every program or project, every contract, every grant, every loan involves the complex process of authorizing the spending of funds, and the actual mechanics of making payments. In order to prevent, or at least mitigate the looting of these funds, several important protections are needed. First, the number of officials who can officially authorize payments should be very limited, and they must be held to strict procedural accountability. It should always be clear who authorized the deployment of money. Second, those who compute the sums that must be spend must also be held to strict, well defined ground rules for how bills are computed, and there needs to be an independent evaluation of these computations. No big unknown costs; no big cost overruns; no excessive costs ($100 screwdrivers), no huge, vague overhead charges, no payment for work not performed; no payment for "phantom" employees. Corruption is the life work of smart, active and clever people, so there is no end to the threat—ever.

A third factor in the administration of public programs is the question of what impact any program really achieves. The history of every government is one in which, if the truth were understood, hundreds of programs would be recognized as useless, pointless, obsolete, duplicative or of high cost but low value payoff. Must of this waste is political. Lobbying groups and special interests press politicians for some payoff, while narrow programs may make the lobbyists happy, they have little value for the general population. Once such programs are in place, it is almost impossible politically ever to abandon them.

An effective anti-corruption campaign must be holistic and should include, at a minimum one or more independent and powerful specific anti-corruption organizations, linked with auditors and inspectors in each government ministry. These auditors and inspectors must have authority to demand any/all information and data. Investigation of corruption must be extended to all political officers and not just to career people.

As part of this extension, laws on campaign finance and political fund raising must be put in place and enforced, and they should be extended to include nepotism and the acts of family members. No form of corruption should be exempt just because it is considered minor or acceptable. That's how small corruptions get to be big. Therefore, there should be strict clampdowns on all forms of petty corruption generated by the delivery of public services (police protection, health care, tax collection, licenses and permits; inspections, etc.). In addition, there should be a focused campaign against organized crime; a root-and-branch reform of the procurement system; a reform of land allocation; the establishment of an effective judicial dispute resolution system; full disclosure of the value of public assets; careful monitoring of banks; control of money flight." It is an absolute necessity that the courts and chief prosecutors be independent, with long term judicial appointments. Special anti-corruption commissions sometimes work if they are truly independent, concentrate on the really significant problems, and have the power to investigate and to arrest. Stiffer penalties are needed, along with much more forceful enforcement. Current results seem pitiful. The U. N. anti-corruption convention is said to be really enforced only in seven countries, and only another nine more do even moderate enforcement. None of these sixteen countries are Muslim. But sadly, in many Muslim countries the possibility for reform is seen as political wishful thinking.

The Future

The greatest need for governments in the Muslim world is to find ways to resist the grip of centrist power elites and to broaden the base of power sharing. This diffusion of power involves the structure of governments: the role of the chief executive, the legislative bodies, the courts, and the military, and the powers of government agencies. Yet most Muslim governments have a full array of such apparatus, ostensibly designed to balance power and restrain excess, but it is obvious that the mere existence of this apparatus is not enough, nor is the rule of law really alive and well.

All too often centrist power simply overwhelms everything and everybody else.

A new philosophy of government must be designed, adopted and implemented. It must emerge from and be largely defined by Islam's holy documents: the Quran, the Sunnah and Hadith. This new philosophy cannot be provided either by centrist power holders or by narrow religious interpretation. It cannot be a mere imitation of the political philosophies of the West, nor can Western influences insist on any preferred pattern. The new philosophy must arise from within the Muslim community—and in fact, from many Muslim communities. The idea of a single political philosophy for all Muslims around the world is unreal and would be dysfunctional.

But the new diffusion of power is also beginning to arise outside of the controlling apparatus of the government, among the people themselves, acting in hundreds of ways to form a more pervasive civic community which can influence government and mitigate its excesses. The pace of the emergence of civil society has often been slow and uncertain. Part of this is the enduring agricultural economies and cultures in the Muslim world which remain very conservative and often reactionary. Only recently is there a real shift toward urbanization, but Muslim cities were not ready or able to absorb huge gains in urban populations. Most Muslim cities have large slum populations and informal economies.

The Arab Spring is perhaps the most hopeful sign in the history of Islam about the emergence of this civic community sturdy enough to have real influence. As Robin Wright puts it, "New players are shattering the old order. The sleeping majority is awakening. The wider Muslim world is increasingly rejecting extremism. The Arabic world is where "the many forms of militancy—from the venomous Sunni creed of al Qaeda to the punitive Shiite theocracy in Iran—have proven costly, unproductive, and ultimately unappealing. Jihadists have failed to provide anything constructive. There are counter-movements which are unfolding in the wider Islamic bloc of 57 countries, as well as among Muslim minorities worldwide. These movements reject violent groups and influences as well as the general principle of violence to achieve political goals. Every reliable citizen poll since 2007 shows steadily declining support for the destructive and disruptive jihads. The counter-jihad has been especially evident among Sunni Muslims, who account for more than 80% of the Islamic world."

Feldman says that there is a distinctly Islamic political vision.[8] After WW II and the great wave of liberation, many Muslim states turned to State Socialism as a replacement for the "Old Model", but this movement has petered out mostly because of two things: first, clashes with Muslim religious leaders who see Communism and State Socialism as Godless apostasy; and second the failures of state socialism in economic development. But again, this failure did not lead to a surge toward a democratic state as it has done elsewhere, but rather to an Islamic movement which says "Islam is the Solution", and urges a return to the good old days of Sharia law. Islamists argue that Sharia law is "an all encompassing structure that precisely orders social relations and facilitates economic justice." But the sad truth seems to be that the problems of Muslim states (as with many others) are so enormous and intractable that it is innocent to believe that the mere adaption of more Sharia law could be "the solution."

But if there is an institutional model for a future Muslim political structure, it is probably the Muslim Brotherhood (MB). This movement is really a whole range of Brotherhoods in many countries and not just in Egypt. While they are linked, they set their own courses, but many have multiple "product lines" like the Brotherhood:

a. They are significant providers of social services. b. They serve as public interest groups or sponsors of such groups over a broad range of subjects from social critique to political lobbying. c. Many see their role as requiring the peaceful propagation of the Faith. d. Increasingly, they form the basis for legitimate political movements, and many have been elected to office or serve in important posts in government ministries. e. Others are organizers and suppliers of militant wings, or separate militant groups. f. Some form fighting groups—often as subsidiaries of other groups, and some of these groups employ terrorism.

The nature of Brotherhood "affiliates" in any country is determined by local circumstances, and not some form of tight central control, and they are usually a very mixed blessing. None of the Muslim Brotherhood groups have ever taken control or run anything until their recent election in Egypt. Like all Islamist organizations, the Brotherhood is an iceberg: 80% of it is deliberately concealed, and it tells "the people" only what it wants them to hear—much of it very self-serving and much of it misinformation. Its three main leverages have been public respect, backing of the middle class, and good works. It is not aimed primarily at starting wars or propagating terrorism.

The Muslim Brotherhood role in Middle Eastern and North African (MENA) countries is as follows:

1. Egypt: The birthplace of the Muslim Brotherhood (MB) which initially started out as a charitable organization with emphasis on helping the poor and advocating programs for youth and mothers. It has long been banned as a political party, but it has always remained a powerful and influential organization. It is now the largest political party and it won the recent election and has formed a government. The MB still has many conflicts, both among Muslim interests and with non-Muslims, secularists, and business interests. It is still a moderate organization, willing to abandon its more militant product lines.
2. Morocco: King Muhammad V had earlier appointed the head of the MB party, the Justice and Development Party as the Prime Minister, and that party is now in office.
3. Libya: MB militias were among the most active in the overthrow of the government. It is not clear how willing and able they are to become a political party, and what its political stance would be. Meanwhile, more extremist Islamic groups are growing up which oppose both the government and the MB.

4. Syria: MB elements have been active among the opposition to the regime. The MB and the Syrian regime are deadly enemies since the Baathist purge of MB followers in the 80's, and it is also anti-Hamas because its headquarters is still in Damascus and can be attacked there, but not in the Gaza Strip. It is too early to tell the outcome of the civil war.

5. Jordan: The Islamic Action Front, the MB organization in Jordan, has been one of the two strongest parties in the country literally for decades. It acts as a political party and not as a militant organization, and has generally been able to get along with the regime.

6. Iraq: The Islamic Party (MB) worked first with Saddam Hussein and then with the Americans after 2003. The MB is Sunni and has guarded relationships with the current Shia government.

7. Bahrain, Kuwait, Yemen: In all three countries, there has been long standing political activity by the MB, including parliamentary representation for at least 30 years.

8. Sudan: The National Political Front (MB) backed the military coup in 1989, and has held many cabinet posts since then, but this stance is seen as increasingly untenable and unpopular because of the horrible performance of the Sudanese government.

9. Gaza Strip: The MB was the sponsor of Hamas and helped it to get into power and to stay in power, but the party strategy is more against Israel rather than liking for Hamas.

10. Tunisia: Nahda, an MB affiliate, won the election of 2010 and supports a non-Muslim national president, and it holds several cabinet posts.

11. Turkey: The MB is only one group in a general coalition of Muslim interests that won the last two elections and has the sitting Prime Minister. Generally the MB here is considered moderate.

There seems now to be a far greater willingness to reject the traditionalist assertion that the Quran cannot be interpreted, and that the Muslim religion must be frozen into the definitions demanded by the clergy. The tide running seems to be to examine such interpretations (except possibly for an immutable basic core of the Quran) with a broader vision, and various forms of more moderate interpretation are gaining ground. For example, it is increasingly realized that the view of women's place in the world is not immutably set by the holy documents, but by longstanding male ground rules which often run counter to these documents.

The constant pressure for religious conformity has acted to stultify intellectual freedom and make education very narrow and defensive. This stultification was not only over the introduction of new technology, but over any concept of CHANGE. In truth, change happens whether the conservative leadership wants it or not, and the values of the new things of the world (computers, cell phones, TV, autos, refrigerators, independent thinking, self determination, etc.) is eagerly absorbed by Muslims along with everybody else. Graham Fuller defines the new view: **"Think not what Islam used to be; think what it can become."**[9] The historic Muslim religion and historic Arab culture seem very conservative by modern standards elsewhere. This contributes heavily to the slow pace of change in both the Middle East and Far East where India, Pakistan, Bangladesh, Indonesia and China hold about 650 million Muslims, or almost half of all the Muslims in the world, and are not preoccupied with the Arab view of the world.

The ultimate question: will Muslims themselves take primary responsibility to control their radical elements? Many governments have had to do so, but to save their own skins. But it is not clear how much the average Muslim is willing to do, admittedly against long odds. This would not really be an attack against religion. Most terrorists are motivated by nationalistic issues (usually Arabism), but they cloak themselves in religion, and as "liberators". It must be recognized that a large part of terrorist activity is sponsored by the governments themselves, and thus it is particularly risky to oppose them. Terrorism can't be handled by regular police/military because terrorists hide themselves in the general population, creating the risk of a lot of collateral damage. It is helpful to note that fundamentalist Islam has succeeded to power in only three cases—Iran, Afghanistan and Sudan, (and very recently perhaps in Mali), and all three came to power by undemocratic means. All have bred eternal conflict and pain, and none have offered any real solutions for people's needs.

If Islamic politics is to succeed, it must largely abandon its more conservative aspects, accept cultural diversity, accept the challenge to carry its popularity into power without turning dictatorial—in other words, learn how to be relevant to a far broader constituency. It must stop thinking of non-believers as barely tolerated inferior infidels. It must also learn to mitigate its internal conflicts, some of which have been painful for 1400 years. To date, none of this seems to be happening among Islamic organizations, but it is happening among the people themselves. Again, all of this is perfectly consistent with the holy documents, but not with the interpretations of reactionary leaders. Examples of the ability of Muslim regimes to coexist are India, Turkey, Egypt, Malaysia. Rival claimants as sources of authority in Islam are expanding exponentially, with independent and self appointed religious opinions being issued through multiple forms of media, including <u>fatwa</u> centers all over the world. Originally, the *fatwa* was seen as a local authority issued by an Imam for the guidance of his own flock. The "electronic *ummah*" or collective Muslim world community, can be both a vehicle for the encouragement of diversity and broader public participation, or a device to rally the faithful to the wrong causes. The imposition of Sharia law is not supposed to apply to non Muslims, but if it becomes the official law of a country, this concept is negated.

Muslim governments seem to be finding themselves in a situation where the world is increasingly pluralist, not all citizens are Muslim, not all Muslims are the same, not all are religious, and where Muslim theology and interpretation has failed to take into account what exists in the real world. Conservative interpretations can be too rigid, failing to meet the acid test of politics which is negotiation and compromise, and being a drag on economic development. How can a Muslim citizen and family lead a devout Muslim life while still getting all of the advantages of a modern society and economy? State Socialism/Communism failed this test.

Some version of relaxed Islamism is possible, and it is increasingly recognized that the force of secularism is growing globally, while reactionary Islamism is acquiring an evil reputation. In the last analysis, religion in Muslim terms has always been subordinate to the State—even now in Iran. People grow tired of old theology and now increasingly want Islamist theologians to stop thinking of "democracy" and "materialism" as threats and start thinking of them as desirable goals.

What is the Western challenge? Islamist apologists like to make it sound like the challenge is military, political or economic. In fact, much of it is cultural, and not deliberate. Muslims who are deprived are now seeing and hearing too much about the successes of <u>people</u> in the West to continue to believe the propaganda handed out by their governments—or by Islamist liars. At some point, Muslims in many countries will start to realize that the source of their problems is not the U. S., but themselves. Lee Smith points out "Arabs are deeply confused about the United States and their own feelings toward it. In any mall in the Arab Gulf states, teenage boys in bright white dishdashas, baseball caps, and Converse All Stars wait in line for first run Hollywood action films, while their teen age sisters in black burkas and designer sunglasses balance armfuls of shopping bags from American retail outlets while chatting on their iPhones."[10]

Robin Wright says that "Muslims are learning that 'women's lib' does not really come directly from the West, but is coming through Muslim women themselves and is taking place well within the framework of Islamic movements. Thus, the women's movement is anti-clerical. Women want clerics to stop supporting inhibiting customs invented by men, really outside of the meanings of the Quran and Sharia. A perfectly good example is the prohibition in many countries against women driving cars, which is totally unrecognized and unsupported by Islamic law, and is ignored in 90% of the Muslim world." (11)

SOURCES

Brown, Nathan J., "When Victory is Not an Option", Cornell U. Press, 2012.

Casey, Roane (Ed.), "The Other Israel", New York, The New World Press, 2002.

Chehab, Zuki, "Inside Hamas", New York, Nation Books, 2007.

Esposito, John L., 'Unholy War: Terror in the Name of Islam", Oxford U. Press, 2002.

Feldman, Noah, "The Fall and Rise of the Islamic State", Princeton U. Press, 2008.

Foreign Affairs Journal, "The New Arab Revolt", May/June, 2011.

Gause, F. Gregory III, "Why Middle East Studies Missed the Arab Spring", Foreign Affairs Journal, 2011.

Friedman, Thomas L., "From Beirut to Jerusalem", New York, Anchor Books, 1995.

Fuller, Graham E., "The Future of Political Islam", New York, Palgrave Macillan, 2003.

Hayek, F. A., "The Road to Serfdom", U. of Chicago Press, 1944.

The Global Competitiveness Report, 2010-2011, World Economic Forum, Geneva, Switzerland, 2011

World Development Indicators: Vulnerability, Women in Development, Size of Economies, Enhancing Security; Washington, D. C. World Bank, 2012

Foreign Affairs Journal, Abramowitz, Morton, and Barkey, Henri J., "Turkey's Transformers: The AKP Sees Big", November/December 2009

Rosenberg, Matt, "Capitals of Every Independent Country", About.com.geography, Sep. 4, 2011

Foreign Affairs Journal, Shah, Aqil, "Getting the Military Out of Pakistani Politics", May/June 2011

Islam by Country, Wikipedia, March, 2007

The Economist, "Doing Well on Parole: Tunisia's Islamists have survived a shaky first 100 days in power", April 7, 2012

Organization of Islamic Cooperation, Washington, D. C., Organization, policies, and listing of member states, 2011

United Nations Development Program Monthly Turkey newsletter, Issue 10, October, 2006

Bener Law Office, Istanbul, Turkey, "A Comparative Overview of Public-Private Partnerships With Those in Turkey, 2011

The Economist, "Dreaming of a Sultanate: Thailand's violent south", May 5, 2012

The Economist, "An Unholy Alliance: secession in Mali", June 2, 2012

The Economist, "The Sword and the Word: Sunni-Shia strife", May 12, 2012

Islamic World.net, "Islamic World Countries", 2012

Wholesome Worlds, Ross, Stephen, "The Harvest Fields: Statistics 2011"

WWW.geographic.org, World Muslim Population Projections, sourced from United Nations Population Fund, May, 2005

The World Factbook, "The World's Most Populous Cities, Metropolitan Areas, Urban Agglomerations, 2008

The Economist, "Put Faith in Writing: Islamists and Arab Constitutions", March 31, 2012

Wikipedia, "Islam by Country", March, 2007

Wikipedia, "Muslim World", September, 2011

SperoNews, Samir Kalil Samir, "Violent Fatwas Worry Muslim Governments", September, 2006

Esposito, John L., "Practice and Theory: A Response to Islam and the Challenge of Democracy'", Boston Review, April/May 2003

Front Page Magazine, Locke, Robert, "Islam: A Defective Civilization", Feb. 28 2002

World Policy Journal, Ross, Dennis, "Counterterrorism: A Professional's Strategy", Spring 2007

About.com, "Bahrain: Shia Islam", March, 2011

Washington Post, Charney, Craig, and Dobbins, James, "Change Afghans Can Believe In", April 1, 2011

World Policy Journal, Lewis, David, "High Times on the Silk Road: The Central Asian Paradox", Spring, 2010

World Policy Journal, Ottaway, Marina, "The More Things Change . . . Political Reform in the Arab World", Summer, 2009

The Jamestown Foundation, Kaussler, Bernd, "Sunni Terrorists Strike Shi'a Mosque in Iran's Sistan-Baluchistan Province", June 12, 2009

Freedom House, Freedom Country Ranks 2011—Country Rankings, February, 2011

Islamicpopulation.com, World Muslim Population, 2006; American Muslim Population, 2006; Oceanian Muslim Population, 2006; European Muslim Population, 2006; Asian Muslim Population, 2006

The Economist, "Under Threat Form all Sides: Palestinian Democracy", August 14, 2010

Wikepedia, "Saudi Arabia", Aug. 27, 2010

Wikipedia, "History of Egypt under the Muhammad Ali Dynasty", July, 2011

The Pew Forum, Pew Research Center, "The Future of the Global Muslim Population", January 2011

The Economist, "Banyan: More Black Tea than Jasmine", March 5, 2011

Foreign Affairs Journal, Danin, Robert M., "A Third Way to Palestine: Fayyadism and Its Discontents", January/February 2011

The Economist, "What Happens if Assad Goes?", May 21, 2011

Huffpost World, Keath, Lee, and Hendawi, Hamza, "Egypt's Al-Zawahri Likely to Succeed Bin Laden", May 2, 2011

Kennedy, Hugh, "The Great Arab Conquests", Philadelphia, Pa., Da Capo Press, 2007.

Kepel, Gilles, "Jihad: The Trial of Political Islam", Cambridge, Mass., The Belnap Press, 2002.

Kinger, Stephen, "Crescent and Star", New York, Farrer, Straus and Geroux, 2008.

Lamb, David, "The Arabs", New York, Vintage Books, 2002.

Levitt, Matthew "Hamas", Yale University Press, 2006.

Makilisi, Saree, "Palestine Inside Out", New York, W. W. Norton and Co., 2008.

Nasr, Sayyed Hossein, "The Heart of Islam, New York, Harper One Publishers, 2004.

Rashid, Ahmed, "Taliban", Yale University Press, 2000.

Rutberg, Robert I. (Ed.), "When States Fail", Princeton U. Press, 2004.

Said, Edward, W., "The Question of Palestine", New York, Vintage Books, 1992.

Smith, Lee, "The Strong Horse", New York, Anchor Books, 2010.

Takeyh, Ray, "Hidden Iran", New York, Times Books, 2006.

Viorst, Milton, "Sandcastles", New York, Alfred A. Knopf, 1994.

World Political Almanac, 4th Edition, New York, Checkmark Books, 2001.

CHAPTER II

ECONOMIC DEVELOPMENT

"FIFTY MILLION NEW JOBS": MISSION IMPOSSIBLE

Many less developed country (LDCs) governments including those in Muslim countries adopted policies that were socialist in outlook and approach, or heavily influenced by conservative religious doctrines both highly centrist and controlling. This conservative thinking led to the dominance of the central government in planning and controlling both the economy and the social contract. This led to a predominant pattern of state ownership and control of productive institutions in the form of state owned enterprises (SOE) (sometimes called public enterprises or government corporations). It also led to the "cradle to grave" commitment to government control of most important social services. Social theory centered around the poverty of the population and their inability to take care of themselves; and the parallel theory that the role of the private sector was ominous and anti-social. Most of the LDCs started with rudimentary private sectors with the expectation that the private sector would rapidly strengthen.

But socialist governments seldom intended to permit the growth of strong private enterprises; many seriously inhibited the private sector, largely for doctrinal reasons. Many have elite ruling classes which tend to be conservative and defensive. This led them to keep their countries too long in a basic economy, and many such countries were slow to get into the modern industrial/commercial world. As a result, the Muslim countries of the Middle East and

North Africa (MENA) find themselves with an impossible gap between the number of people needing jobs versus the ability of their economies to create jobs. The total population of the MENA countries is approximately 415 million people. Within this population, about 210 million are of working age, and perhaps 190 million are actually in the workforce. That means that at this time, there are already about thirty million potential workers who cannnot find jobs; they are unemployed, or not active in the workforce. Many of these inactives are women who are seriously inhibited in Muslim countries from constructive employment. Others are young: there are perhaps ninety-five million youths under the age of 15 who are, or will shortly be seeking jobs. In sum, 54 percent of the population is unemployed, not active in the workforce, or not in school.

This situation is rapidly getting worse. In addition to the paucity of jobs for new entrants into the workforce, most MENA countries have been suffering from serious long term unemployment so bad that the unemployment rate for the region is the worst in the world. The "dependency ratio"—the number of people who are working and thus support those who do not—is also the lowest in the world. Combine this with the fact that the populations of all of the MENA countries has been growing very rapidly, and it becomes clear how really desparate the general workforce situation has become. The World Bank in several of its reports has estimated that these MENA countries somehow must find a way to create fifty million new jobs by 2020 to rescue their people from economic collapse and widespread poverty. The World Economic Forum agrees with this kind of assessment, but it believes that one hundred million new jobs is the real necessity.

At the same time, political leadersship throughout the region has been ineffective and inconsistent; they are best understood as being composed of the "INS" and the "OUTS". The Ins tended to form around elites; the outs tend to be reformist. Few have been compelling examples of representative democracy. The population is undereducated politically; labor unions seldom really represented worker interests but were usually controlled by the government and were a rallying point for political power. The real politics is the politics of power brokering and special interest negotiation. In most, the military is a dominant force in the government and even in the civilian economy.

Most of these countries are "regulation intensive"—regulations are most often used to control the economy in detail and to protect the government's position. Yet regulation of public health and safety and the environment is relatively weak.

In most, the primary industries (agriculture, mining, forestry, fishing) are all marginal. But lack of industrial/commercial jobs has led to a policy of keeping people in these marginal industries until manufacturing or commercial growth can absorb them. But this has meant that the government has deliberately acted to perpetuate a poor peasantry. Retailing is sub optimal, the distribution system is old fashioned and inefficient, and much commercial traffic is illegal including smuggling, weapons sales, and drug trafficking.

Most suffer from chronic underfinancing. Local economies are not able to generate sufficient investment capital, and their owners and managers stoutly resist government taxation. There has been heavy reliance on external financing, both public and private. This in turn has led to the "structural adjustment" intervention of creditors. Most also suffer from chronic underfinancing of public programs—social services, education, health care, housing, infrastructure.

Most are characterized by a rapid shift to urbanism, which has put great pressure on cities. The percentage of the population which is rural in 2000 was as follows: Sudan = 41.1 percent; Pakistan = 26.7 percent; Syria = 22.8 percent; Iran = 17.7 percent; Egypt = 16.7 percent; Turkey = 15.4 percent; Morocco = 13.5 percent; Tunisia = 12.3 percent; Jordan = 2.2 percent.

Mosques are a traditional and still widely used alternative to the provision of public services by governments. The religious leadership has always known that the provision of services equals credibility, and thus they might actually resist the expansion of government provided services.

MUSLIM ECONOMICS (1)

SECTOR %S OF MUSLIM ECONOMIES

	Industry	Services	Agriculture
Egypt	33.1	50.2	16.7
Iran	33.3	49	17.7
Jordan	24.8	73	2.2
Morocco	32.2	54.3	13.5
Syria	28.7	48.5	22.8
Tunisia	28.8	58.9	12.3
Turkey	25.3	59.3	15.4
Pakistan	23.1	50.2	26.7
Indonesia	47.1	35.9	17
Sudan	18.5	40.4	41.1

In the Global Competitiveness Index (2010-2011), these are the rankings of 15 Muslim countries: (total of 139 countries ranked)

Saudi Arabia	21
UAR	25
Tunisia	32
Kuwait	35
Indonesia	44
Turkey	61
Jordan	65
Iran	69
Morocco	75
Egypt	81
Algeria	86

Lebanon	92
Syria	97
Libya	100
Pakistan	123

The older mercantile tradition is gradually fading as the basis of national economies. There is nothing really wrong with this centuries old system except that it could not adapt to encompass modern business and increasingly became non-competitive, unable to deal with great size and complexity.

Modern Muslim economies suffer from a whole range of characteristic weaknesses. **(3)**

- Muslim countries tend to be poorer than non Muslim countries. 2000 figures showed non-Muslim average income at $5987, but Muslim counties at $3335. The Muslim share of global population is nineteen percent, but its share of global income is just six percent.
- GDP grew more slowly in Muslim countries, and there is much evidence that the situation is gradually getting worse rather than better. Muslims also now face new challenges not from the U. S. or Europe, but from China and India where cheap labor and better leadership has produced the kinds of strong economies that Muslim countries only dream of.
- Muslim governments have been slow to develop and support modern economic growth and to provide crucial public goods, social infrastructure, policies and practices conducive to business growth, and a stable legal and economic environment. Government intervention in the economy, in terms of a state socialist control tended to hamper economic growth, and was significantly more prevalent in Muslim countries than in non-Muslim countries outside of Europe. Muslim regimes have tended to ignore or oppose the expansion of the private sector both because of conflicts with state socialist policies, and because they fear a loss of their own power. Public regulation has a

bad reputation. It is either unnecessary, or vastly overdone by a pushy bureaucracy; or driven down into unnecessary levels of detail; or poorly administered; or riddled by corruption.

- Too much of the capital assets of the country are under the control of the governments, and there is a serious underdevelopment of capital investment, capital markets, a productive banking system, and savings. Over long periods, enormous value in assets have been locked up in *wakfs*, or charitable endowments, which support valued services but have constrained the wealth available within the economy for new or innovative or high payoff investments.

- In most Muslim countries, the banking system was dominated by the political meddling of the regime, and they were "extraordinarily inefficient" and misallocated available funds away from the most productive uses. The desire in some countries to introduce Islamic banking (no interest) has had little impact on the gross inefficiency of the whole banking system.

- In general, economic development in Muslim countries is strongest in East Asia and the Pacific, less productive in the Middle East, and worst in African countries. Of the three Islamic economies, two are horrible—Afghanistan and Sudan—and the third, Iran is more solid but being hurt by politically mandated interventions.

- The low level of economic achievement is one of the key factors creating huge and ominous public opposition. The others are injustice, and a lack of social services. Part of the outrage about injustice is the "vicious circle of corruption" that fills the whole Muslim world. It is difficult to see how any country could develop a morally superior society defined by religious principles when the public, the government, the military and the mosques are riddled with corruption, and the corrupt know exactly what they are doing.

- Muslim countries waste human capital through neglect of the true potentials of women in both society and the economy, and the congenital inability to provide value-making jobs for the young, especially college graduates. What has seldom occurred in Muslim societies is the emergence of broadly based research and technology organizations with staffs of sophisticated talents creating high value products and services. Nowhere in the Muslim world are there first rate research universities or private laboratories to develop a cadre of engineers, scientists, technicians and managers capable of producing high value/high quality products and manufacturing organizations. Nor are there world class manufacturing plants, information technology firms, sophisticated chemical producers or superior transportation facilities found elsewhere.

These reports make it more clear what is needed in Muslim countries: first and foremost, the expansion of the economy making greater use of an influx of foreign investment. This must lead to development of more and sturdier industrial and commercial enterprises, based on a higher use of modern technology. There must be a greater tolerance for dissident Muslims and non-Muslim people and ideas. Muslim leaders seem not to recognize that economic development is competitive between countries, and Muslim countries are losing.

State Owned Enterprises (SOE)

After WW II, State Owned Enterprises (SOE) were seen in a large number of countries as a middle ground between a standard government ministry or bureau and a true private sector organization. The key is that the SOE is supposedly designed so that it could function like an independent private organization in the economy, but would still be under the policy direction of the government so that each would implement some defined public purpose. Socialist theory argued that somehow, government officials would always act correctly and that public decisions about the use of national resources would always be "right", in contrast to the greedy and self serving private sector. Government ownership could vary from total government control, to government as majority stockholder in SOEs that had been given corporate structure, down to sufficient minority ownership to give the government dominating influence. In almost all cases, the government's interests were exercised by some ministry exerting detailed control of SOE activity. Ministers usually appoint members of SOE boards of directors, approve SOE business strategies, approve business lines and markets, and control finances. Funding plans require approval, especially where the government is the principal source of funds, and the guarantor of SOE deficits.**(4)**

The relationships between a government and its SOEs have almost never been strictly business-like. Instead, they become complex webs of political and economic tactics and strategies which define who really hold ultimate economic power and profits most financially. SOEs gain a lot of political power for themselves and can often end up in competition with their supervising ministries. While SOEs are supposed to generate profits which are added to the government's revenues, in fact, there is a broad world-wide history of SOEs that proved to be so inefficient and ineffective that they have operated at congenital deficits, draining funds from other government programs. In most developing countries, the banking system has also been primarily SOEs, and they have been used by the government to control the whole national banking system, as a means to grant further advantages to SOEs including subsidizing banking loans, preference in lending over private companies, government loan guarantees, and overdraft privileges.

According to Waterbury, "the empirical record shows that managers of public enterprises doctor their books, hoard goods, evade taxes, hide profits, and collude with other enterprises to defraud the government. So many enterprises ran forever as loss makers that the cost of propping them up contributed greatly to the fiscal troubles of their governments, and their failure meant that often decades of real potential economic development were wasted in the fruitless task of attempting to make SOE work."**(5)**

These experiences were shared in the Muslim world. At some point, it became clear that SOEs were mostly weak or even failed institutions and that government development of economies was seldom successful. If the private sector was weak, the real answer would have been to pursue government policies that strengthened them in every possible way rather than substituting the government for the natural roles of the private sector. So now, policies of state ownership and control are gradually fading, governments have shifted in the direction of strengthening their national private sectors, import substitution has been abandoned and export stimulation has replaced it. Even in the agriculture sector, governments are trying to reduce public subsidy and encourage production for export. The sectors of the economy that have most frequently been SOEs are:

- Power generation, telephone/telegraph
- Railroads, ports, highways, urban transport, auto/truck production, railroad rolling stock, airlines, shipping.
- Radio, TV, media and book publishing
- Agriculture, irrigation, fertilizers, food and beverage processing, agricultural credit, crop purchasing,
- Construction, heavy engineering, machine tools, electronics industrial credit, small business credit
- Defense related industries
- Specific industry sectors of local importance such as textiles, iron and steel, aluminum, copper, petroleum and petroleum products, petrochemicals, electronics.
- Consumer durables and nondurables, retail and whole trade, hotels, tourism, food and beverages.
- Foreign trade, banking and insurance.

One of the characteristics of the SOE world is that it is often monopolistic or oligopolistic by government design. Governments want more control by putting "their" industries in a dominant position. The public/SOE payroll may be from 25 to 55 percent of the national workforce. For example, public enterprise outlays as a proportion of GDP are 6-10 percent in the United States, France, U.K. and Sweden; about 20 percent in Latin American countries; 34 to 35 percent in Peru, Mexico, and Venezuela; 24 percent in India; 49 percent in Turkey, and 61 percent in Egypt.

The Record of State Owned Enterprises

In relatively poor developing countries with weak private sectors, import substitution was seen as a means to build up the domestic economy and reduce the flow of money out of the country at the same time. Most governments were committed to socialist policies and populist motives for government programs centering around the alleviation of massive poverty. This clearly led to the need for economic expansion to generate more national wealth and absorb chronic unemployment, and for expansion of the public sector to provide a social safety net. Governments felt that they had to step in and force the pace of economic expansion since the private sector could not develop fast enough, nor could private sector motivations solve critical public problems. In most cases, governments were interventionist on a broad front and made heavy commitments to the use of government owned and controlled State Owned Enterprises (SOE) and a broad range of socialist laws and policies assuring a firm government grip on the economy.

This in turn meant that, in many instances, strengthening the public sector has been accompanied by the need to downplay and constrain the private sector—i.e. to "protect the public from private greed", or to fill gaps in the economy that the private sector could not or would not undertake. Such socialist policy commitments led to mandated multiyear planning, heavy regulation of all economic activity, administered prices, control or modulation of normal market forces, subsidization, cross subsidization, partial or even total control of banking and lending, heavy government oversight of enterprise performance, and the "politics" of state control.

But the track record is one of disappointment in the performance of SOEs—chronic losses, inability to avoid import reliance, the high cost of sheltering both industries and labor, and a growing realization of the failure to capitalize on export development potentials. But governments found it hard to act on this reality. In order to keep SOEs afloat, governments subsidized their energy costs (through control of energy sector SOEs), forced the provision of supplies and materials at low transfer costs, gave SOEs preference and preferential rates in the borrowing of money, kept labor rates down, and in every way concealed the true costs of SOE shortcomings from the public.

Political corruption drained SOEs of resources to fund perverse political actions, make payoffs to politicans, and syphen off funds for personal accounts. Challenges to failing policies has led to heavy defensiveness, or at best modest reforms instead of fundamental change. Often, the continuation of this policy defensiveness could be sustained only by becoming excessively reliant on external lending, which simply ran up external debt and led to spasms of "structural adjustment" which usually involved retenchments of popular public programs and a lot of political hand wringing. The current problems of European nations such as Greece, Spain, Ireland and Portugal are cases in point. Regimes simply could not bring themselves to admit that the policies that they had created and stoutly defended were dead wrong.

Excessive use of SOEs creates an elite class of public managers and very rich or powerful interests within these SOEs which tend to be very self perpetuating and reactionary. They all display the symptoms of emergence of a public sector managerial elite and dependent, privileged labor organizations which defend their entrenched positions against change. There is a lot of evidence that these elites are too short sighted, inflexible, and self-serving, and too inclined to let the "politics" of the economy override economic reality.

The centrist use of state enterprises requires heavy commitments for enforcement of the government's policies. This cost of enforcement is monetary and fiscal and societal. The cost of such enforcement will always be exorbitant, and it substitutes itself for the more normal mechanisms of market discipline and self enforcement. SOES proved highly vulnerable to corruption and pathological government policies and practices. The rate of unemployment in Muslim countries under this SOE system is stagnant at about 10% of the workforce, which is the highest of any economic region in the world. The youth unemployment rate is always just short of crisis, and an estimated one out of four youths in the labor market is unemployed. Even more critical, the employment-to-population ratio in 2010 was at just over 45%, meaning that fewer than one out of two persons of working age are actually working. The greatest cause for this failure is the fact that only about one out of every five women in the region works, a record which is twice as bad as the global average. These same problems extend to the Muslim countries in North Africa as well.

In the Global Competitiveness Index published by the World Economic Forum in 2011, ranking 139 countries, Muslim countries ranked as follows: Saudi Arabia, 21st; United Arab Emirates, 25th; Tunisia, 32nd; Oman, 34th; Kuwait, 35th; Bahrain, 37th; Indonesia, 44th; Turkey, 61st; Jordan, 65th; Iran, 69th; Morocco, 75th; Egypt, 81st; Algeria, 86th; Lebanon, 92nd; Libya, 100th; Pakistan, 123rd. In effect, there is a group of countries that are fairly competitive, and another group that are seriously bad.

In the Economic Integrity Report published by the Center for International Policy in Washington in 2012, Muslim countries were ranked as follows (maximum = 100 points):

Indonesia: 81
Bangladesh: 70
Turkey: 68
U.A.E.: 68
Jordan: 57
Morocco: 56
Kuwait: 55
Egypt: 54
Algeria: 54
Lebanon: 53
Iraq: 53
Tunisia: 45
Qatar: 42
Yemen: 33
Syria: 29

Note that any score less than 70 is considered "weak", while any under 57 is considered "very weak". By comparison, the U. S. is ranked at 85, Italy at 78, India at 70, and China at 64.

Transport

Since ancient times, the primary mode of transport has been by water, and primarily for the movement of goods in foreign trade, so most Muslim countries have been part of the "global economy" long before the contemporary version of that concept. Waterways were far less useful for internal country movement because of their limited access in many areas. The second wave of transport became the railroads, and they too were designed for limited range because of their expense, and they were initially intended to serve a few critical places: mines and factories, ports, key cities, and key military locations.

As economies matured and grew more sophisticated, most countries tried to keep up by expanding their transport capabilities, and the primary demand now became to develop networks of roads across the country to be utilized by trucks and cars. But poor countries often lacked the national wealth to make this road network adequate, and the road network once again concentrated on a few of the most vital corridors of freight movement, especially to ports providing import and export access. In most cases, the development of transport systems was beyond the capabilities of weak private sectors, and was generally seen as the responsibility of governments, and, in the name of state socialism, hundreds of State Owned Enterprises (SOE) were created in both the MENA and in the Muslim countries of the Far East to build and operate transport facilities such as railroads, airports and airlines, shipping ports and cargo ships, roadways and trucking enterprises, and bus companies. But in a pattern common around the world, a large number of these SOEs proved highly inefficient and operated at a deficit which had to be made up by diverting government budget funds from other programs.

Few Muslim countries have solved the problem of extending adequate transportation to rural areas. The main problem is the inability to extend the road system into less populous locations. What roads exist tend to be very bad, and often impassable in rainy periods, and this hurts movement not only of people but more importantly the movement of goods, especially agricultural products, especially those that are intended for export. But still, roads carry more than 90 percent of both passenger and freight in almost every Muslim country. Half of the countries in Africa are land locked, and the cost of transport might represent 75 to 80 percent of the value of exports. Rail density in Africa and most of the Middle East is among the lowest in the world, and the safety of travel on regional air carriers is suspect; 25 percent of air accidents worldwide occur in Africa. Road travel ranges from bad to murderous, few countries can be said to pay due attention to maintenance and repair. For example, Iran, with just 11 million vehicles of all kinds ranks # 1 in the world in road accidents, with more than 38,000 per year by 2010 and 2011. By comparison, the total number of accidents in the United States in 2011 was just over 32,000. As Muslim countries have become more urbanized, most accidents now occur in these larger cities which have totally failed to keep up with the growing demand. Traffic in most cities is gridlocked most of the time, and huge amounts of money, time and gasoline are wasted while urban atmospheres become increasingly deadly. Many cities have turned to the construction of subway systems to help solve this problem. Turkey has five cities with subway systems and Iran is aiming for six. In addition, Turkey is constructing a new, very modern high speed rail system between Istanbul and Ankara, and plans to extend service from Ankara to Konya, but the government is heavily criticized for making huge investments in these lines when other parts of the national transport system are in very bad shape.

Turkey sees the development of the energy and transport sectors of the economy as vital keys to future economic growth. The main priorities for transport include the need for improvement of railway infrastructure, the upgrading of maritime infrastructure, and the general effectiveness of management and increasing actual results from the money spent. Specific planning targets include:

1. The need to build or upgrade a comprehensive and environmentally friendly transport system serving all of Turkey in a more balanced way.
2. Make Turkey a key element of regional transportation of all kinds through 16 large scale logistics centers linked to ports and rail services and offering free trade zones.
3. The country's five main ports are all state owned; the railroads are state owned and operated; the highway system is state built and controlled; basic telephone systems are state owned. In recent times, there appears to be a new willingness to consider privatizing some of these transportation assets.

Sudan may have the worst road system in the world. It is extremely limited, really serving only a few main corridors. Little of it is paved, all is neglected, and much is impassable when it rains—which is often. The Arab Muslim government deliberately neglected South Sudan and Darfur, and this neglect, along with many other outrages contributed to the insurrection in the south. Port Sudan is a major deep water port on the Red Sea and it is far more important for transportation purposes than the Nile River. It includes a major pipeline for the transport of petroleum to the capital in Khartoum and beyond. The rail system is an old out of date decaying single track service which has operated primarily in the Arab north and east, and it is operated by the state owned Sudan Railways Corporation which is highly inefficient. The air service monopoly on domestic service is provided by Sudan Airways Company, which however is really another state owned enterprise, but it loses money, lacks enough skilled staff, and has a hard time coming up with the funds to buy spare parts or guarantee meeting maintenance schedules. International air service is mostly by foreign carriers.

Iran has a fairly good road system connecting all cities and most larger towns, and two thirds of the roads are paved. Transport is inexpensive because of the government's major subsidization of the price of gasoline, but there are negative consequences. Drivers are wasteful of gasoline, the costs of the subsidies are huge, and there are corrupt ways in which the cheap gas is sold illegally in neighboring countries. And yet, travel on these roads remains highly unsafe, creating one of the highest accident rates in the world. Road deaths have reached a level exceeding 38,000 per year, and they account for a majority of deaths in Iran.

There are almost 7,000 miles of rail track, with good connections between ports and urban and industrial areas, and service is well connected with other systems in the area. All large cities have mass transit systems and there are bus connections throughout the country by private bus service. The government has ambitious plans to add to the current Metro subway system in Tehran, and to construct systems in six other cities.

One notable fact is that the Kharg oil terminal handles about 98 percent of Iran's crude oil exports, and Bandar Abbas in southern Iran handles more than 90 percent of the country's container throughput, which means that Iran's export capability is highly vulnerable to potential attack in the event of either embargoing or military action.

By contrast, Morocco has a transport sector which is both efficient and pleasant. The road system is fairly well developed if somewhat frantic. Trains are comfortable, inexpensive and efficient and represent the management of a really successful government enterprise. Local bus systems and shared taxi services are popular and well run and are designed to connect with intercity trains. Intercity buses are cheap and well liked. Many were formerly state enterprises but have now been privatized to their advantage. Air flight connections to Morocco are very good.

The Economic Impact of Sharia Law

This issue is half government and half economic—plus a real question of how the law relates to each national culture. Despite the often exaggerated fears expressed in the West, there is little to fear or reject in Sharia law. Its roots are in the holy messages, which share a common heritage with Christian and Hebrew humanist concepts and cultural context. Sharia law as it has evolved is always seen as a strong, valuable element of any Muslim national legal system. There are persistent criticisms of a few elements of Sharia law, but no legal system in any country is free from criticism.

To the lead question "Would the adoption in some form of Sharia law be a bad thing for governments?" the answer is clearly no unless it is applied in some vicious and corrupt manner.

Has Islam created a concept of government and of the law that can satisfy the demands of the modern world? If not, can Islamic thinking really adapt fully enough to produce one, given the rigidities of much of Islamic thinking? Muslim governments have, in the past displayed several major tides:

1. A useful but obsolete history of mercantilist trade, buttressed by adequate but narrow interpretations of Sharia law. There are elements of traditional Islamic economic concepts involving such things as the zakat, which a special tax usually allocated for charitable works; or rules against usury, or from benefitting from money lending or from the incidence of change events such as insurance.
2. A penchant for economic centrism a la Communism, which involves close centrist and prejudiced control of any legal system.
3. A history of failed State Socialism, also highly centrist in character.
4. Strong religious/cultural opposition to secularism and westernization.
5. A history of choosing—or suffering from—centrist dictatorships.

One of the key elements cited by insurgent organizations is the stated need to mandate the use of a "pure" form of Sharia Law. The most fundamentalist attitudes about the Quran view its contents as immutable, of divine origin, and thus not subject to any form of interpretation. And yet, most religious scholars themselves accept that the Quran contains not only matters that are eternal but also matters that change with circumstances. Scholars have classified adherence to these statements as obligatory, recommended, neutral, not acceptable and forbidden. Thus, Quranic principles show a considerable degree of flexibility and pragmatism, and they have been adapted in different countries in many different ways. The fact seems to be that Sharia law is fundamentally sound, and is almost always combined with other elements of law drawn from other sources in ways that are very facilitative of economic development. Sharia law may include elements of ancient custom, the results of reason or common sense, or the consensus of legal interpretation. The distinction between public and private property is often blurred. Private property may be used to engage in commerce, industry and trading, and may involve contracting, the hiring of labor, the extraction of minerals such as iron ore or copper, and other activities as long as they do not endanger the general public interest or do harm to others. Sharia law has, since its earliest days encompassed concepts of intellectual property protection including patents, trademarks and copyrights.

Narcotics Traffic in the Middle East and North Africa

Much of the economy of Afghanistan consists of the narcotics crop and the fine arts of drug smuggling. As much as 25 percent of Afghanistan's heroin production is exported through Central Asia. Drug trafficking is financing terrorist and insurgent groups. There are regular clashes between Iranian counter-narcotics units and drug smugglers, in a murky world of corruption and official protection. In Afghanistan, the Taliban now demand a tax from both farmers and traffikers, on the rationale that "only nonbelievers use drugs" and they deserve to be ruined. It appears that trafficking money is lubricating the trade. The more drugs that are trafficked through Central Asia, the lower the levels of drug related crime. Seizures of opium and heroin by the police have actually fallen from 1997 to 2007. Of an estimated 128 tons of heroin, less than four

percent has been seized in the region. In Afghanistan, the number
is about one percent. Government efforts, aided by outside interests
have not begun to stem the tide.

Much of the drug trade started out as local cottage industries, but
recently, larger and more vicious organizations have stepped in as
international gangs now control distribution. Many of these groups
are Russian or Chechen, and in places like Turkmenistan, the
government itself has taken over the trade. The drug trade helped
to finance a bloody civil war in Tajikistan, but gradually a reformist
government has reduced trafficking to about twenty percent of its
old level. Uzbekistan is said to have a high level alliance between
traffikers and top government officials. Kyrgyzstan however, shows
that popular disgust with corruption can lead to rejection of the
government and a new regime that recognizes that corruption and
trafficking are linked, and both must be cleaned up. Not easy.

Thus, the record of the Middle East is one of trafficking conducted
with the active connivance and support of state institutions,
controlled by senior security officers, government officials, and
parliamentarians, who have effectively nationalized drug transit
through the region. They have brokered lucrative deals with Turkish
and Russian criminal groups and with Afghan suppliers, many of
whom also benefit from close relationships with state structures in
their countries.

Prevention efforts are cynical and mostly for show. Many of the
police and security organizations are corruption pyramids, with
illegal funds widely collected, some of which ascends the pyramid.
Thus, there is a whole complex set of relationships between
governments, organized crime, terrorist organizations, and radical
extremists. UN and EU efforts to mitigate these efforts are pompous
and ineffective. Such things as training for law enforcement officers
or public education programs are laughed at.

Country Economic Conditions

Afghanistan

Afghanistan is land bound, and lacking infrastructure, industry, and trained human capital. 85 percent of its people still depend on agriculture, and much of that is illegal. Interminable conflict has ruined much of the country, sanctions are still in force, and its credit has largely been suspended. The country is a basket case, with little going for it. The whole nature of the Afghan economy is dictated by the catastrophic military and political conflicts of the last 35 years—or 350 years. The economy is an artificial creation: the government functions with two types of budget: an internal operating budget, and a donor "development budget" which is donor provided and administered deliberately outside of government control. The development budget provides 75 percent of public expenditures; in addition, much of the internal budget is actually outside money, so that in total, outsiders provide more than 90 percent of government expenditures.

The economy of Afghanistan has improved a great deal from its depths largely because of major international assistance and money sent home from expatriates, and very strong improvements in agricultural production, after several years of drought. The major concern is that, as U. S. and other country forces withdraw from the country, the levels of this foreign assistance will decline drastically and the Afghan economy will probably collapse. In fact, exports did suffer a significant collapse in 2009/10, and the financial gap then had to be made up by increased donor payments. The withdrawal of foreign presence will include professional governance assistance, and the current perception is that no Afghan government will have the will or the skill to avoid disaster, and there is already increasing concern about the deterioration of the current government. Afghanistan now has the second worst corruption rating among the one hundred and eighty countries surveyed in Transparency International's Corruption Perception Index. There seems to have been some progress. Candidate cabinet ministers must now reveal their economic assets—maybe. New laws govern the production of fuel and minerals and force more transparency—maybe. There has been a tightening up of controls of government income and expenditure transactions—maybe.

An important conference was held in London in January of 2010 in which the Afghan government laid out a major plan for national development. **(6)** The government of Afghanistan and donor and other government participants agreed:

1. To develop a plan for a phased transition to Afghan security leadership, province by province.
2. Targets for significant increases in domestic Afghan army and police forces, up to a total of over 300,000.
3. International forces to support the training of Afghan forces would be significantly increased.
4. Measures would be instituted to tackle corruption, including the establishment of a new Office of High Oversight.
5. Development assistance would be better coordinated and increasingly channeled through official government organizations.
6. A "surge" in civilian assistance and new leadership in international leadership.
7. Support for a Peace and Reintegration Trust Fund to offer alternatives to those who renounce violence, cut links to terrorism, and agree to work within the democratic processes.
8. To support increased regional co-operation to combat terrorism, violent extremism and the drugs trade.

But here again, as so often is so many places, these noble thoughts which represent ideal solutions will probably never really come to fruition.

But at least, the agriculture sector of the economy continues to enjoy a surprising rebound—except that a large part of agricultural "exports" continues to be illegal traffic in heroin. The service sector of the economy continues to grow in double digit figures, including government, banking and transport. Manufacturing however has been sluggish; mining has increased by nearly thirty percent in the last two years. At the same time, the government seems to have rediscovered the ability to collect its own taxes and fees, and it achieved an exceptional increase of more than fifty percent in 2010 over the previous year. But the government has proved very fumbling in its use of funds provided by donors through the development budget, spending less than forty percent of the funds already available. But still, the national financial system has ceased to be a total disaster and is merely now inferior. But the government owes something like $2.3 billion to the World Bank, the International Monetary Fund, Russia, and various other international banking institutions.

With all of these confusing and shifting trends, Afghanistan remains a very poor country, and very torn by intractable internal conflicts, many of ancient origin. The poverty rate is estimated at 36 percent of the population below the official poverty line, but if "near poverty" is included, this number is more than half of the population. There is clearly not enough money anywhere to deal with even critical needs including infrastructure development, housing, education, health care and coping more effectively with corruption and the highly addictive drug trade.

The great dilemma remains that the government can afford either adequate military security, or vital social services, but it cannot afford both. Nor is it clear that the government can defend itself from the Taliban as it attempts to develop its natural resources of oil, natural gas, coal, gold, copper, and other minerals—resources estimated to be worth more than one trillion dollars. Many of these assets could be quickly developed. For example, the government has already signed an agreement with China's Metallurgical Corp. of China to develop its copper resources, and barring militant attacks, this project can be in production is three to five years. Another major prospect is the Hajigak iron ore mine, with companies from India, Turkey and China already interested. Natural gas export which, in the past, had been mainly exported to the Soviet Union, has been largely restored, along with oil production, and a deal with the China National Petroleum Corporation has been signed for new oil exploration.

Egypt

A new Parliament has been seated, with the Muslim Brotherhood (MB) having the leading presence, having won forty-seven percent of the vote in recent elections. The new group has terminated the interim government set up by the military which was considered illegitimate, incompetent and guilty of mismanagement of both political and economic issues. There appear to be two conflicting theories: one seems to be based in centrist political tendencies, old style state socialism, and conservative religious views. The other is more pragmatic, led by business people, those who favor a market based economy, and a whole new generation of citizens who are willing to take a powerful active role in national affairs for the first time. If there is a general public view, it centers about rejection of conservative religion, the urgent need for more health and education programs and funding, and a sense of outrage against greedy business men and corrupt government officials who resist calls for serious reforms. The Freedom and Justice Party, the political arm of the MB, seems to favor option two with emphasis on export promotion (vice previous import substitution); greater control over government budgets and deficits; serious efforts to reduce the hugely excessive and unproductive civil service, an increase in the minimum wage, a more progressive income tax and ceilings on fat cat tax exemptions. There is a soft attitude about Islamic banking and Sharia law; Islamic banking is not threatening, and has never been more than about four percent of total banking, and Sharia law has long been used, mostly for religious matters, family matters such as divorce or inheritance, and for merchant business. Sixty five percent of banking is now private. But where will the needed money come from? Important proposals include the review and renegotiation of oil and gas contracts, cuts in public and industry subsidies, making the voluntary charitable contributions (zakat) compulsory, and taking back some state owned land that was misappropriated and could be resold at far higher prices. One deep pocket is seen as the military. There is little guts to tackle their budget directly, but an interesting idea is to prune away the military's irrelevant holdings: production of consumer goods, ownership of condos, resorts and hotels, selling of transport services, etc. There is also a lot of hope around the idea of big increases in tourism. The Muslim Brotherhood needs to separate itself from the ultra-conservative Salafi religious fringe. The two main economic objectives appear to be economic stability and support for business interests; and doing something real for the poor at the bottom of the scale. Another priority is to provide more jobs at a level suitable for recent school graduates. But again, the real solution lies in economic expansion. In fact, the reduction of poverty between 2005 and today is above 12 percent.

Indonesia

Indonesia is the one of the most populous countries in the world, with more than 250 million people, a huge workforce approaching 120 million and perhaps the most extraordinarily varied and complicated economic, ethnic, racial, religious and linguistic mix of citizens of any country in the world. For long periods of its history, it has been a very poor nation, not really able to keep up with the growth of its own population, much less the demands for economic and social improvement. It also suffered from rule by its two long term dictators, (Sukarno, 1945-1965, and Suharto, 1966-1998) and a state socialist economic system which, as in an almost universal pattern in the developing world, was seriously flawed and ineffective. And as with so many other countries in the Muslim world, the gradual abandonment of failed state socialist economic policies and the movement toward a more market driven economy has totally turned the economy around. Reforms included major changes in the financial system to emphasize capital market development and much needed cleanup of the tax and customs systems. Indonesia still suffers from high poverty, totally inadequate public infrastructure, overregulation, and the vestiges of its former special interest politics, linked with persistent corruption. But during the recent financial crisis, Indonesia did better than most of its neighbors and continued to attract solid levels of foreign investment.

If this pattern has a real threat, it is in the arena of the country's infrastructure, much of which remains old, crumbling, obsolete and totally overwhelmed. The capital of Jakarta is a transportation nightmare; a real mess at all times, and a massive gridlock during its tropical downpours. The national road network and the rail system are both shoddy and seriously inadequate. Indonesia may be a good place to invest, but it is not yet a good place to travel, and most cities are overcrowded, dirty, noisy and scarcely livable.

Iran

The Iranian economy has been very weak, but has been improving. Inflation and unemployment are serious. The eight year war with Iraq was a disaster, with an estimated 300,000 killed and 500,000 injured. Yet despite this, the population has increased from about 23 million in 1960 to more than 65 million now, with about 34 percent of the population under the age of fourteen.

The economy relies too much on oil, and the whole energy sector is in fact an integral part of the government, controlled by the National Iranian Oil Company, the National Iranian Gas Company, and the National Petrochemical Company. Almost all power generation and distribution, including nuclear power is under direct government control. Seventy percent of industry is controlled by the State or by a religious foundation. The banking sector is dominated by ten state owned banks. Even tourism is controlled: most of the tourist visits are to religious sites run by religious associations, which also own the hotels where tourists stay. Foreign direct investment is weak except perhaps from Russia and China, and Western sanctions have had significant impact.

The government has been trying to beef up the weak areas, but the economy still can't meet the job demands of new workers and the greater number of women in the workforce. Exceptional portions of the economy are in the hands of the military Revolutionary Guard, and in unique religious foundations, said to make up more than thirty percent of national government spending. Feeble attempts have been made to shift away from centrist control of the economy, either by the government, the military/intelligence community, or these religious foundations. There are constant promises to upgrade the education system to make it more relevant to the real demands of the economy.

Public subsidies have been an expensive way to buy public support or at least tolerance of the regime. Iranian authorities have reached broad internal consensus even as political differences sharpen around the urgent need to advance forms of reforms necessary to meet economic and social challenges. Iran is perhaps a good example of a bureaucracy trying to do their jobs while the politicians quarrel. The economy is underpowered and suffers from lack of employment opportunities, high and rising inflation, and structural impediments to private sector development. A large SOE sector dominates manufacturing (60 percent of output), and public banks still dominate, while some privatization efforts are gaining. The Constitution defined huge segments of the economy that had to be state owned, but in 2006 a new policy has permitted privatization up to eighty percent of authorized stocks. This includes the downstream oil sector, utilities, much of the financial sector, and large industrial and commercial enterprises not critical to State control. Public subsidies are not only expensive but fail to target the real poor; a lot of money destined for the poor is the victim of corruption or misappropriation of funds. Extensive subsidies, including energy subsidies and credit subsidies are excessively large and skewed toward the rich. Subsidies for bread and medicine are highly untargeted, and the richest members of the population get far more of the gasoline subsidy than the poorest. **(8)** Housing is particularly bad, with one million units needed, especially for low income families. Economic growth is running at about five to seven percent per year. Non-oil exports are rising, and public debt is reasonable by regional standards, but unemployment is about eleven and a half percent over all, and more than 20 percent for youths. The government budget is about 8.6 percent of GDP. **(9)**

Jordan

Jordan weathered a series of crises in the Middle East up through the nineties, and when King Abdullah ascended to the throne in 1999, he initiated a vigorous program to expand the economy, lure back expatriates, enhance foreign direct investment, expand tourism, and make Amman a center for regional banking and investment management. He has also moved very far in the privatization of state owned enterprises, which, as in most other Muslim countries, had proved to be a drag on the economy. During Abdullah's regime, the economy has sparkled, and there is general feeling of a reasonable, stable government at work. He has eliminated most of the populist but unproductive fuel and agricultural subsidies, and by agreement with the U. S., he has phased out tariffs culminating in the almost complete elimination of duties by 2010.

The system of a monarchy linked with a two tier parliament (the upper level Senate is appointed) along with a Prime Minister as head of government and a Council of Ministers seems to work well. There are twelve local states headed by Governors, and these governments have a good deal of real power. Political parties were authorized in 1992, and Islamists have been very active in the country, with varying results. Conflicts with the regime caused them to boycott the elections of 1997, but they did very well in the elections of 2003, lost a lot of ground in the elections of 2007, and seem to be looking forward to the elections of 2012. Jordan, along with every other country in the region, still suffers from too many political subsidies, an excess of funding for the military establishment, and widespread corruption.

During most of its history, Jordan had been an agriculture based country; but in a sense, this kept it poor because lack of good land and the lack of consistent rainfall meant that much of agriculture was of high cost and low value added. The government has spent a lot of effort trying to upgrade its agricultural sector, but in truth, it is now less than 2.5 percent of GDP, and it no longer employs many people: only about four percent of the total workforce. This is not a bad outcome. It has freed many people in marginal agricultural occupations to come to the cities and work in higher paying industry and services. Potash and phosphates are old time sources of export and income, and Jordan continues to rank as the third largest producer of phosphates in the world.

In recent years, construction has been growing as a part of the economy, and now manufacturing and industry are about 26 percent of the economy. Perhaps the greatest impediment to the development of the Jordanian economy continues to be a shortage of energy production. The government has ambitions to increase output from both nuclear and renewable sources, but oil remains the principal fuel source and most of it must be imported, primarily from Saudi Arabia which has replaced Iraq as principal supplier. Some natural gas is now coming to Jordan through the new Arab Gas Pipeline from Egypt, under the Gulf to Al Aqaba and then to Jordan. The transport sector looks healthy as well, and Jordan is a major transit point for goods flowing in and out of Iraq these days.

But the fact is that the service sector has emerged as the heart of the Jordanian economy, and it is now 70 percent of the GDP and employs nearly 75 percent of the workforce. Banking and insurance are sophisticated and profitable. Real estate investment had a real splurge during the seventies and eighties, driven heavily by investments by expatriates, and while it has cooled off somewhat since, it is still vigorous, in part because of the stable economy and politics of the country. Money continues to flow in from other places in the Middle East, especially from Saudi Arabia, and also from Europe and the U. S.

Major problems other than the energy shortage are concerns over the cost and influence of the military establishment, the inability to control the government's budgets, and an excessive reliance on foreign financing. Another confusing element is the fact that there are now more than one million seven hundred thousand registered Palestinian and other nationality refugees living in the country and they are expensive to maintain. It is not clear what will be done about their long term fate.

Libya

Huge upheavals have left the country in uncertainty; a new transitional National Council is in charge, and this is enough to allow foreign aid to be committed, and get the release of other funds that had been blocked. People are now learning how to cope with the incompetent, bumbling and corrupt consequences of Gaddafi rule. Oil revenues must start to flow immediately. The international community is ready and willing to provide critical help. The GDP now is about $90.6 billion, and the rate of economic growth a respectable 4.2 percent. But the recent attacks on the U. S. Embassy in Benghazi and the death of the American ambassador there have forced the recognition of the ominous presence of vicious terrorist elements in the country.

Morocco

Morocco has a lot going for it these days. It has the fifth largest economy in Africa, it is ranked as the second most competitive economy in N. Africa (after Tunisia), and the Economist Intelligence Unit ranks it at the top of its Quality of Life Index. **(10)** Much has been done not only to grow the economy but to diversify it, and the service sector, including off shoring, now accounts for more than half of GDP, with industry accounting for another twenty-five percent. In addition to traditional manufacturing, mining, phosphate production and construction, there has been a lot of growth of the telecommunications and textile sectors. Agriculture has been rehabilitated, but it is still too dependent on inadequate rainfall, and it still is of relative low value added. But it cannot be ignored since it still employs forty to forty-five percent of the national workforce. Much of the economy is pointed at exports and business relationships with other countries, and along with Egypt, it is a major balanced economy not heavily dependent on oil. But then, the high cost of importing fuels, along with persistent droughts (1995, 1997, 2000, 2007) are perhaps the two most important deterrents for the economic development program. Unemployment remains high at around ten percent, and like most

Muslim countries it cannot find employment for all of the young people coming out of school.

Pakistan

The country suffers from income inequality, crushing poverty, high illiteracy, rural underdevelopment, underlying serious tensions and conflicts within the country, and a growing estrangement from US aid and support. Possession of nuclear weapons by a shaky regime with Taliban supporters in the military and the ISI is highly disturbing. Pakistan, like many other Muslim countries is heavily dependent on outside countries, even when the government does not acknowledge it. In the competition for scarce funds in recent years, economic development has always won against the development of social services, and the military has demanded an inordinate share of the national budget. The government seems to get weaker and the fundamentalists seem to get stronger.

Saudi Arabia

The petroleum sector accounts for about 55 percent of GDP, 45 percent of fiscal income, and 90 percent of all export earnings. Of a workforce of just under seven million, five and a half million are foreign workers, so the remittances from these workers prop up other countries.

Business Monitor International reports that robust growth will be seen in the Saudi Arabian economy in at least the next two years, and the country will continue to be a strong magnet for foreign direct investment (FDI). Targets for investment include public infrastructure, the energy sector, natural gas development, much of which will be through government contracting, and improvements in health care and education.

Saudi Arabia strangely benefits from some of the very conflicts it helps to instigate because it is getting money that might have been invested elsewhere but for the widespread conflicts. If sanctions constrain Iran oil shipments, Saudi Arabia is the only country with excess capacity, and they will make up the shortage. The country has seen big up-surges of economic development in the late seventies, a big decline in the eighties, another in the late nineties, and now a substantial surge again. Plans now must include huge sums ($46 billion) to expand and modernize oil industry production and refining capacity. Enhanced oil revenues are being immediately fed into the economy through a big new housing program, and increases in pay for government workers—most of whom work for the government in some fashion.

The Saudi government has been one of the most determined in the region to develop coherent economic development plans and then work to bring them about. Five Year Plan #1 for the 1970s sought mainly to catch up with population growth, and to deal with old neglects. Plan #2 in the 80's shifted substantially to major emphasis on building public infrastructure: roads, ports, airports, power generation and distribution. Plan #3 for the years 1980-85 shifted some money to education, health care, social services. Plan #4 for years 1985-90 for the first time really opened up the economy to private interests. Some of the state owned enterprises were sold off, and new policy was initiated to encourage foreign direct investment. Plan #5 for 1990-95 initiated defense modernization, and managerial upgrading, and means for developing more effective social services. It also moved to allow more latitude for local governments to pursue regional development, and it sought to reduce the number of foreign workers in favor of employment for nationals. Plan #6 for 1996-2000 included some difficult choices for cutting government costs, and furthered the policy of greater economic diversification. Plan #7 for 2000-05 is leading a policy of pushing toward stronger economic growth results.

Sudan

Sudan's history, for the last fifty-five years since independence (1956) has been heavy favoritism for the Arab north, and oppression of the Christian and Animists in the south, and Darfur in the west. This favoritism, neglect, and actual tyranny against these peoples produced heavy conflict and serious fighting for thirty years. As a result, public infrastructure, along with all other social services, was deliberately neglected and is in desperate shape. The last few years have seen the greater development of oil resources, but the major production areas are right at the border between the north and the south. The economy grew by 4.5 percent in 2009 and by 5 percent in 2010, and is projected for over 5 percent again in 2011 and 2012. This led to the ability of the government to increase public spending. More of government spending is financed by borrowing, and more comes from increased oil revenues. Private sector development has languished because of the world financial crisis and the constant conflict in the country.

The government has been relieved of a substantial responsibility for the now departed south (new South Sudan), but they had never spent much there anyway. In the north, the government continues to make very large subsidy payments for fuel and electricity. Inflation is very high: 11 percent in 2010 and up to 13.8 percent in 2011. The national road network and electricity generation have been upgraded in recent years. Yet, Sudan remains one of the world's least developed and most indebted countries. Poverty increased dramatically in the period 1990 to date. It is as high as 90 percent in most of the country, including all but portions of the capital of Khartoum. And there is growing concern that the new wealth coming from oil production increases is not working its way down to the poor, and too much of the new money has gone into pursuing the wars in the south and in Darfur; in paying off huge foreign debts; and in losses to corruption. Bottlenecks in infrastructure, lack of social services, corruption, incompetence, and a horrible human rights record seriously inhibit capital investment.

Sudan has shifted its friendships. It deals less with the West and more with developing countries who don't care much about human affairs. The oil industry is a big target for these countries, especially China, Malaysia and India all of which have made heavy investments. The Arab government in the north has finally had to make a deal with the new South Sudan to split oil revenues and jointly protect the oil fields. Income distribution problems are rampant in all parts of Sudan and South Sudan. Loss of oil revenues when the South split off have severely tightened Sudan's fiscal situation and it has had to reschedule its large debt to China. It has also stepped up its gold exports to generate cash.

The U. S. and others have offered some debt forgiveness if Sudan will guarantee an end of fighting with S. Sudan, but the real problem in S. Sudan right now is vicious internal fighting between various clans and tribes, which the Arab north does not control.

"According to "Global Integrity 2011", **(11)** the Sudanese government continues to be absolutely riddled with corruption. Any kind of inspection carried out by authorities will be in an arbitrary and uneven fashion and may involve bribery. Many public services that require licenses, seals, stamps, or authorizations are reportedly up for sale at "negotiated" prices. Billions of dollars in funds were embezzled during the south Sudanese government's food reserve program in 2008. According to an article in Sudan Tribune, many contractors allegedly forged false claims for delivering over 10 million bags of maize and dura in all ten Southern Sudanese states, in what was called "the most costly corrupt practice the region had ever witnessed." Both northern and southern Sudan are notorious for siphoning money off the system through "phantom" projects. The World Bank finally refused to fund road projects because the level of corruption was so severe. Those mechanisms designed to protect against fraud are themselves corrupt. There are in fact, legal barriers against outside access to government information of any kind.

Syria

Syria under its previous president Hafiz al-Assad was a state socialist nightmare. To quote the Middle East Quarterly **(12)** "Its economy is centrally planned, rigid, backward, impoverished and dilapidated." An all powerful central planning bureaucracy fixes prices and owns the bulk of industry in the country. As with the Soviet Union, Syria has a Central Plan with Five Year Plans that mandate most of the critical elements of the economy. The central government controls resources, operates large governmental monopolies, serves as the main employer (40 percent of the workforce), controls all of the imports and exports of the country, owns all banks and insurance companies, regulates every financial and most commercial transactions, owns all big industry and much of small industry, controls ordinary wholesale and retail trade, and controls agricultural markets. Nationalized manufacturing continues to be mismanaged and money-losing with gross over-employment and featherbedding. Repeated assurances that the government will undertake reforms always prove to be hollow rhetoric.

Economic development was not the only failure of the regime. An example is the fact that babies were seldom born in any health facility, and few women had any medical care during pregnancy or birth. By any kind of comparison, Syria has had seriously deficient heath care, education and other social services for the whole thirty year tenure of Hafiz al-Assad and of his son Bashar al-Assad who succeeded him in 2000. The government control of prices has not prevented severe shortages of food when local production is hard hit by drought. Education has been limited, and even today most women over fifty are illiterate.

When Bashar al-Hassad succeeded his father, he recognized that the economy was in big trouble, and a great part of that trouble stemmed from the failed State Socialist structure patterned after the Soviets. His father never got it, but Bashar did, and set out to draw back from this failed pattern toward a more market based economy. To begin with, he addressed the all crucial agricultural sector of the economy which has eternally suffered from droughts and lack of water. Huge irrigation projects were undertaken in the areas of highest reliance on annual rainfall. This was accompanied by massive investments in public infrastructure in rural areas, input subsidies, and favorable price supports. The result has been substantial: Syria is now largely food self sufficient and is a net exporter of cotton, fruits and vegetables. But many crops such as wheat, barley, sugar beets are still classified as "strategic" and thus under government production and price controls which, as in dozens of other countries, heavily subsidize farmers to the disadvantage of urban consumers.

Syria is a small producer of oil, but the revenue from its sale is vital to the economy, accounting for more than 25 percent of government revenues. Despite this importance, oil production declined because of oil field neglect under Hafiz al-Hassad so Bashar has had to initiate major upgrades that are expected to develop new fields and achieve higher production. State control however, remains substantial. The state owned Syrian Petroleum Company directly controls about half of the national oil production, and is a fifty percent owner in any deals with foreign companies in the petroleum industry.

Similarly, electrical power generation and transmission was neglected, and the current government is trying to play catch-up, with major expansions of generating capacity, but at very high costs. The transmission system is in particularly bad shape with transmission losses estimated at more than twenty-five percent because of poor quality of both wiring and transformer stations, and from theft from the system.

The banking sector had been strictly a government preserve, but private banks were made legal in 2001, and have prospered since, largely in retail banking. As of 2010, there were thirteen private banks including two Islamic banks. But the government continues to operate six "specialized" state owned banks: the Central Bank of Syria, the Commercial Bank of Syria, the Agricultural Cooperative Bank, the Industrial Bank, the Popular Credit Bank, and the Real Estate Bank. These banks receive preferential treatment by the government, and they manage a major slice of total lending. As a result, many private banks and individual borrowers must go to other countries, especially Lebanon. The economy entered 2011 in relatively good shape, with oil revenues and tourism at very high levels, but of course, the raging civil war and even the whole process of sanctions by the international community against Syria has hurt its banking systems and the rest of the economy in major ways, with no end in sight. Inflation has increased, the currency has weakened, and the whole economy has sunk into recession. The vital tourist industry has all but disappeared, and hotels have few bookings for the foreseeable future.

Sanctions have caused dollar transactions into and out of the country almost to disappear as well, and many foreign banks are refusing to do business with Syrian companies. Europe, which accounts for ninety-five percent of Syrian oil exports, has now imposed a ban on such imports. Turkey, after some hesitation, is now defining sanctions of its own. Help is expected, and has been promised, by Iran, but little has materialized. The Syrian economy, never very strong, has suffered losses of both wealth and credibility that make take a very long time to recover. The revolution in the country is undoubtedly going to change it forever, in many disastrous ways.

Unfortunately, the agriculture sector suffered a major setback because of a crippling drought which cut crop production, and sent hundreds of thousands of farmers and farm workers into the cities looking for work or relief. Widespread hunger and malnutrition contributed greatly to the sense of outrage against the government and to the masses participating in the national uprisings.

Each year, another 200,000 new workers enter the economy looking for jobs, and even before the insurrections and international sanctions, the Syrian economy could not supply these jobs. The unemployment rate is usually around 18 to 20 percent (officially, 12.6 percent). Sixty-five percent of the population is under the age of thirty-five, and 40 percent are younger than fifteen. Most work is in the services sector of the economy, and about 30 percent are in public sector organizations, and are very poorly paid. Some 700,000 households, three and a half million people, have no stable income. And yet, Syria's economy began 2011 in relatively good condition, with tourism looking strong and higher prices for oil exports. It has taken less than a year and a half for Bashar al-Assad's horrible mistakes to all but ruin the national economy.

There are dozens of international organizations, and most Muslim governments are members, but they seem to have little or no effect on the most serious issues and problems. Syria, for example, which is now under heavy sanctions by the UN, the Arab League, and other countries is nevertheless a fully authorized member of the following organizations:

1. Arab Bank for Economic Development in Africa
2. Arab Fund for Economic and Social Development
3. Arab Common Market
4. Arab League
5. Arab Monetary Fund
6. Council of Arab Economic Unity
7. Customs Cooperation Council
8. Economic and Social Commission for Western Asia
9. Food and Agricultural Organization
10. Group of 24
11. Group of 77
12. International Atomic Energy Agency
13. International Bank for Reconstruction and Development
14. International Civil Aviation Organization
15. International Chamber of Commerce
16. International Development Association
17. Islamic Development Bank
18. International Fund for Agricultural Development
19. International Finance Corporation
20. International Labor Organization
21. International Monetary Fund
22. International Maritime Organization
23. INTERPOL
24. International Olympic Committee
25. International Organization for Standardization
26. International Communication Union
27. International Federation of Red Cross and Red Crescent Societies

28. Non-aligned Movement
29. Organization of Arab Petroleum Exporting Countries
30. Organization of Islamic Cooperation
31. United Nations
32. UN Conference on Trade and Development
33. UN Industrial Development Organization
34. UN Relief and Works Agency for Palestine Refugees in the Near East
35. Universal Postal Union
36. World Federation of Trade Unions
37. World Health Organization
38. World Meteorological Organization
39. World Tourism Organization

None of these 39 organizations seem to have taught Syria anything.

Turkey

After suffering a serious downturn in 2001, the Turkish economy has come back strong and it has grown an average of 6 percent since—one of the highest sustained rates of growth in the world. And there is general recognition that this is largely the result of good monetary and fiscal policy, and significant structural reforms, including a substantial retreat from state socialism. These actions are viewed with favor in the World Bank and the IMF, which have been very supportive. Turkey has pushed administrative streamlining, reduced burdens on the screening of investments, strengthened intellectual property rights, and eliminated double taxation. Many State Owned Enterprises (SOEs) have successfully been sold off, and there are buyers because the private sector knows they can be more effective and profitable than the old SOEs. The government has also slowly relinquished price controls and allowed more market based pricing.

The traditional reliance on agriculture is finally being altered. Now, more than 70 percent of Turks are urban. The economy is approximately 10 percent agricultural, 26 percent industrial, and

64 percent in service sectors. The labor force however, is 30 percent agricultural, 25 percent industrial, and 45 percent services. As is a common pattern in Muslim countries, there is high unemployment generally at 12 percent in excess of 25 percent for youth. Inflation runs about 8 percent.

There are, however, serious concerns in the energy sector. Fossil fuels provide 90 percent of the energy needs and almost all of it has to be imported, which is not only costly, but adds a lot of uncertainty to the stability of the economy. Yet Turkey is increasingly a link between customers at home and in Europe with new sources in the Middle East. The Baku—Tbilisi-Ceyhan pipeline, on line since 2006, is now at full performance. The South Caucasus Pipeline for natural gas runs from Azerbaijan to Turkey, and a branch to Greece was opened in 2009. There are agreements being worked out for another natural gas pipeline running to Austria. In telecommunications, the SOE Turk Telecom was sold off in 2005, but it remains as a monopoly in fixed line service.

Foreign trade is shifting from the European Union (down from 56 percent to 47 percent after 2008), to the Middle East, North Africa, Russia, and increasingly China. This is in large part because efforts to dump the old Socialist economy have succeeded in broadening the industrial and service base, thus attracting more and different customers.

Turkey experienced military coups in 1960, 1971, and 1980. These coups were not only disruptive, but there has been little confidence in the stability of the government generally, and little confidence that the military leaders knew what they were doing. The current regime, elected in 2007, is "semi-Islamic", but has proven to be moderate and competent, and this has bolstered Turkey's reputation and stimulated foreign direct investment (FDI).

In general, the quality of transportation infrastructure is low. Improvements have been made but they are not sufficient and they still fall behind population growth. Highways are critical, but they carry too much of the traffic including 92 percent of freight movements and 95 percent of passenger miles. The Minister of Transport was reappointed for a third term, which is unheard of in the cutthroat political environment. And as usual, there are the pompous, self serving government announcements of noble things to be done, not tied to any reality. As an example, the Ministry announced that an increase of 11 percent for the next year in rail freight was planned in 2011—and then in fact, traffic shrank by four tenths of one percent. The transport plan promises to:

* Build a safe, fast, environmentally friendly and economically sustainable transport system throughout Turkey.
* Balance all modes of transport and prioritize projects that will support this.
* From east to west, from north to south, make Turkey a logistical base with ports, free trade zones, logistics centers and all modes of transport. At least 16 locations will be large-scale logistics centers.
* Transport infrastructure (motorways, airways, seaways) will be controlled with modern information technologies and security.
* Tranport master plans will be integrated into city-level transport master plans.
* Commercial vehicle drivers will be trained to increase their capacity and awareness.

Since the 1980s, the government has been working on the Southeastern Anatolia Project—twenty-two dams along the Euphrates and Tigris Rivers in nine different, largely Kurdish provinces. (13) This is the first segment of an even more massive plan to build ninety dams and sixty power stations on the two rivers. The main objectives are, as usual, power generation and water for irrigation, with the hope that the increase in agricultural production will result in greater exports. The debate over this plan precipitated a lot of national and international objections, mostly about environmental consequences and human displacements. The government issued a number of "social, ecologic, cultural and internationally mandated standards", most of which have not been fulfilled. As a result, governments of Germany, Austria and Switzerland have cancelled their export credit guarantees, and at least one dam construction project has been halted—but not cancelled.

Shipping plays an important role. Five ports, all state owned handle most of the sea freight. They are in Istanbul and Kocaeli on the Sea of Marmara; Izmir on the Aegean, and Mersin and Iskenderun on the Mediterranean. Iskenderun also serves both the domestic and Iraqi pipelines.

Railways, on the other hand, are one of the weakest elements of the economy. There are 6,800 miles of track, but only 1,300 are electrified. Railroads are SOEs and have been neglected and out of date, are badly in need of renovation and repair, and have lost out to trucks for most goods except heavy bulk commodities going long distances.

The telecommunications giant Turk Telekom has been a State Owned Enterprise, and has been undergoing steady expansion, but is has been slow to switch to cellular service, and the government now has a plan to sell of most of it to the private sector, hoping to increase both investment and operating effectiveness. The government still owns about 30 percent of the enterprise.

Rapid urbanization and strong economic growth have led to one of the fastest growing power markets in the world, but too much of it is imported: more than 60 percent now and expected to climb to 75 percent in 10 years. Here again, the system can just barely keep up with the increased demand, and seen from this prospect, the Southeastern Anatolia Project is seen as "the most crucial public project in Turkey."

SOURCES

World Bank Global Economic Prospects, 2013, Middle East and North Africa (MENA) Annex.

World Bank Report "Jobs for Shared Prosperity", 2013

World Bank Report "Urban Challenges in the MENA Region, 2013

U. S. Department of State, Bureau of European and Eurasian Affairs, "Background Note: Turkey", December 9, 2011.

IndexMundi, "Turkey Economic Profile 2012" (Source: CIA World Factbook), 2012.

Al Arabiya News, "Turkey's Economy Roaring but Euro Crisis May End Party", January 1, 2012.

U. S. State Department, Country Background Notes, "Turkey: Economy", May, 2011.

Kuran, Timur, "The Religious Undercurrents of Muslim Economic Grievances", Social Science Research Council Essay Forum, 2011.

Morocco Economy Watch, Series of Economic Notes, 2008 (http://moroccoeconomywatch.blogspot.com)

Beauge, Florence, "Fragile Morocco Weighs Its Economic Priorities", Guardian

Waterbury, John, "Exposed to Innumerable Delusions: Public Enterprise and State Power", Cambridge U. Press, 1993.

Weekly, 11 October 2011.

Education for All, Global Monitoring Report, "Pakistan Declares and Education Emergency", March, 2011.

Sulehria, Farooq, "Pervez Hoodbhoy: Miracles Are Needed to Rescue Pakistan", Economic and Political Weekly, January 29, 2011.

Hardoon, Deborah, and Heinrich, Finn, "Transparency International Bribe Payers Index, 2011, Transparency International, 2011.

Wikipedia, "Economy of Morocco", February, 2012.

http://afghanistanhmg.gov.uk/en/conference, "Afghanistan Economic Update", April, 2010.

Rubin, Alissa J., "World Bank Issues Alert on Afghanistan Economy", New York Times, November 22, 2011.

Sambridge, Andy, "Robust Growth Will Be Seen in Saudi Arabia's Economy", Arabian Business, Aug., 2011.

Towson, Jeffery, "Saudi Arabia's Economy is Experiencing Its Largest Boom in Years", Business Insider, March 23, 2011.

Wikipedia, "Economy of Saudi Arabia", February, 2012.

El Dahshan, Mohamed, "Where Will the Muslim Brotherhood Take Egypt's Economy?", Yale Global Online, Feb. 6, 2012.

Modern Egypt, "Economic Reform in Egypt", 2012.

Reuters, U. S. Edition, "UPDATE 1—Sudan Delays China Debt, Exports 400 Million in Gold", February 18, 2012.

Wikipedia, "Economy of Syria", 2011.

Plaut, Steven, "The Collapsing Syrian Economy", The Middle East Quarterly, September, 1999.

Albawaba Business, "Syria Should Brace for a Financial Collapse", December 29, 2011.

Wachman, Richard, "Syrian Economy Weakens Under Strain of Insurrection and Sanctions", The Guardian, September 28, 2011.

New York University Center For Dialogues, Conference on The Islamic World and the West, "Session II—The Impact of Globalization on the Muslim World", 2006.

Kuhn, Anthony, "Indonesian Economy Booms, Its Infrastructure Groans", NPR, January, 2012.

IndexMundi, "Indonesia Economy Profile 2012", July, 2012.

Manurung, Norvida, and Utami, Widya, "Indonesia's Economy Grows at Fastest Pace Since 1996 as Investment Climbs", Bloomberg Queue, 2012.

Kuhn, Anthony, "Indonesian Economy Booms, Its Infrastructure Groans", NPR, January 4, 2012.

Wikipedia, "Economy of Afghanistan", 14 February, 2012.

United States Library of Congress, "Jordan: The Economy", http://countrystudies.us.jordan, 2012.

U. S. Department of State, "Background Note: Jordan", December, 2011.

Al-Khalidi, Suleiman, "Arab Spring Exposes Jordan's Economic Policy Rifts", Reuters, October 12, 2011.

Wikipedia, "Economy of Jordan", February, 2012.

Embassy of the Kingdom of Morocco, "Economic Report", 2009.

African Development Bank, "Morocco: Transport", January, 2012.

Wikipedia, "Transport in Turkey", March, 2012.

TWARP.com, "Turkey Transport", 2007.

Aldridge, Justin, (http://rindzany.blogspot) "Public Transport and Driving in Morocco", 2012.

Wikipedia, "Transport in Iran", 2008.

Encyclopedia of the Nations, "Turkey: Infrastructure, Power and Communications", 2011.

Wikipedia, "Transport in Sudan", 1991.

Beltrametti, Silvia, "The Legality of Intellectual Property Rights Under Islamic Law", Digital Islam, February, 2011.

IMF: World Economic Outlook: Recovery, Risk and Rebalancing", Washington, D. C., 2010.

Wikipedia, "Economy of Iran", August, 2011.

Michigan State University, GlobalEdge, "Iran Competitive Rankings", 2011.

Encyclopedia of the Nations, "Iran: Country Overview", 2011.

Wikipedia, "Islamic Economic Jurisprudence", August, 2012.

Goldstone, Jack A. "Islam, Development, and the Middle East: A Comment on Timur Kuran's Analysis", George Mason University, June, 2003.

Chaney, Eric, "Islam, Institutions and Economic Development", VOX, September, 2010.

USAID, "Economic Growth in the Muslim World", Issue Paper Number 3, 2003.

Today's Zaman, "TOBB Head Urges Muslim Countries to Increase Economic Cooperation", April, 2012.

Srinivasan, Thirumalai G., "Afghanistan Economic Update, April, 2010.

Middle East Quarterly, "The Collapsing Syrian Economy", 1999.

Christian Science Monitor, May, 2008

CHAPTER III

THE ROLE OF SHARIA LAW
IN THE MUSLIM WORLD:
THE SEARCH FOR JUSTICE

The Muslims of the world are among the world's most emotional people, and one of the things they are most passionate about is their religion. Most Muslims seem moderate and balanced, with wants and needs not very different from other peoples. But perhaps ten percent of the Muslim population is filled with high emotion—part religion, part ethnic and national pride, and part a yearning for power and perhaps "impact". Only two groups of humans in modern times have been driven by such a great collective passion—the fundamentalist Muslims, and the Chinese of the Mao Zedong era.

There are more than two hundred countries in the world today. Fifty-one of them have Muslim populations in the majority, and twenty-one of them have Muslim governments—defined as countries where the population is predominantly Muslim and the national government is officially or de facto Muslim. **(1)** In addition there a number of other countries which have a large but minority Muslim population. **(2)** In all of these countries, the religion of Islam is deeply important and influential at four levels:

1. It guides individuals and families in the conduct of their own lives.
2. It creates a culture which transcends borders and languages and national identities. In most cases, this Muslim culture

is in addition to, and not instead of national or community identity. But for some small but passionate minority Islam is everything.

3. Islam is also the basis for a political program, and for the advocacy of government policies or programs. Islamic politics may deal with the broad general interests of the nation, or it may be more specifically an advocacy for Muslim interests.

4. Islam may also be the basis for aggressive and violent assertions of power, ranging from terrorist acts to full blown insurrections and wars. Most of this aggression goes far beyond the desires of the general Muslim population, who are dragged along in the wake of an aggressive minority.

In Muslim countries, there are several layers. First are the ancient local populations who usually had developed a stable functioning society and economy, with a basis of common laws and settled ways of exerting control. The common basis was not usually a nation but a tribe or clan or village. To an important degree, the culture of Muslim countries like Afghanistan or Morocco or Sudan remains anchored "from the bottom up" in these old tightly retained relationships.

Second came the layer of authoritarian power structures, initially kings or caliphs or sheikhs, and later presidents, prime ministers and dictators. The earlier tribal and village world was (and remains) very diffuse and disaggregated. The world of sultans and presidents is <u>always</u> very centrist and enforced.

The third wave was a wave of Muslim incursion, starting in the seventh century and still in progress. The spread of Islam was through trade, conquest and religious propagation, and once it advanced, it seldom ever retreated, and the cultures of Islam were in conflict with the local cultures.

The fourth wave was at least two tides of colonialism. The first was by the Muslims themselves, in the period from the seventh century on. The next was by the European nations, beginning in the early fourteenth century.

Fifth is a wave that, in the Muslim world, has not yet quite arrived. It is the wave of representative democracy. But when one steps back and looks broadly at the world, there is the sense that this tide is slowing rising. Just a few years ago, it was felt that this tide would never reach the shores of Muslim countries, which makes the current "Arab spring" all the more extraordinary. In case after case, what is becoming highly significant is the universal perception that Muslims everywhere have been repulsed by the failures of their governments, and they hate the violence and terror that extremists have forced upon them. There is no reason to believe that Muslims cannot generate democratic and effective governments and economies. Yet when one hundred and eighty countries were ranked by Transparency International, # 180 was Somalia, Afghanistan was # 179, Sudan was # 176, Iraq tied for # 176, Uzbekistan was # 170, Turkmenistan was # 168, Iran was tied at # 168, and Yemen was # 154.

These successive waves produced public policies and legal systems that are themselves thoroughly layered and confusing and kaleidoscopic in nature and they have seldom produced what most people would regard as *justice*. There is no nation, not even Iran, which has a purely Sharia based legal system. Even where there are formal constitutions, there is little settled and unchanging legal bedrock. Formal constitutions have proved easy to amend. For example, Pakistan, which suffered coups d'états in 1958, 1973, 1999 and 2007, has rewritten or amended its constitution in 1936, 1962, 1973, 1985, 2003 and 2007. Further, most of these valuable documents have emerged as confusing and often self contradicting blends of native common law, Islamic Sharia law and Western secular law.

These constitutions and the thousands of secondary laws, regulations and policies that evolve around them are in a constant state of flux, and yet they often represent a core of stability in a sea of confusion and uncertainty. When "the people" are really asked what they think, they are usually clear: they want an honest and effective government, protection from the violent elements of their country from whatever source, and they want work and an adequate income. They also want crucial social services such as education, health care and a secure old age. In other words, they want peace, justice and jobs.

But there are other forces at work in all of these countries. There are political parties or dictators or ruling elites who want to control and broker power. There are powerful groups that pursue specific agendas, and in Muslim countries, the most powerful of these groups are primarily Muslim religious interests. And increasingly, there are terrorists full of zeal for power or loot. And again, in Muslim countries these terrorists are usually Islamic zealots. All Muslim nations are centrist in character, and most have leaders who are absolute rulers. All Muslim governments resist internal opposition, and are not hesitant to crush it.

Since their independence achieved in the nineteen fifties and sixties, the most serious conflicts in Muslim countries have been internal. If one looks at the three pillars of national leadership, the people themselves, as revealed by countless public opinion polls and millions of electronic exchanges tend to be secular, pragmatic and democratic. The political leadership, however they achieve power, tends to be dictatorial, centrist, and power based. Islamist politicians share these characteristics and may also be religiously dogmatic, aggressive, intolerant and narrow minded. Thus, Muslim governments experience congenital conflict not only with the majority of their own citizens but with Muslim Islamic extremists, and the people hate all of these power hungry seekers. The religion itself is far nobler than its leaders. Muslim political leadership has, for fourteen hundred years, divided themselves into Sunni and Shia. With more than 80 percent of the Muslim population as Sunni, they have tended to hold the power and have not always dealt equitably with their Shia minorities. Only Iraq, Iran, and Afghanistan have Shia majority governments. Turkey and Egypt declare themselves to be essentially secular.

The whole complex pursuit of the exercise of power in Muslim countries has been colored, and often dominated by the conflict of zealous religion based power seeking, and in some places, the destructive consequences of these conflicts has all but eliminated the exercise of responsible national leadership. Economies may founder, health care facilities may wither and die, schools may deteriorate, roads may decay—but the political leadership cannot rise above their own incestuous battling. Other political concepts are tried but fail. Communism, State Socialism, and representative democracy are all ground down in implacable, relentless self destructive power conflicts that never seem to produce either peace or justice.

Muslim legal systems have thus attempted to develop in an environment increasingly perceived to be behind the power curve in terms of individual rights, civil rights, personal freedom, public education, employment rights, economic infrastructure, and property rights. Thus, the problems of Islamic law are very serious. These laws stemmed from a general premise of the dictatorial nature of the interpretation of the Quran and Sharia, their immutability and resistance to interpretation and their attraction for maintenance of a small ruling elite using religion as justification. This in turn provided the perfect cover for tyranny and corruption.

Yet in the long run, it is clear that the economic evolution of Muslim countries is becoming more important than theological conflicts, and that economic development is very much tied to the outside world as well as with internal national capabilities. Said another way, the common fallacy of countries like the Soviet Union and China was to seal the borders and keep out the world. When this nonsense was abandoned, the emerging links with the outside world and foreign direct investment (FDI) galvanized their stagnant economies. Much the same thing happened in many Muslim countries.

Any legal system faces a number of ubiquitous problems: laws are perverted, or they can be ignored, or indifferently enforced. And most can be corrupted. As stated earlier, legal systems in Muslim countries fit one of two general patterns:

1. They may be essentially secular, with varying incorporations of Sharia law.
2. They can be based primarily on Sharia law, with varying degrees of secular law added.

And the legal systems of <u>all</u> Muslim countries are in constant flux, good and bad. Court systems may be unitary or there may be two parallel and identifiable court structures for secular and Sharia law. There is a widespread pattern of conflict between these two legal frameworks, as well as a mutual overlapping with older and more local common laws and customs. But it has also been shown in many countries and in many ways that the purposes and intentions of these three legal frameworks prove to have much in common, and can be made to coexist, and in fact, be reinforcing. In fact, it is usually not the role or the meaning of Islam as a religion that is debated, but rather how it is interpreted and by whom. Here there are two antagonists seeking to secure control of the courts and the responsibility for interpretation of the laws. One has been an extensive and very influential population of learned Islamic clerics with a tradition of legal interpretation going back centuries. The second adversary is the political leadership of a country, whatever its genesis and character. All seek the control of the sources of power, including the courts and the creation and interpretation of laws and regulations.

Ultimately, it would seem that there is nothing in Sharia law that fatally impedes reconciliation with the kinds of secular laws that many Muslim countries have absorbed, mostly from European sources. Recent trends have been for increasingly powerful elites to lock in ultimate authority over the courts and the laws, despite the powerful resistance of a slowly retreating religious fraternity and network. As legal systems advance and become more sophisticated, there is a natural tendency to codify laws and regulations, usually using ground rules as defined by the political leadership. This in turn has reduced the value of interpretation of laws by individuals, and even Islamic scholars or judges. When leaders choose, they will sacrifice Sharia law in favor of their own legal authority. When the people can choose, they may prefer the more traditional laws and practices.

But the business of interpretation and codification over centuries created a whole world of ambiguity which in turn led to the emergence of four main Sunni schools of jurisprudence, each contributing their own interpretations of Sharia: the Hanifi, the Shafi, the Maliki and the Hanbali schools. These schools have become concentrated in different geographical areas, the Hanbali becoming predominant in the Arabian peninsula, the Maliki in north and west Africa, the Hanafi in the rest of the Middle East, and the Shafi settling in the Far East in such countries as Indonesia and Malaysia.

A form of working compromise appears to have emerged from these conflicts and the introduction of more secular laws. The trend has been toward a single national court and legal system, but often with an integrated but semi independent system of Sharia courts, often concentrating on the arenas of family law and personal property and inheritance, where Sharia law has always been strong and accepted. Constitutions and broad national policies may assert inclusion of Islamic principles, and recognition of Sharia law, but in a practical sense, the useful compromise that has emerged has seemed to satisfy this official posture. All laws may be examined to determine whether they are "consistent with" or "in accordance with" some Sharia base. Finally, as with any country, the real import of national laws may be distorted by the lack of enforcement, flawed application or blatant defiance of the laws by elements in society—especially crooks and zealots—and politicians.

The long term political structures in the Muslim world have almost always been centrist and power driven, from kings and caliphs to presidents and dictators. The balance of influence has shifted from the mosques and Imams and madrassas to more or less secular governments that design their own power systems outside of that of the religious establishments. This has been a slow evolution, and for a long period of time, these two power structures have been intertwined in very complex ways. For example, the Sultans of the Ottoman Empire were also the Caliphs of the Muslim religious world.

This evolution has produced a perpetual conflict between the more traditional Islamic view that insists that Allah can be the only source of authority and direction for Muslims, versus the political power seekers who are constantly looking for ways to enhance their own authority. These political power seekers ironically find great political leverage in cloaking themselves and their policies in the garments of the Islamic religion. But the great majority of Muslims are morally and intellectually somewhere in the middle of this conflict. They do not want either dictators or religious zealots, and they seriously reject vicious and extremist Islamic movements. All too often they see such zealots as rigid, aggressive, limited in outlook and unwilling to use the major political tools of negotiation and compromise.

From time to time, governments in the Muslim world have dealt with waves of Communism, State Socialism, Pan Arabism, and more representative forms of governance. All of these have advanced and then faded. Most have foundered on the resistance of powerful leaders, or the Islamic view that such forces represent Godless unbelievers. Politics is also forced to react to the great traditional conflict between Sunni and Shia movements, and a world in which tribes and clans and villages still hold major social and political leverage such as has been seen in Afghanistan. While these complex political conflicts preoccupy the leadership, nobody really seems very interested in running the country, and public services and infrastructure suffer.

The gaps between Sharia law and the needs of the Muslim world are perhaps most serious in the arena of economic affairs. Sharia economic laws are really very limited. They arise from an older simpler economic life of individual merchants and traders. Modern economic development has grown far more complex and sophisticated and is far broader in scope, dealing with large multi dimensional corporate structures, complex banking and investment activities, a bewildering array of financial instruments, more sophisticated commercial and production capabilities, transportation and marketing. Sharia law seems most prevalent in the narrower arenas of the rules governing usury and the charging of interest, the rules of contracting, and the obligations of business people to contribute to a religious charitable tax called the zakat, which is one of the specific objectives imposed on Muslims by the Quran.

The great concern for Muslims is whether it is possible to honor to some large degree these economic provisions of Sharia law and still deal with the rest of reality by adopting the most useful elements of secular economic law and practice. Two interests are vital. First, it is vital that Muslim countries not fall farther behind other countries in developing and maintaining a modern, highly effective economy. Second, if possible, Muslim countries should come to recognize that they can benefit greatly if they can attract foreign investment in their countries. But realistically, this will not happen in a legal system solely of Sharia law. None of these Muslim countries, even those with oil to sell, can boast of the strength of their economies, or their attractiveness for foreign investors. This, of course is not solely because of their legal systems, since most countries are in constant turmoil.

The great stronghold of Sharia law is, as intended, in its guidance for individuals and families. The Sharia system reflects, and to some degree defines, a whole way of life based on the teachings of the Quran, beyond being just a legal code. Its great strength is that it most closely translates the Quran and the Sunnah, and represents a bridge between the human desire to live a devout life, and the need to live a practical and successful life. In the crucial arenas of marriage, divorce, inheritance, the status of women, and the general rules for business association, the Sharia laws have remained so strong that many governments have been very reluctant to intervene. What has most frequently emerged is some melding of Sharia and secular law, and indeed with two or three exceptions this seems to have served very well.

But the exceptions are major and of vital concern, both within Muslim communities and in their complex relationships with the broader and increasingly internationalized world. First and foremost is surely the role and status of women across the whole range of economic and cultural concerns. The Quran itself requires that women be given equal status with men, and the Prophet Muhammad urged such equality. But Muslim men have perpetuated a far different reality. There are many Muslim leaders and women's groups who are serious advocates of reform within the Muslim world, with a good deal of success. In fact, the status of women varies widely from country to country. It is in this arena that Sharia law is seen as most at odds with the far greater freedoms enjoyed by women in other countries, and it is here that Sharia law is most under attack. It is increasingly obvious that even women who are devoutly religious are still increasingly questioning the male designed inhibitions against them, which they see as contrary to the language and intent of the Quran and Sunnah. Muslim nations have ratified international treaties and protocols mandating greater latitude for women's rights, but many have signed only if granted waivers or limitations in situations where women would be given rights that appear to run counter to Sharia law. Those who look to the long haul may feel that women's full rights and equality will ultimately be realized, but the pace of change is exceedingly slow, the resistance to change seems as implacable as ever, and the reputations of the Imams and the governors is ever more tarnished.

A second great change taking place in the Muslim world is the shift in responsibility for social service programs from the mosques, and religious leaders and the extent of reliance on voluntary charity. It is not that these approaches are bad; it is just that they are inadequate and they are being overwhelmed by the needs of rapidly growing populations. There is a lot of public confusion because in some cases like the Muslim Brotherhood in Egypt or the Hezbollah in Lebanon, these organizations operate substantial charities and social welfare programs, but they are also sponsors of disruption and terrorism. The great tradition of a voluntary tax, the zakat, paid to religious organizations, has increasingly been converted into an official tax collected by some government, but usually still paid to support religious institutions and activities.

Another great change in the Muslim world has taken place in the arena of criminal justice systems. In general, with two or three notable exceptions, Sharia law and secular law regard the same things as crimes and the same punishments are considered appropriate. In western countries, executions have been widely used on the premise that death was the ultimate visible deterrence for the next perpetrator. But this premise seems much discredited and the practice is waning. Similarly, in Muslim countries some punishments long mandated in the Quran or Sharia law, such as whippings and chopping off the hands of thieves have also declined. Of the long term traditional crimes defined by Sharia law (extramarital sex, false accusations of infidelity, robbery, theft, the abuse of alcohol and apostasy), only apostasy might be seen as beyond the range of the defined crimes in other countries. And yet, the civil crime of treason might well be regarded as the equivalent of the religious crime of apostasy.

Health care obviously has become far more complex and demanding, and citizens in Muslim countries should not be deprived of the benefits of modern health capabilities because of reliance on weak and outmoded practices, or by the failure of their governments. Health care is now so complex that it must be provided and funded by governments, or sophisticated private corporations working closely with governments. The well being of workers and the level of wages, salaries and benefits now demand a level of protection that cannot be guaranteed by employers' devout good will.

And finally, the Muslim world has now entered a crisis over education. The older tradition has been rote learning only of passages from the Quran, taught by religious Mullahs in mosque based schools (*madrassas*). This is not seen as improper in itself, but increasingly as inhibiting the ability of young people to learn the things that will allow them to succeed in the far broader real world. It is untenable to believe that learning science and technology is somehow ungodly. It is not practical to be unable to study modern economics and business theory and practice because these things are said to violate ancient Sharia law. It is not feasible to try and reject any understanding of modern political science and public administration on the premise that no secular authority of any kind can be allowed to exist. It is increasingly inexcusable to fail to meet the social services needs of any country for any reason, even including religious interpretations. As these imperatives become more powerful, both Muslim theology and Sharia law are in a constant struggle to rebalance their human rights and their basis of law.

"Secularism" is Not the Enemy

Both Muslim and other nations argue that there is inevitable conflict between Islam and some forms of something called "secularism". Yet many of these arguments are confused because the meaning of secularism is confused. Every society of any complexity has norms with the force of law that derive from multiple sources. The interpretation of the Sharia by a body of scholars gave some degree of stability and some degree of predictability to laws. The Sharia and the interpretation of the scholars opposed unjust rulers, and offered some degree of validation to rulers, but of course they could be swept aside or suborned by dictators. But the tides of change made the Sharia too narrow, as determined by Muslim regimes themselves, and gradually, legal systems were expanded and made more sophisticated by the introduction of new forms of law coming from the West, and generally labeled secular. But it also became common practice to bemoan the loss of the purity of Sharia law, and to blame any and all failures of regimes on this ominous secularism. But secularism scarcely really exists as a finite quality. The secularism of the Communist USSR or China is much different from the secularism of the US, or Brazil or Japan or France. At the same time, comparisons between Western secular principles and hard core fundamentalist Islam are not the same as with largely secular Muslim countries like Turkey or Egypt or Indonesia. Here are some views about the nature of secularism.

In the U. S., the heart of secularist conception is the official separation, in the Constitution, of Church and State. But in countries like France or China, religion is officially subordinate to the state. This subordination may be soft, or implacable as in China or the old Soviet Union, but no religion is free to direct its own affairs. Therefore, those countries that are Muslim states tend to be neutral toward the U. S. form of secular interpretation, but in conflict with the French or Chinese interpretation. In the most fundamentalist Islamic theological terms, all governments are illegal, immoral, and infidel, and there is no force in the world that is recognized except the will of Allah.

Secularism also stands for the idea of the objective pursuit of knowledge, the preferred employment of rationalism, and the importance of technology. But the essence of these points is this: under this interpretation, change is a good and desirable thing, and the ethic is not only to accept change, but actively to pursue it. Change is inevitable in this world, so why not accommodate to it? In the fundamentalist version of Islam, this whole view is false and threatening. Their view is that Allah has defined the ground rules for the world's people in the holy documents, and these ground rules are holy, fixed and immutable. To advocate change is to advocate apostasy.

On the other hand, the great bulk of Muslims—as opposed to religious leaders—are perfectly willing to accept change and do not see it as opposed to the Muslim religion, nor do they seem to see the secular origin of the expanded legal structure as any ominous plot. Many want to see change take place within the framework of Muslim doctrine and practice, but this is perfectly possible and acceptable, and in fact, is happening all the time. For example, over time, law enforcement became more sophisticated, with more defined crimes, a broader range of penalties, greater enforcement, and a more realistic set of standards for proof, not because of some Western pressure but by Muslim adoption. Most of the most radical changes from traditional Sharia law were made during the long rule of the Ottoman Empire.

A "modernist" Islamist view is emerging which is both open to greater freedom of interpretation within the religion, and more open to the best characteristics of what secular philosophies have to offer. This modernist view is expressed along the following lines:

1. God bestowed on mankind the power of intellect, and clearly expects humans to exercise these powers, including for their own benefit.
2. No one can be compelled into belief, nor can the State impose an interpretation of Faith on individuals. The Quran says explicitly: "There is no compulsion in religion".
3. Human understanding of God's message in the Quran has changed, and will continue to do so. It is richer now than in the seventh century.
4. No one can claim to possess a monopoly of understanding God.
5. A democratic state offers maximum opportunities for freedom of study, discussion and debate—a process that best enables the individual and society to understand God's message and its relevance in constructing a just society.

The Ottoman Empire changed the ground rules for the entire Muslim world. It relied more on the formal government and the official courts to the detriment of the religious scholars. The Sharia was codified, including the adoption of many elements borrowed from European practices. The codifications established that Sharia laws and regulations had legal force only because they were incorporated into an official legal document issued by the State. Islamic scholars could participate in the drafting of laws, and could be consulted on the meaning of the laws, but they were no longer accepted as the sole and single official interpreters.

Another aspect of the debate is to ask: who gets to set the ground rules? In the West, the answer is the establishment of an elaborate system of governance and a structure of laws, defined essentially by the interpretation of elected officials, judges, and the apparatus of government. In the most fundamentalist of Muslim communities, this approach is wrong and immoral. Their view is that only Islamic scholars and priests should be allowed to interpret what is right and wrong. In more moderate communities, there tends to be a combination of secular and Sharia law which is generally seen as workable and not inconsistent. The most likely debates are about the correct mix of each form of law.

Inherent to the design of any system of laws is the question of the extent to which the government should mandate, and the extent to which individuals are free to determine things for themselves. The fundamentalist view is that people have latitude only within the framework of close adherence to the dictates of religion. More moderate interpretations of Islamic law find a great deal more latitude. But the same problems exist in the secular world. Some secular governments such as the USSR and China have been among the most dictatorial and tyrannical in modern history.

Seccularism gives value to diversity, tolerable controversy, disagreement, and enduring differences in any society. Government systems are expected to incorporate the right to be different, and the State should be both guarantor and protector. But the Muslim faith, in almost all of its manifestations absolutely demands that the world be seen as divided into two groups: the Faithful, and the infidels, and infidels are by definition, inferior. Fundamentalists concede no diversion whatever from their own interpretation of Islam, and even millions of Muslims who do not agree are themselves branded as infidels and apostates. Some diversity can be recognized within either the Faithful or the infidels. In fact, equality is encouraged within the Muslim religion, but never achieved because of the immutable conflicts between Sunni and Shia. In secular thinking, the ostensible purpose of governments is to serve the people, to figure out what they want, and to help them get it. This view is widely shattered by tyrants. In much of Islam however, the basic purpose of the State is to impose the Will of God.

A further assessment of the role of science and technology is seen to include the adoption of logic, the processes of rational thought, and acceptance that these approaches can and will suggest change—in addition to the change that naturally occurs in human society, planned and guided by no one. In fact, it cannot be said that somehow, change is the product of secularism. The difference is that secularists accept change, and fundamentalist Islamists try to reject it because they fear that it will undo their theological control. But the inevitable march of change refutes the fundamentalists, and forces recognition of the processes of secularism. And in fact, many "Muslim" governments are already heavily secular, and most Muslims in this world live in secular nations. This really destroys the validity of the argument that somehow Islam and secularism cannot co-exist. For most of the Muslim world, that is exactly what is happening.

National System Use of Sharia Law

Sharia Law in Egypt

There are now national courts developed along side of religious (mostly family) courts, not only for Muslims, but for Christians and Jews. Laws designed to deal with other matters began to be formed in the 1880s dealing with civil, commercial, criminal and procedural law. As civil courts evolved, Sharia courts were subject to increasing reform. This was based on the Sharia itself and not just adaptation of Western models, and many felt that European societies and laws were close to the ideals stated in the Quran. Modifications involved the right of people to make their own interpretation of the Quran and Sharia, some liberation of laws governing marriage and divorce, and a general relaxation of laws affecting the status of women in general. One of the forces that motivated people was a higher degree of secular nationalism. The Muslim Brotherhood was created in 1928 by Hassan al-Banna, and was initially a charitable organization with nationalist tendencies. The Brotherhood went on to establish offices in Palestine, Jordan, Syria and Sudan.

There was a steady trend to codify all laws, and this has had the effect of sharpening the debate as what the law should be. Women became more active in their own defense, objecting not so much about the laws themselves, but about the male interpretation of those laws, much of which seemed incorrect.

The revolution of 1952 which brought Abdel Nasser to power initiated a wave of state socialist reforms. Nasser nationalized the banking, insurance and industrial sectors, redistributed much land, liberalized provisions about the status of women, and introduced free education and health care, but he also introduced the foundations of what was to become a police state. Local religious courts were abolished; the religious laws largely remained but were now interpreted by state courts. Nasser set out to subordinate all institutions in the country including mosques and schools (including the famous university al Azhar), and religious foundations. This led to serious conflict with the Muslim Brotherhood which continues to this day. The Emergency Law was invoked in 1956 which gave the President, the police and the military extraordinary dictatorial powers. It has yet to be revoked; the "emergency" has lasted more than 56 years.

Nasser died in 1970 and was succeeded by Anwar Sadat who tended to Islamize the government. Islam was established as the official religion of the country and "the major source of legislation". And yet, it seems that little change really took place. The enforcement of new laws was ineffective and laws were widely ignored even by the government. For example, Egypt signed the U. N. Convention on the Elimination of All Forms of Discrimination against Women (CEDAW), but then internally declared that it was inconsistent with the provisions of Sharia Law.

Hosni Mubarak came into power in 1981, and his tenure was marked by a very heightened sense of "push" and conflict for the Islamization of society, but an increasing opposition to violent Muslim extremism. This was also a period when a movement for economic liberalization and democratic reforms expanded and provided a greater challenge to the Islamization process. But the period of the 80s was one of the religious revival of Islam—in movies, literature, dress, music—in part as a form of Islamic political correctness. The courts were flooded with law suits against people and organizations for "un-Islamic" actions or content. Yet, family law is still the only law in Egypt that is based primarily on Sharia law. The Brotherhood continued to be popular, largely through their humanitarian programs, which tended to show off the failures of the state.

A key event in 1997 was an attack by Muslim extremists who massacred 63 tourists at Luxor. This swung the government and most of the outside world against not only terrorist organizations, but unfortunately against all Muslim organizations in general. Yet the Supreme Constitutional Court which emerged as the only entity that could rule on the compatibility of Egyptian laws and the Sharia has tended to take a more relaxed view of such interpretations. Human rights organizations were brought under the supervision of the Ministry of Social Affairs. Increasingly, business matters have found that, in commercial matters, the Sharia "has not proven to be an obstacle to the enactment and implementation of laws that complied with the modern financial world." [3] In short, the Egyptian world of law has found great use of phrases like "consistent with", or "not contradictory with" or "compatible with" or "in accordance with", in reconciling Sharia and secular law.

Egypt passed laws that prohibited any political activity based on religion or a religious frame of reference. One exceptional accommodation passed as part of a new law defining a standard marriage contract was provision for women unilaterally to divorce their husbands. Again, women were less interested in changing the interpretation of Sharia, but more concerned with altering male interpretations.

The Egyptian Constitution was adopted in 1971 and amended in 1980, 2005 and 2007, and has been amended once more in 2013 under the new regime of the Muslim Brotherhood. The main thrusts of the later amendments has been toward democratic reform and economic liberalization. The Constitution provides for the structure of government, the definition of the People's Assembly and an independent judiciary. It lays down the basic rights and freedoms of citizens including beliefs, religious rights, and freedom of expression and of the press. There is a Supreme Constitutional Court, and it is the final determiner of legality. Laws are drafted by the People's Assembly and must use the principles of the Sharia as the primary legal source for all legislation drafted after 1980. The courts seem to interpret "the principles of Sharia" fairly restrictively as relating only to those principles that are "fixed and immutable", which technically means those mentioned explicitly in the Quran or the Sunnah. However, the new government amendments to the Constitution in 2013 gave extraordinary powers once again to the Egyptian President.

Where the Sharia is cited, it normally is defined by the Hanafi school of law. Most inheritance laws are very close to Sharia interpretation. Criminal law, while citing vestiges of Sharia law, is primarily developed from Italian law. However, interpretations of the law have been substantially confused by the existence of the Emergency Law which has been in effect, with two short breaks, since 1956, justified by the fight against terrorism and "Islamic extremism".

Laws defining economic policies and practices have been seriously developed since 1996. Many are retreats from Socialist centrism promulgated by Nasser, and all are supposedly "in accordance with Sharia", which primarily deals with usury and charging of interest. Somehow, Egypt has both modern commercial banking and Sharia banking side by side.

Egypt has not accommodated well to the modern wave of human rights for two reasons: first, there are some Sharia principles that are not consistent with UN human rights policies and treaties, especially relating to the status of women. Second, the regime has used the Emergency Law to justify oppressive practices in the name of fighting terrorism and Islamic extremism. The Emergency Law has been (will be) cancelled as a result of the recent uprisings that ousted Sadat. Of particular concern is female circumcision which is banned by UN treaty, but still practiced on ninety-five percent of Muslim women.

Sharia Law in Indonesia

Indonesia, with a population of about two hundred and thirty-five million is by far the most populous Muslim nation in the world. Muslims, mainly Sunni, make up 86 percent of the total population.

Islam reached Indonesia about the thirteenth century, but Hinduism had arrived much earlier. The legal system started with local common laws and practices (*adat* laws), added laws promulgated by princely courts, added some from Hindu practices, then added an overlay of Sharia law, primarily from the Shafi school of legal jurisprudence. Then finally another overlay of European legal concepts was added, first by the Dutch East India Company in 1747, then by the Netherlands government as colonial ruler after 1800. Under Dutch rule, courts were mainly regional administrators acting as judges. In 1830, a ruling applied the codified legislation of the Netherlands to Indonesia. In fact, there was a dual legal system, largely because the Dutch had no clue about the actual impact of either native (*adat*) nor Sharia legal practices and influence. In 1882, the government did attempt to rationalize the administration of Islamic legal elements, mostly around the three main topics of marriage and divorce, inheritance, and the administration of religious endowments (*wakaf or zakat*).

Starting around 1900, there was a strong tide running to base the legal codes more on *adat* law; but this was also seen as an effort to undermine Islamic law. The high uncertainty and confusion combined with growing opposition to the incumbent dictatorship slowly led to growing resistance within the country, leading to a surge of Islam/nationalism starting in the 1930s. In 1937, the government established a series of *panghulu* courts led by religious scholars, and an Islamic Court of Appeals was also established. Despite these efforts, the Islamic community became increasingly dissatisfied.

Indonesia became independent in 1945, and established a government that was democratic, led strongly from the top, and primarily secular and modernist. The five basic principles laid down were:

- Belief in the One and Almighty God
- A just and civilized humanity
- National unity
- Popular sovereignty governed by policies determined by deliberation and representation
- Social justice

In 1946, a Ministry of Religion was established, and a series of local bureaus were established around the country.

In 1965, the army foiled an attempted leftist coup, and used this to launch a huge attack on the Communists, backed by Muslim groups. In the end, hundreds of thousands were murdered, imprisoned or fled. But in the process, Sukarno lost so much authority and credibility that he was deposed by the military, and power passed to Suharto. Sukarno ruled from 1945 to 1966; Suharto in turn ruled from 1966 to 1998. Between the two of them, Indonesia experienced fifty-three years of heavy handed centrist dictatorship. Suharto had used a secular mass organization created by the army to fight the communists called GOLKAR. During his rule, GOLKAR was not just a political party but became the chief negotiator with special interests. Indeed the regime was one of the best examples of a country running on special interest deals rather than any form of people's representation.

The Judiciary Act of 1970 created four types of courts: general, administrative, military and religious. But the religious courts dealt only with Muslims. However, the senior Religious Court and subordinate religious courts were subject to the oversight of the Supreme Court. Suharto also created a new National Council of Religious Scholars (MUI) which was entitled to "assess the religious quality of laws, and could issue independent legal opinions (*fatwas*) which were often conflicting and confusing, but a Compilation of Islamic Law made in 1988 was very constructive. Having made these accommodations, the Suharto regime ruthlessly stamped out any serious opposition, Islamic or otherwise.

An important shift of emphasis then took place when the Islamic community began to concentrate on cultural Islam rather than political Islam. Suharto meanwhile began to need the backing of Muslims (because of the large scale corruption of his family and friends), and caused him to embrace a more pro-Islam stance. Muslim schools became more wide spread with more students; mosques prospered and got more financial support; Muslim intellectuals were more persuasive.

Suharto finally resigned in 1998, the victim of revulsion against his dictatorial and corrupt regime. He was succeeded by Bacharuddin Habibie who initiated a wide range of legal changes featuring democratization, social justice, liberalization, decentralization, and easing of some controls from the central government. At the same time, there was a more liberal package of Muslim based procedural laws which allowed Muslims greater freedoms of choice. In the subsequent elections in 1999, the new President Wahid further restricted the role of the army, strengthened human rights and press freedom, and provided new safeguards for the judiciary. Religion dealt more promoting interreligious harmony than in the unilateral advance of Islamic politics.

Decentralization in fact emerged as one of the most important tides running in the country. Aceh and Papua were given special autonomy authority, and the other thirty one provinces were also given many forms of relief from the strangle hold of the central government. What emerged was a revitalization of *adat* laws and not aggrandizement of Islamic law.

And yet, Islamic forces became more violent. There were major clashes between Muslims and Christians in the late nineties. In 2002, there was a serious terrorist attack in a nightclub in Bali, and many Indonesians and Australians died. In 2003 the Marriott Hotel in Jakarta was attacked and in 2004 the Australian Embassy became the target of Islamic terrorism. More softly, minor accommodations to Muslim legal demands became more frequent, Islamic banking and insurance expanded, and polygamy laws were stretched. Despite these accommodations, no general movement toward Islamization ever took place. In fact, in the elections of 1998, an overwhelming majority of Indonesian Muslims came out in favor of secular and nationalist parties, and this was confirmed again in the 2004 parliamentary and presidential elections.

President Yudhoyono transferred supervision of the Religious Courts to the Supreme Court, thereby reducing the role of the Ministry of Religion to an advisory one. It appears that the Islamic movement is one of specialized political advocacy rather than a deep tide running among Muslims in the country. Yet, the Religious Courts, in their own jurisdiction, seem to have been a success. They continue to have three main areas of jurisdiction: marital relations, inheritance issues for Muslims, and the affairs of religious endowments. Indonesia does not have any national legislation dealing with inheritance. Interfaith marriages are permitted by national law but forbidden by Sharia law as defined by *fatwas* issued by the MUI. The laws governing repudiation have been modified to allow women the right to seek divorce, but only on application to a judge. Polygamy laws have been modified to permit a man to marry more than one wife only with the approval of a judge, and with the wife's consent. In practice, it appears that many Indonesians take measures to ensure that their property will be divided equally between sons and daughters because they consider this to be fairer than the prescriptions of Islamic inheritance law. Similarly, the great majority of cases coming before the Religious Courts are brought by women, and judges most often rule in their favor.

While religious courts are state courts, most of the judges have been trained as religious scholars studying law. The Compilation of Islamic Law still remains the chief source of legal precedent. It is drawn from five sources:

1. Standard texts from the Shafi school of jurisprudence.
2. Additional texts from other schools (Hanafi, Hanbali, Maliki)

3. Scholarly legal opinions (*fatwas*)
4. Existing case law.
5. Sources from other countries

Indonesia has signed several international agreements dealing with civil rights/human rights matters, but there remain several major areas of contention: first, the rights of women which are still largely defined by classic Sharia law; second, the failure to officially permit atheism or polytheism; third, the rights of minorities including the Ahmadiyya, and other religionists; and fourth, areas where Muslims are given some advantage or privilege not given to others.

The current criminal code is based on the French-Dutch legal tradition and does not incorporate *hadd* crimes (i. e. as defined in the Quran), Islamic corporal punishment or retribution-based sentencing. There are laws against extramarital sexual intercourse, which is interpreted to include homosexuality, but there are real doubts about how rigorously they are enforced. Attempts at religious conversion are prohibited, and pornography is illegal.

A Compilation of Economic Sharia Law was prepared in 2006, dealing with interest, taxation, banking, religious charitable foundations, and contracting. Islamic banks are part of the national banking system and subject to supervision. The same applies to insurance, brokerage, mortgages and other forms of credit. The general intent is to allow those who want to follow Islamic business practices to do so within a well defined legal basis. There is no law requiring zakat charitable contributions.

Sharia Law in Morocco

France held a protectorate in Morocco from 1912 to 1956, and much French law and movement toward more centralized authority was adopted as an overlay onto traditional customs, Muslim law, and the decrees of the Sultan. After independence, legal provisions were codified, based primarily on the French model. Muslim law has been marginalized, but it has recently returned as a renewed basis for political debate. The country has 33 million people, almost entirely Muslim. The basis of Muslim law was mostly from the Maliki school, but within the Muslim community, there is considerable interest in both the Hanbali school and the more conservative principles of Wahhabism. Many *fatwas* had been codified. The role of the Sultan is that of a direct descendant of the Prophet, and thus highly regarded.

The French were the instigators of a long term trend to modernize the legal codes, including a code of contracts in 1913. In fact, what has emerged is a complex of French law, Islamic law from the Maliki school, rules issued by the Sultan, customary law for Berber territories, and Jewish law applied by rabbinical courts. Islamic law however was frequently modified by the French to reflect a native preference for customary law over Islamic law. But there was a period of Muslim reformism and nationalism as Muslim activists protested against what they perceived to be anti-Islamic policy, foisted on the country by foreign colonialists.

When King Hassan took over the throne, he wanted to transform Morocco into a modern state. The Constitution passed in 1962 was heavy with great authorities for the King, and unfortunately, this led to an authoritarian rule, short on human rights. The army revolted in 1971 and 1973. The economy remained weak, a privileged elite emerged, and the regime became more oppressive. The vast majority of the population in rural areas and in fast growing cities, continued to live in serious poverty. Hassan saw the Iranian revolution of 1979 as a big threat, and it led to persecution of Islamic opponents and critics.

The legal system was finally rationalized and unified in 1965, still largely based on French precedents, but it was seen as too unwieldy and confusing, and was again reformed in 1974. The courts functioned at four levels: local courts, first instance courts, courts of appeal, and the Supreme Court. The fact that Muslim law was being increasingly codified gave it greater weight without major change in its use. Major amendments of the Constitution were enacted in 1992 and 1996 favoring a two chamber parliamentary system and some opening of democratic practices which seemed to satisfy nobody. Islamists saw them as ominous, and others thought them too limited. The regime (of 38 years) got into the most trouble over its civil rights stances. International pressure was substantial and the Muslims cunningly used this record against the King, despite that fact that Muslim law was itself deficient. As in so many cases, State management and ownership of the economy had proved inefficient, and Hassan sold off many state owned enterprises to the private sector, and tried to promote foreign investment. The vicious civil war in Algeria, in which Islamist groups played an important part, scared the Moroccan public—many felt that even a kingship, with all of its faults, is better than such savage conflict.

1999 was a key year for Morocco. The elections of 1997 had brought a more liberal party into power, and by 1999, they had prepared a new agenda calling for drastic reforms. Then, Hassan died and was succeeded by his son Mohammed VI, who saw himself as a reformer, with a special interest in the status of women in the country. However, major reforms proposed in family law produced extensive public protests, saying that reforms were both "un-Islamic" and "un-Morroccan". This debate was pursued almost entirely in Islamic terms, but in 2003, there was a shocking series of terrorist attacks in Casablanca which badly hurt the Islamist voices and led the king to crack down on their more extreme elements.

A new family law was passed in early 2004 and was widely accepted, in part because it was really an expression of the consistency between the more moderate interpretations of the Sharia and modern Western thinking. Traditional Maliki law and the more conservative forces of Wahhabism lost out to more centrist religious views. More freedoms for the press and for public utterance were allowed. Yet, in the final analysis, Morocco is still essentially a centrist authoritarian establishment, and reforms have been more marginal than fundamental. Moroccans are guaranteed equality before the law, equality of the sexes, more political rights in a separation of powers form of government. Family law remains a moderate form of basic Maliki jurisprudence which seeks to promote the nuclear family. However, it remains illegal for a

Muslim woman to marry a non-Muslim man. There are measures to limit polygamy, prevent fathers from forcing daughters into unwanted marriages, and to defend the woman's right to her bride price. Inheritance laws however are little changed from Maliki practice. As in most Muslim countries, family law remains the most important form of Sharia law, and the most likely to retain Muslim interpretations. Criminal law is based mostly on French law, and the application of classic Muslim law is limited to the interpretation of religious practices or any attempts to "undermine the Faith". Hadd punishments (defined in the Quran) involving corporal punishments are not mentioned.

Morocco still does not have a comprehensive civil code, but it does have a code of contracts on the French model; a trade law, an insurance law, a real estate law and a banking law. There is no prohibition on charging interest, and no legal enforcement of the collection of the zakat. Much remains open to royal decree which covers a vast terrain and is seldom codified.

The official stance on human rights is favorable, and it is premised officially on the position that Islamic norms are compatible with international definitions. Morocco is a member of the UN and the signatory of dozens of UN treaties, covenants, and conventions, with few reservations, mainly with respect to the application of Sharia based family law. There are some other limitations dealing with the fight against terrorism, but they have little to do with Islamic law. Yet Shiites are still seen as direct threats to authority. Part of the problem is that opponents of the regime seize on any perceived human rights violations and use them for political purposes.

Sharia Law in Pakistan

The Republic of Pakistan was created through independence from British India in 1947 and it was initially composed of West Pakistan and East Pakistan, but following a war, East Pakistan declared their independence in 1971 and became Bangladesh. Pakistan has a population of about 170 million; 97 percent are Muslim and 77 percent of these are Sunni. The official language is Urdu, but few speak it; the real languages are English, Punjabi (44 percent) and Sindhi (14 percent). The region has supported civilizations for 4,500 years, and Muslims began to populate the region around the early seventh century. But it was not until the advent of the British that the legal system began to take on any coherence, and as usual, it was a blend of old traditional law with modern European adaptations. In the case of Pakistan (and India) common law arose out of both Hindu and Muslim usage exercised through tribal or community councils or tribal eldership. The East India Company remained primarily a commercial organization and so retained local law structures and customs. The exception was in criminal law and in commercial law where broadening was needed, and was modeled after English practices. But as the East India Company progressed, it took on more of the authorities of a government, especially around land ownership or usage.

The slow progression seems to have been from native Hindi and Muslim customary law, to a more formal codification of them plus English secular law overlays, to a full set of English law when the Mughal empire and the East India Company were replaced in 1858 and India became a crown colony.

The urge to create a Muslim state began early—at least by the 1920s, and it led to a sort of three cornered conflict: the English regime, the Congress Party representing mostly Hindus, and the Muslim League. When the Congress Party rose to the top in the 30's, it largely refused to share power with the Muslims, and their opposition became implacable, and frequently resulted in combat and terrorism. Finally, in August of 1947, Pakistan east and west became an independent state—the same date as did India. This meant that all things in Pakistan had to be Muslim if only to separate and distinguish them from things Indian and Hindu in India. But that does not mean that there was clear consensus or even understanding within the country as to its future and intentions. The Constituent Assembly was formed and set about drafting an "Objectives Resolution" to try and answer such questions as whether Pakistan was to be a Muslim state with an overlay of secularism or whether it would be a full bore Islamic state; and especially what would be the status of non-Muslims. What emerged was a sort of "quickie" draft constitution which put a Muslim overlay across what remained the legacy of the previous Indian law framework. But a serious problem also emerged in the disparities between West and East Pakistan. The Constitution finally adopted stated that "the legislature shall not enact any law which is repugnant to the Holy Quran and the Sunnah." But it also provided that the Supreme Court alone should have jurisdiction for determining whether or not a particular law is repugnant.

But this Constitution lasted only to 1958 when the government was overthrown by the military under Ayub Khan, who immediately declared martial law. He immediately set out to "de-Isamize" the Constitution to some degree. The name of the country was changed simply to the Republic of Pakistan; the authority of God was no longer directly cited as the ultimate authority for the country, and the nature of these changes vitiated the constitutional basis for the enforcement of many Islamic laws or rules. An Islamic Research Institute was cleverly created as advisors to the leadership, thus helping the government loosen the grip of the clerics on the interpretation of laws.

But in the period of 1960-1971, Pakistan was in the grips of two wars: one with India over Kashmir; and the other one in which they lost E. Pakistan, with India's help, to become the new country of Bangladesh—for which India has never been forgiven, at least by the Pakistani military. Pakistan's attempt to take over the Indian state of Jammu and Kashmir escalated into a full scale war resulting in a humiliating defeat and back down by Pakistan. In the process, Ali Bhutto and the Pakistan People' Party emerged as the new political force. Their success in the elections of 1970 led to drafting of a new constitution in 1973. It returned the pendulum toward recognition of Islamic commitments, based on the recommendations of a new "Council of Islamic Ideology", and Islam was once again declared the state religion.

The Constitution of 1962 did protect from judicial review the most important of Islamic laws, family law, through the creation of the Muslim Family Laws Ordinance of 1961. But when the constitution was rewritten in 1973 it reflected the increasing strength of the Islamic political forces, exercised through control of the streets. Part of the growing influence of Islamists stemmed from interference from activists from outside of the country, especially in the areas bordering Afghanistan. Islam was now declared to be the official religion of the country, drinking alcohol was officially banned, Friday became the official holy day, and other Muslim policies were recognized. Meanwhile, the turmoil in the country and the general incompetence of the Bhutto regime meant that little was done to improve the economy or the delivery of social services. Everything was just bad politics. Finally, in 1977, Bhutto was unseated by another coup d'état. General Zia immediately declared martial law and began a relentless drive to make Pakistan an Islamic state.

But the Soviet invasion of Afghanistan in 1979 turned everything upside down. Suddenly, Pakistan was the favored ally of the U. S., and Islamization became a noble tool to fight Soviet Communism. Pakistan took in millions of Afghan refugees and supported Afghan fighters against the Soviets, thus inviting thousands of new fundamentalist fighters into the country. Further, after some time, the typical, almost universal strains between Sunni and Shia became more compelling, and ethnic rifts opened wider in Punjab and Sindh. The politics were horrible; another new constitutional amendment was passed in 1985 taking more power back into the central government. The position of women and minorities worsened. An election won by the Pakistan Muslim League was dismissed. Then Zia died in a plane crash in 1988.

Against this total confusion, the judicial system tried to stagger along, coping with dictatorship, martial law, rapid constitutional change, big gaps between what the law said and what could be enforced. Zia fired many, curbed others, and created a new Federal Sharia Court (FSC) in 1980 which was given authority to review the validity of laws, excluding only the constitution. The crimes of murder and various forms of assault became Sharia crimes, and many things once again became "repugnant". Even Sharia family law ultimately came under FSC authority.

But on the other hand, the death of Zia seems to have precipitated a period of "democracy", meaning more two party political catastrophes. Thus, when Musharraf's coup in 1999 occurred, there was surprising public support. As usual, he suspended the constitution (1973) and made everything legally subject to "Orders of the Chief Executive". The political assemblies never met again until 2002. Once again, affairs turned in his favor after 9/11. Musharraf was forced into making some serious constitutional changes in 2002. The power to dismiss the Parliament was limited; a new Legal Framework Order 2002 was issued which reversed this trend and restored draconian powers to the President. All of this was passed in 2003. All was vague, and gradually the judiciary rebelled and began challenging regime actions. Despite this, he won reelection in 2007—by an overwhelming majority. Yet again, the politics were horrible. The two main parties boycotted the election, which ultimately solved nothing. Fearful that the Supreme Court would not allow him to take office, Musharraf declared a state of emergency, suspended the constitution and removed a large number of judges. But faced with serious threats of impeachment, he resigned in August of 2008.

Yet in retrospect, except for the rise of Taliban and fundamentalist tribes in the northwest, Pakistan was elsewhere experiencing revulsion against harsh Islamization and was buoyed by the passage of the Protection of Women Rights Act in 2006. Efforts to make the legal system more Islamic simply paused and petered out. Newspapers became more assertive in reporting about secular issues, and the government of Bangladesh removed references to Islam from its constitution.

During the long period from 1960 to today, Pakistan has been in a state of continuous political turmoil and chaos and almost little has been done by the political leadership actually to run the country, provide social services or improve the economy. The legal system reflects this turmoil and it has vacillated up and down from Islamic pressures to secularism and back. It is doubtful whether anybody really understands what the basis of law really is, and the religious scholars would disagree with those of European tradition. Indeed, the country has not yet decided. And yet, elsewhere in the Muslim world, many countries have learned to live with a blending of Sharia, traditional and modern secular law. Pakistan could too if it could get everybody to calm down. The tide seems to be running that way if the country does not collapse before something happens.

As of now, what does the Constitution say? First, "loyalty to the state is the basic duty of every citizen". In turn, it guarantees the fundamental rights to freedom, life, liberty, freedom of religion, freedom of expression. The Supreme Court and the provincial high courts have the final authority to declare laws void. Article I does state that Pakistan is an Islamic republic and that Islam is the state religion, but this is said to be of a declaratory nature and has little legal effect in the development of Pakistan's legal system. In fact, Pakistan shows that "the harmonic interplay between Islamic principles and human rights is possible, and that references to Islam do not as of necessity result in a violation of basic freedoms."

The Federal Sharia Court has eight members: the Chief Justice, four judges, and three religious scholars, and the court can examine any law as to whether it is "repugnant to the Injunctions of Islam, as laid down in the Holy Quran and the Sunnah of the Holy Prophet." The FSC is the court of appeal for all cases involving Hudood (Hadd) Ordinances of 1979. (but stoning and amputations authorized under these Ordinances have never been executed in Pakistan). But exempt from FSC jurisdiction are the constitution, procedural laws or regulations, and Islamic personal status and family laws.

Since the late 90s, there has been wide consensus that, without exception, all efforts centering around Islamization must be aimed at making Islamic laws more gender-sensitive. This has usually meant making the interpretations of Islamic law more harmonious with constitutionally-guaranteed fundamental rights, and to a lesser degree consistent with international standards. In fact, the violations under Musharraf were mostly political, anti-terrorist, and anti-extremist, rather than anti-Islam, and many were local tribal "honor killings". But this national accommodation to women's rights did signal the steady decline of the movement toward radical Islamization marked by the Zia years. Yet all of this seems once again to have been "blown" by the surge of Taliban activities again in 2008 to the present.

As to Muslim family law, the base has been the Muslim Family Law Ordinance of 1961, which was a moderate codification, especially relating to divorce and polygamy. Husbands may not easily repudiate their wives, and wives may seek judicial divorce themselves. Inheritance law remains governed by classical Sharia regulations, although never codified.

Criminal law from British India remains the basis of Pakistani criminal law, and the classic Hudood (Hadd) laws as stated in the Quran as always remain in force, but the most violent of punishments have seldom been used. But now, rape and fornication are no longer Hadd crimes but come under the civil penal code. The blasphemy code is very heavy: "Whoever by words either spoken or written, or by visible representation, or by any imputation, innuendo or insinuation, directly or indirectly defiles the sacred name of any wife or members of the family, of the Holy Prophet (Peace Be Unto Him), or any of the righteous Caliphs or companions of the Holy Prophet (PBUH) shall be punished with imprisonment of either description for a term which may extend to three years, or with fine, or with both." Imprisonment for life has been stipulated for the willful damaging, defaming, abusing, denunciation, and improper use of a copy of the Quran." **(4)**

Classical Islamic law provides redress for the family of victims in murder and assault cases: monetary compensation (blood money); criminal punishment including the death penalty; or pardoning. The Shariat Act of 1991 directs that the state must establish "an Islamic economy", including the intent to abolish interest, set up a zakat (charitable) tax, and maintain trusts to finance mosques. The Supreme Court ruled against the prohibition of interest payments, but on procedural grounds. To date, the issue is unresolved. A

2.5% zakat is imposed on the estate of every Muslim, and there is a "religious tax" on agricultural proceeds.

Sharia Law in Saudi Arabia

Saudi Arabia is an absolute monarchy with a population of more than 28 million, almost all of whom are Arabic, and 90 percent are Sunni. The "default" legal basis is Hanbali jurisprudence and the other schools can be consulted only where the Hanbali is recognized as inadequate. The prevalent religious philosophy is the very conservative Wahhabi school, but under the monarchy, there has been a long term trend toward the modernization of the country and the economy. According to the Wahhabi doctrine, rulers are permitted to promulgate necessary legislation for government policy providing it is complementary to and not in contradiction with Sharia, and serves the public interest. From the 1930s onwards, many specialized tribunals or committees have been created to adjudicate matters in certain areas such as labor law and commercial law and to apply new regulations defining the authority of the central government, under the supervision of some ministry. Thus, even the ultra conservative Saudis step back from sole application of Sharia law and have attempted to be more modern and more flexible.

Saudi Arabian leadership has long feared the kind of nationalist Islamic wave encouraged by Nasser, and they have set out to create a worldwide campaign to spread Wahhabi Islam, largely in conflict with Shia influence out of Iran. In the 1950s and 60s, Saudi Arabia gave political asylum to thousands of Egyptian Muslim Brothers, only to find that they have become the supporters of some of the more radical elements of Saudi society.

Saudi Arabia has, since 1953, had a Council of Ministers that effectively runs the country on behalf of the king. It has authority to formulate policies relating to domestic, foreign, financial, economic and civic affairs. Even royal decrees cannot become law until approved by the Council, and now all laws must be made public knowledge by publication in the official gazette. The *ulama* (religious leaders) have had no official role in the legislative process but are widely consulted for both political and religious reasons. In 1971, a Council of Senior Ulama was established to represent that advice, but even today, the conservative religious leaders remain highly suspicious of the king as a "secular" leader. The Supreme Judicial Council has supervision of the courts, and can establish general principles and declare precedents that must be followed by the courts.

The period under King Faisal was a time of great modernization, especially in education where dozens of both religious and secular schools and universities were founded, and thousands of Saudis were sent abroad for education. Ministries of Commerce, Industry and Electricity were created and staffed by the new highly educated elite. A heavy counter force was the *ulama* establishment who succeeded in negotiating the separation of the sexes in the classrooms and elsewhere, and who succeeded in getting the creation of the Committee for the Promotion of Virtue and Prevention of Vice, which operated what became known as the religious police, across all of society including all public places, shops, restaurants, buses and any other places where people gather. Its purposes include dress code enforcement, separation of the sexes, shop closings during prayer time, and denial of the propagation of religious beliefs by non-Muslims. In addition, Saudi Arabia has developed what is perhaps the best national health care system in the Muslim world. The regime has spent many millions of dollars on the building of mosques, Islamic centers, and schools, not just in Saudi Arabia but around the world. But this did not fully stop the development of a relatively small group of young radical Islamists, five hundred of whom attacked the Holy Mosque in 1979, which in turn charged up the government to take more drastic measures against such radicals.

The Quran, the Sunnah and the Sharia are officially "the constitution of the country." And yet, the "king shall be the final resort of all authorities." A new consultative council was established in 1992 authorized to lay down regulations and bylaws to meet the public interest. The public interest is a very useful phrase, as is "consistent with—" and "in accordance with—". All are ways to seem visibly to be implementing Sharia law, while allowing the King and government officials some added authority. While terrorism is outlawed, it persists, most often against western targets.

Saudi Arabia's economy has deteriorated substantially since the golden days of top oil prices. Now, there are enormous debts, trade deficits, a doubling of population in the last twenty years, high unemployment, especially among youth, and a quandary about what to do about six million migrant workers in the country.

When elections were held at the provincial level, the conservatives usually won. The adamant attitude against women was all too obvious. But when King Fahd finally died in 2005, his son Abdullah emerged as a true reformer; he had been behind most reform efforts during Fahd's last years. Yet critics are still negative and pessimistic. A Supreme Court and several special tribunals for family, criminal, labor and commercial law have been established. Thus, the Saudis have the traditional three separated authorities, but the king is still the unchallenged final voice. Sharia law is still not codified, and judges and prosecutors still consult Hanbali *fiqh* (statements of law) books. Many cases—as high as 90 percent—are resolved by some form of mediation, often Sharia based. Religious leaders still issue *fatwas* (pronouncements by religious leaders) which are not law, but are often accepted anyway, especially by their congregations. Administrative regulations have the force and effect of law, and everybody gets very confused when they conflict with Sharia interpretations or royal decrees. There are three levels of courts as usual—first instance courts, appellate courts, and the new Supreme Court. There is a second judicial branch—a Board of Grievances. In general, it deals with appeals about administrative regulations, and issues dealing with foreigners. Judges are often very much independent authorities, not bound by many laws or legal precedents, or by regulations or even Sharia interpretation. They are charged to resolve disputes, and they can do it any way they like. But only graduates of a Sharia college may become judges or serve on the Board of Grievances. Recently, new law schools have been established by the government, perhaps to create an acceptable alternative to the Sharia schools.

Family law is very heavily based on the Hanbali school of jurisprudence, and deals largely with marriage, divorce, family maintenance, inheritance, and interpretations of Sharia stipulations. Criminal law is still largely un-codified, heavily reliant on Hanbali Sharia law, and has only recently begun to be modified by new regulations stemming from French and Egyptian law. Saudi Arabia, perhaps more than any other Muslim country, still actually performs most of the punishments defined by Sharia law (*Hadd*), including blood money. But other offenses defined by Sharia law not *Hadd* are being superseded by new regulations dealing with bribery, counterfeiting, drug abuse, trafficking, smuggling, and official corruption. These cases are tried by the administrative committees and appealed to the Court of Grievances. The king retains enormous discretion.

Commercial law remains at its root Hanbali *fiqh*. But the special committees have developed regulations based on western examples, especially dealing with corporate legal standing, taxation, laws of contract, intellectual property, stocks and bonds, commercial paper, and banking. This has meant a good deal of confusion for all as to which set of laws really apply, and what laws 'will actually be enforced. Saudi Arabia remains a huge banking market; some of the biggest "Islamic" banks are Saudi banks. Zakat taxes are fully enforced.

Basic human rights are seen as inherent in Sharia law, but these principles and practices are often in some degree of conflict with international laws. Saudi Arabia has signed many UN treaties and conventions, but often makes special reservations to retain Sharia interpretations. For example, Saudi has signed the Convention Against Torture, but it retains the interpretation that whipping, stoning or cutting off hands are not "torture" but God defined responsibilities. Saudi signed the UN Convention on the Elimination of All Forms of Discrimination Against Women, again with some reservations where the Convention is judged to be in contradiction with Sharia norms. Nor is Saudi Arabia willing to submit any such dispute to the International Court of Justice. Further, the press is under tight control, and few civil rights organizations are permitted if they seem to advocate views in contrast with Sharia law.

Women are still barred from voting, driving a car, traveling alone, or traveling without the permission of their male guardian. Women and men are segregated in travel vehicles, schools, universities, hospitals and health care facilities, and work places. Women cannot obtain a license to practice law, or become an architect, engineer or accountant. Technically, women can choose their own education, open a business, execute financial transactions, inherit, get elected to public office or hold a government position. But in fact, all of these things are deliberately made difficult and regarded as irreligious. Again, as in other countries, the law as executed is more a question of male interpretation than any hard and fast position stated in the holy sources.

Meanwhile, the process of reform, started under King Abdullah in 2005, proceeds at an uncertain and glacial pace.

Sharia Law in Sudan

The Sudan got its independence from Egypt and the British protectorate in 1956. Its population prior to the separation of South Sudan was about 41 million of whom 70 percent are Muslim. The rest of the population is mainly Christian or Christian/animist. The country is very divided with 19 major ethnic groups, almost 600 identifiable sub groups, speaking more than 100 languages and dialects. Most in the north are Arabs and Muslims, and many are of recent arrival. The south is mostly blacks of many tribes. When the south broke off and became independent in 2011, these internal divisions were mitigated, but have not really gone away.

Arabs gradually turned up in Sudan initially as traders and slavers. Ottoman/Egyptian rule extended from 1820 to 1881 during which the country was politically consolidated but never really united. While there was a set of local administrations, legal cases or disputes often had to be referred to the highest legal body in Cairo, and most laws were administered by Egyptian administrators. But there was a new set of secular courts established in about 1850, including a penal code that was not based on Sharia law. As a consequence, it appears that Sharia law has been largely limited to personal law, land rights, and religious matters. Those elements of the legal system derived from Egyptian law, however have been derived from the Hanafi school of jurisprudence.

But all of this changed with the advent of the Mahdi who conquered Khartoum in 1885 and who instituted a series of personal *fiques*, often eccentric, and usually out of conformance with any of the traditional schools of jurisprudence. Then, in 1896-99, the Anglo-Egyptian army conquered Sudan, and they instituted another complete revamp of the legal base. The British did concede to popular demand by allowing the creation, in 1915, of a series of Mohammedan Law Courts to apply Sharia law to personal, family, and land issues. In the period 1900-1920, Islam had a good deal of latitude, and prospered with many mosques built and arrangements made for the Hajj, the compulsory pilgrimage of the Faithful to Mecca.

This is a typical situation: from the customary law of the sixteenth century, an overlay was applied first of Sharia law, then of Turkish and Egyptian law, then British colonial law and then modern law drawn mostly from Egyptian sources. As elsewhere, where Sharia law has been applied, it is seen as in conflict with modern interpretations of civil rights and the rights of women. Sharia based law was utilized by the 20 year rule of the military regime, but the current regime is not interested in further expansion. Starting about 1920, native courts became more important as the country moved toward independence, but they tended to replace the Sharia courts, especially in the application of a penal code.

At independence, the new Constitution provided for a parliamentary system, multi-party politics, and free elections. The country was dragged through three military takeovers, and got "revitalized" after each, which meant that it was in a constant state of confusion. Conflict in the country was four cornered: first the Muslim clergy and the Sufi sect, very conservative; second, the Nasserites, then Baathist political party, Arab nationalists and those who wanted Sudan to become part of the pan-Arab Egypt; third, the modernists and pragmatists who wanted a sensible final version of the Constitution; and fourth, the black African south who were mainly against forced Islamisation and too much centrism.

The first military dictatorship (1958-1964) led to a wave of "democracy" and fiddling with the Constitution. But democracy meant a weird combination of Islam and State Socialism—all of which regarded the black south as second class citizens who were guilty twice: they were Muslim apostates, and they resisted Socialist centrism. When the second military dictatorship took over in 1969, it was led by the Nasserites, communists and Baathists (another weird combination), and the government immediately outlawed all other political parties, revoked the Constitution and began a huge purge of all political or civic opposition. When the communists attempted their own coup in 1971, it was bloodily terminated and another purge ensued, backed by Egypt, Saudi Arabia and the U. S. This military dictatorship in turn fell in 1964, and the new government returned once again to "democratization". But it was a thoroughly confusing "democratic Socialist republic under the protection of Islam", and it again turned the Christians and Animists in the south into second class citizens. A new constitution was drafted but could not pass, and then was abandoned after another coup d'etat in 1969. What followed was essentially a heavy conflict between an ultra Islamist group vs. a Nasserite socialist group. But still, they were all Muslims and all Sunni. The Numeiri party, consisting of a motley group of communists, Nasserite nationalists and Baathists won out, and the new President Gaafar Numeiri immediately banned all other political parties and killed hundreds of opposition people of all kinds. Again, a new Constitution was undertaken, drawing heavily from the Egyptian Civil Code which meant a shift from loose common law to a more European legal basis. In one description "the commission proceeded to copy with impunity and with trivial and sometimes meaningless amendments, section after section and chapter after chapter from the Egyptian Civil Code of 1949, flavoring it here and there with a slightly modified or differently phrased version from the Iraqi, Syrian or Libyan Civil Code as well." During the ensuing dozen years, President Numieri catered increasingly to Islamic interests as a populist political ploy. And it succeeded in garnering backing from the Muslim Brotherhood and it weakened the position of his opponents. He also backed off from any attempts at reconciliation of the south and advocated breaking the territory up into three provinces.

Internal conflict continued to be fierce, and in response, Numieri turned to the introduction of an agenda of Islamic laws in 1983. But again, the result was totally confusing—a residue of common law, a good deal of the Egyptian type civil code plus a new overlay of Sharia law which nevertheless was seen as out of kilter with traditional Islamic jurisprudence. Implementation of Hadd punishments crept back, and again, the communities in the south were totally opposed to the whole mess. Only the Muslim Brotherhood continued to back the Numeiri regime, but it cost them much support of their own. The implementation of Sharia law, or almost any law, became almost impossible in the south, and eventually war broke out in the spring of 1983. Numieri attempted to tighten his control by "Islamizing" the Constitution to provide him with a life time role as "commander of the Faithful", and reducing the Parliament to a consultative body. The leader of the Republican Brothers, Mahmud Taha, was arrested and hanged for "apostasy". The Muslim Brotherhood then finally broke from the Numeiri regime. Numeiri then dismissed all Brotherhood members from any official position, arrested their leader along with two hundred others including the then president of the People's Assembly—in other words, a slide to all-out dictatorship.

In March of 1985, Numeiri abolished subsidies for bread and fuel. He then flew to the U. S. to meet with Reagan, but even while he was flying home, a military coup seized the government. The new Military Council abolished Numeiri's constitution and restored the transitional constitution of 1956, restoring political freedom, political pluralism, separation of powers, and suspending Hadd punishments. A new political party was formed that included Muslim Brotherhood, Sufi, tribal leaders, *ulema* (religious leaders), and current and former military officers. Power was returned to a civilian government in mid 1986. Several political parties had been created, and two of them allied themselves and won a clear majority which did not include the Muslim Brotherhood and its allies.

In retrospect, the 19 year regime of Numeiri (1969-1986) was a total chaotic waste. The country was in constant turmoil, wasting its time and substance on sterile political fighting, creating implacable enemies in the south, and accomplishing practically nothing. And yet, the country continues to be Islamist in outlook, and the retreat from the south does not seem to have reduced this tendency in the north. Bashir dissolved Parliament, declared a state of emergency, and instituted harsh reprisals. More than 60 percent of all judges have been replaced with Islamic appointments, many of whom were inexperienced and unqualified, but loyal. In 1991, a new penal code was enacted which catered more to Islamic standards, including the full range of Hadd punishments. A parallel military/police system was established, relying initially on tribal militias and forcibly recruited students and other young men, and it was used gradually to reduce the regular forces.

It was not until 2005 that some accommodation was made to deal with some of the divisiveness in the country. An Interim Constitution was adopted for a six year period, and an agreement was signed which called for a separation referendum in the South—and in 2011, the south voted to succeed and become South Sudan. The interim constitution states that "Sudan is a multi-racial, multi-ethnic, multi-religious and multi-lingual state", thus refraining from a specific declaration that Sudan is an Islamic state. It also refers to Sharia law, common laws and the legal umbrella of the constitution as the sources of legislation and regulation, but as usual, the whole thing is a total muddle. It is silent on such Muslim traditions as enforcement of zakat, or the banning of alcohol.

Another example is the fact that the interim constitution "guarantees men and women equal rights in civil, political, social, cultural and economic rights", but there is legislation in force that is in conflict with this intent. Another example is family and inheritance laws. Much of this law is based on traditional Hanafi jurisprudence, but particular situations are defined by provisions from the other three schools, or from more secular law. The criminal law codes preserve the standard Hadd offences: unlawful sexual intercourse, false accusations against people for unlawful intercourse, consumption of alcohol, banditry, theft, and apostasy; and whipping and mutilation are still somewhat practiced.

The commercial codes have really only formally recognized traditional Islamic banking practices since the seventies, including a provision that 10 percent of a bank's net profits will be given to charity as a zakat. It appears that the government, or at least many government officials, plus the Muslim Brotherhood are closely connected to Islamic banks, which in turn enriched these people and led to preferential loans to their political parties—often without the expectation of repayment. The financial sector however is very weak, and the Bank of Sudan has failed to protect the public or stop the corruption. So it could be said that the banks are failures as financial institutions, and successes as political patsies.

As for zakat, there is a national system of voluntary donations by companies and wealthy individuals, but in 1984, it lost its status as a religious contribution controlled by religious leaders and became another tax within the regular tax system with the revenues simply going directly into the general funds. There is however, a better government program of good works, ostensibly funded by zakat, which distributes cereals, flour, sugar, dates, lentils and medicines to hospitals, orphanages and schools, and as financial support for charitable or state organizations. There have been lots of criticism, mainly that some of these funds have been stolen or misappropriated by their administrators, including funding for the wars in the South.

As in almost every other Muslim country, there is conflict between local laws of the country with respect to human rights, and the standards set by international organizations to which Sudan subscribes. There has never been any concerted effort to satisfy these standards, and in fact, Sudan has made many reservations about specific provisions, or has said "we are considering them". At this point, there seems to be no great tide running in the near term future that will lead to revision of Islam away from fundamentalism and the past, and toward a new form of Islam that is more positive constructive, and future oriented.

Sharia Law in Turkey

The history of Turkey for the last 500 years was dominated by the long reign of the Ottoman Empire beginning about 1500 and lasting until 1920, which involved highly authoritarian centrist governance, a religious Caliphate, Sunni orthodoxy, a huge restless empire, and a pattern of slow decline. Modern Turkish history is dominated by the advent of Kemal Ataturk who destroyed the Empire and the Caliphate as well. His modernist, secular policies called for the adoption of Western methods of military training, government organization, civil, economic and educational changes, a revamping of the legal system along Western lines, and a forceful secular attitude. Yet, for most of this time, Turkish law was really a blend of religious and secular laws, with wide latitude left for the ruler, and modernization along secular lines which actually started at least as early as the 1800s. The last stoning of an adulterous woman was in 1680.

Increasingly the school system was state provided and designed to teach technical rather than religious knowledge. The Constitution was rewritten in 1876 to include recognition of most of the modernization agenda. Some latitude was left for Sharia courts to handle family matters and Hadd punishments, but then these punishments were formally abolished in 1858. New laws were set up for commercial affairs, including legal charging of interest, despite the ancient Sharia prohibitions. A whole new civil code called the

Mecelle was enacted in 1868. In other words, Turkey, even under the highly conservative Ottoman Empire and the residual Caliph, moved slowly but steadily toward modernization.

In 1871, a new legal system and code came into effect along side of the Sharia courts, and gradually usurped much of their jurisdiction, and Sharia courts became limited mostly to family matters such as marriage, divorce, inheritance, succession and property rights. But even here, there were secular courts that were allowed to deal with the same kinds of matters, especially where one of the litigants was non-Muslim or foreign. By 1917, it was pronounced that the modernization of Ottoman law had largely been completed.

The Constitution of 1876 set up a Council of Ministers, a supreme Sheikh for Religious Affairs, a two house parliament: an elected Chamber of Deputies and a Senate appointed by the Sultan. But in 1907, a military coup swept the military into power, and the Sultan was forced to reinstitute the 1876 Constitution, and to institute a broad reform program which included the secularization of the schools, courts and legislation, first steps in the emancipation of women, transfer of supervision of Muslim courts to the Ministry of Justice and of Muslim universities to the Ministry of Education. Family law was removed from the religious courts, and legal interpretations were required to recognize all schools of jurisprudence and not just the Hanafi.

The Ottoman Empire broke up after WW I and subordinate countries such as Egypt, Syria, and Saudi Arabia were largely taken under Western country supervision. Finally, in the early 1920s, a new wave of secularist reform swept the country leading to the Ataturk regime, starting in 1924. A new Constitution was drafted in 1921, and it stated that sovereignty belonged to the people, and in 1922, the Sultanate was abolished, followed by the abolition of the Caliphate in 1922, and the position of the Sheik ul-Islam in 1924. The entire system of religious schools was abandoned, religious foundations were made responsible to the government, many religious figures were retired, and those who remained became civil servants. Sufi religious orders were banned, as well as the wearing of religious garments. The Penal Code of 1926 made it illegal for "any who, by misuse of religion, religious sentiments, or things that are religiously considered as holy, in any way to incite the people to action prejudicial to the security of the State, or form associations for this purpose—." A new family law replaced the Mecelle, which had been Sharia based. The new laws abolished polygamy and made the sexes substantially equal in rights, especially with respect to divorce.

Many laws from Europe were adapted for commercial activities, civil procedures, and a more extensive penal code. A new Latin alphabet was adopted to replace Arabic. In most schools, religious instruction was removed from the curriculum or made optional as a general subject. In the thirties, women were given the right to vote, to serve in public office, and to have equal access to education and employment. New "Village Institutes" were established as a form of local governance. In 1953, a law was passed prohibiting the use of religion for political purposes. Yet the Muslim faith was not directly attacked, and has always remained deeply imbedded in Turkish society. A military coup took place in 1960, and it was very Kemalist in nature. Yet the elections of 1962 saw every political party citing religion in some context. Military coups have been launched in 1907, 1920, 1960, 1971 and 1980.

The formal legal system was slowly and quietly purging itself of obsolete Sharia elements in favor of secular laws and regulations. The counter thrust was largely seen as religious bigotry. It seemed that the government wanted to establish legal tolerance for legitimate religion, but was increasingly concerned about extremist religion, especially when it turned political. Turkey now has a regime that is mildly Islamic, and not really in conflict with the general secular nature of the government and its legal base. The European Court of Human Rights said "Turkey is by far the worst violator of human rights among the 47 signatory states of the European Convention on Human Rights (6) But the court granted Turkey the discretion to preserve the secular life style, women's rights, and public order in the face of religious movements attempting to impose their world-views. Also, new laws are being considered to preclude mosques from being used for anything but pure religious purposes.

Recent public opinion polls show that the general public is concerned about major things, while the politicians argue trivial pursuits. Major public concerns:

1. Unemployment (39%)
2. Terrorism and threats to national security
3. The increasingly higher costs of living
4. A weak, inadequate, and largely obsolete education system
5. Economic instability

There is little concern about religious dress issues, or the introduction of Sharia law. In fact, the public shows a great deal of confusion about what Sharia law would mean. The public does not see any serious link between terrorism and Islam, and they are overwhelmingly opposed to terrorist attacks against civilians.

Sharia law for family matters is not allowed in the Turkish system. Things like polygamy (banned) and inheritance are defined in secular law which is seen as consistent with the Sharia. Similarly, criminal law has banned the Hadd punishments, and does not relate at all to Sharia criminal rules. Article 10 of the Constitution says "women and men have equal rights, and the State is under the obligation to ensure that this right operates in everyday life."

Thus, Turkey has moved steadily for 80 years toward conformance with European standards, the reduction of Sharia legal positions, but wants to retain a reasonable incorporation of Sharia intent into the secular legal system. In general, there are several sources of law: religious law, constitutional law, case law, and common law, and they are widely intermixed in practice.

Thus, there is no such thing as "the" Sharia; there is no one universal Islamic law; the rules of Sharia law are widely interpreted and disputed. There are said to be four distinct types of Sharia law:

the divine and abstract; the old original classic interpretations; the law as history translated to current times; and a new contemporary set of legal interpretations. The divine interpretation is very fundamentalist: rigid, said not to be subject to interpretation, supposedly tied closely to an interpretation of the life of Muhammad, and closely controlled by a fundamentalist group of religious scholars. Classical Sharia is based on the extensive elaboration and interpretation of the Quran, the life of Muhammad and the codification and development of a set of rules in the first 2 hundred years after the death of Muhammad in 632. Historic Sharia law is the outgrowth of more than 1000 years of usage and interpretation. It is an almost indefinable blend of classic, practical, case law, and changing realities, ranging from personal situations to government policy. It is most similar to the blend of case law and common law that undergirds most Western legal systems.

Contemporary Sharia law attempts to start differently by utilizing legal forms that are actually in use today. These are a blend of historic Sharia law plus heavy inputs of modern secular law, mostly from Europe. They include development of new legal interpretations with which the traditionalists dealt poorly, such as environmental law, contract or business law, information technology, or complex corporations or new forms of human institutions. So the reality is that, as states in the Muslim community developed, the basic issues of law became less anchored in religion and more in state power and authority. Thus, the supremacy of secular laws dealing with the power of the state has been overwhelming the older commitment to religiously interpreted Sharia law. Sharia law became more and more concentrated in the arenas of family matters and of course religious interpretation.

There are four major concerns in the West about Sharia law:

1. What would it be like to have Sharia law as the dominant national legal system?
2. What is wrong with Sharia law as it relates to the rights and status of women?

3. What about the Sharia law that seems to mandate cruel and inhumane punishments?
4. Does Sharia law do violence to modern concepts of human rights?

In general, there is little likelihood that a purely evil form of Sharia will ever emerge, much less get adopted anywhere. In fact, Muslim countries seem to have become very comfortable with combinations of secular and Sharia law, and do not find them in much conflict.

The rights of women are, however, an exception to this trend; or at least, the processes of accommodation are slower and less substantial than other arenas of law. It is constantly pointed out that advances in the affairs of women are spotty and vary widely from place to place, but the general conclusion is that this remains one of the most serious failings of Sharia law. It is also pointed out repeatedly that the real issue is not legal interpretation but rather the unwillingness of men to give up authority.

Classical Sharia law confines hard punishment to six areas: extramarital sex, false accusations about extramarital sex; robbery; theft; consumption of alcohol, and in some places, apostasy (called Hadd offenses). Evidence suggests that practices such as cutting off the hand of thieves are now seldom used. Of greater concern is the growth of new legal interpretations supposedly based on Sharia law, such undefined "un-Islamic behavior", or prejudice authorized against non-believers, and even death or imprisonment for apostasy.

Thus, in developing countries where the legal system is still evolving, the tendency is to make the legal structures more comprehensive, and the hope is that, in human terms, the law that will win out is the one that produces the best human results. Sharia need not be merely an element of the legal system; it was and is and will be guides to living decent, devout lives.

All legal systems suffer to some degree from common problems: first, the rule of law may be perverted if the laws themselves are bad. Second, most legal systems suffer from dysfunctions and shortcomings. Third, dictators and tyrants can ignore the law or pervert it. Fourth, the legal base may be poor or inadequate. Fifth, the law may be corrupt. Lack of recognition of human rights remains a problem with respect to Sharia law, but here again it is difficult to distinguish inadequacy of the laws vs. failures of the legal system in operation. But still, there is little real conflict between the intent of world concepts of human rights and those of Sharia. The rule of law here means:

1. All State actions must be written and published.
2. The law must be clear and consistent in substance, general in its application, and accessible and understandable for citizens.
3. The laws must be influenced in substance and usage by public opinion.
4. There must be self limiting or other means by which abuses of the law can be rectified.
5. There must be an independent judiciary

In general, moderate Muslim regimes find ways to provide the rule of law, but more puritanical interpreters often refuse to accommodate. The most serious debates about the rule of law and other issues are not between Muslims and the West, but within the Muslim community itself. These debates seldom concern the virtues of the Muslim faith, but rather how that faith is interpreted—and by whom. According to the more fundamentalist view, the Sharia must reflect the absolute supremacy of Allah, and must provide a Sharia which prescribes exact rules to which people should submit by strict and meticulous compliance and obedience. These rules can be defined and interpreted only by religious jurists. Moderate Muslims however, believe that, in the moment of creation, God has entrusted humanity with a heavy responsibility by providing human beings with rationality and the ability to differentiate between right and wrong. They must use this capacity to strive to achieve goodness, which includes justice, mercy and compassion. They point out that the Quran itself says "God creates the capacity for you to act, and ultimately it is you who acquire a choice from among the choices God presents."

But this is essentially a religious dichotomy, and the debate always takes place within the context of a broader world. It is this broader world which forces the religious debate into arenas not fully covered by traditional texts or interpretations. Examples are environmentalism, economic affairs, the breadth and scope of education, and who provides health care—and indeed human rights. As Muslim states advanced—even as early as the development of the Ottoman Empire and the state of Egypt—there has been a tendency to expand secular law and retrench the more conservative views of the application of Sharia law, but still incorporating elements of Sharia law into the secular base. As this has happened, the role of religious scholars as interpreters of "the law" has shrunk and more secular forms of interpretation have dominated. In a parallel pattern, the role of the Mosque as the provider of social services has been preempted but not eliminated by the growth of state provided social services. The provision of social services by Muslim groups of all kinds represents one of the best ways of attracting and holding the backing of the people.

The process of developing laws is called *Ijtihad* and it may draw on several techniques: the use of consensus and/or the synthesis of various views; the use of analogy or precedent; elements from the four schools of Sunni thought; elements of Shia thought. The products of these techniques are laws or policies used by governments to conduct the practical work of governance. These laws are also used to define actual working and living relationships between human beings.

Within the Muslim world, the Sharia is mostly seen as universal, but it is also a product of the Arab center, and is not always fully understood or accepted in far flung corners of the Muslim world. The decline of the Sharia is heavily a factor in the emergence of non Arab Muslims in Persia, Turkey and the Far East, beginning as early as the ninth century. Thus, it certainly cannot be blamed on

"Westernism" although Western values are often seen as conflicting with Islamic values.

In fact, it appears that even relatively conservative Muslim scholars believe that most Western laws are, or can be made consistent with the broad principles of the Sharia. Put another way, Sharia laws can be mandated, and they will easily accommodate a wide range of laws dealing with more secular dimensions of governance with little or no moral or ethical conflict as long as they are judged to be "consistent with" the Sharia. Mutually held concepts include the idea of government accountability; some form of the concept of checks and balances; the desirability of an independent judiciary; the concept of equal justice (colored by belief/non-belief); the security of the State; the responsibility of the State to help the needy.

Further, Islamic scholars are criticized when they try to insist that only they can define the final version of laws or policies. Too many of them have been appointed by, or benefited from dictatorial regimes, and too many of them have proved to be so rigid and inflexible that they are not credible. Therefore, while it is generally acknowledged that religious leaders should be part of the law drafting process, they are seldom (except in Iran) allowed the final voice. Other approved voices are public opinion and, increasingly, those with "the most relevant knowledge". In this context, there seems to be a lot of confusion over whether the public includes all citizens or just believers.

Both the Quran and Sharia contain many elements of equality for women in society and in governance. But the failure here is very pronounced. Many Muslim communities keep women in an inferior status as a matter of the traditional male view of that role. But according to the holy sources, that kind of attitude should be impossible! So the continuing failure of Muslim society to make women equal is massive hypocrisy, widely tolerated by the conservative religious leadership as well as government leadership. Similarly, an independent judiciary is mandated by the controlling religious documents—so that if a regime prevents this, they are in violation of holy writ, and this should be impossible. Yet few court systems in the Muslim world are really independent.

Economic concerns are growing, and there seems little comfort in the more traditional Islamic principles. As many as 50 million new jobs are needed if the current unemployment and the large numbers of annual school graduates are to be accommodated, but few of the region's economies can meet this need. There is a growing perception among Middle East populations that democracy is badly needed, and little confidence that current regimes are willing to move in that direction. This is not a direct reflection of Islamist religious positions, but it is another pressure on religious leadership. In Egypt, the linkage is direct: many organized demonstrations (e. g. the Kifaya or "Enough" movement) have had Muslim Brotherhood backing and mobilization of demonstrators. But essentially, Islamic political movements face most of the same problems as their more secular rivals, and it now seems that advocacy of the mandating of Sharia law is increasingly viewed with concern by the public. And as elsewhere, it is not certain that even valid elections will really have much effect.

SOURCES

Dawood, N. J. "The Koran", New York, Penguin Books, 1997.

Esack, Farid, "The Quran: A Short Introduction", Oxford, One World Publications 2002.

Fuller, Graham E., "The Future of Political Islam", New York, Palgrave Macmillan, 2003.

Kuran, Timur, "The Long Divergence", The Princeton Press, 2011.

Mohaddssin, Mohammad, "Islamic Fundamentalism" The New Global Threat", The Seven Locks Press, 1993.

Nasi, Vali, "The Shia Revival", W. W. Norton and Co., 2007.

Nasr, Sayyed, and Tromppert, Leigh (Eds.), Freedom House Study: "Women's Rights in the Middle East and North Africa", Rowman and Littefield Publishers, 2005.

Said, Edward, W. "The Question of Palestine", Vintage Books, 1992.

Sultan, Sohaib N., "The Quran and Sayings of the Prophet Muhammad", Woodstock, Vt., Skylight Path Publishing, 2007.

Tekeyh, Ray, "Hidden Iran", New York, Times Books, 2006.

Zia, Rubehsna (Ed.), "Globalization, Modernization and Education in Muslim Countries", New York, Nova Science Publishers, Inc. 2006.

The Economist, "Swords and the Word: Shia-Sunni Strife", May, 2012.

The Economist, "Putting Fatwas in Writing: Islamists and Arab Constitutions, March, 2012.

Samir, Kahil Samir, "Violent Fatwas Worry Muslim Governments" Spiro News, September, 2006.

Esposito, John L. "Practice and Theory: A Response to Islam and the Challenge of Democracy", Boston Review, April/May, 2003.

Kuran, Timur, "The Religious Undercurrents of Muslim Economic Grievances", Social Sciences Research Council Essay Forum, 2011.

Beltramitti, Silvia, "The Legality of Intellectual Property Rights Under Islamic Laws", Digital Islam, February, 2011.

Chaney, Eric, "Islamic Institutions and Economic Development, VOX, September, 2010.

Landis, Joshua M., "Islamic Education in Syria: Undoing Secularism", Brown University Watson Institute for International Studies, November, 2003.

Otto, Jan Michiel (Ed.), "Sharia Incorporated", Leiden University Press, 2004.

CHAPTER IV

EDUCATION IN MUSLIM COUNTRIES

There is a great element of strength among Muslims in their long tradition of honoring learning and scholarship. The Quran says "Seeking knowledge is incumbent on every Muslim. Seek knowledge from the cradle to the grave." This in turn led to a broad cultural preference where learning was strongly connected with the religious establishment. The leadership of mosques created schools (*madrassas*) all over the Muslim world, and it is not surprising that these schools concentrated on religious instruction, usually to the exclusion of many other fields of study.

But the world expanded and became more complex and sophisticated, and the older educational system began to face new realities. Critical new fields of knowledge evolved, but Islamic educators showed a reluctance to permit what they regarded as secular interference with what they saw as the need for immutable obedience to defined wisdom. Muslims found themselves deprived; they felt entitled to the benefits of modern medicine, modern engineering which could produce crucial upgrades of public infrastructure, new and more modern and complex forms of commerce and industry, and broad new forms of human relations, including cultural diversity, expanding roles for women and minorities, and a new yearning for people to speak for themselves and to be listened to, and not merely dictated to.

Starting largely with the Ottoman Empire from the fifteenth and sixteenth centuries, the roles of government expanded. In education, government schools began to replace the old traditional mosque *madrassas* as the primary source of elementary education. This conflict was a part of a broader conflict between the new secular power of governments vs. the older and more conservative religious establishment. But these conflicts are increasingly three sided, with the "third side" represented by the general Muslim population. People are increasingly disenchanted with governments that have proven to be dictatorial, incompetent and corrupt, nor do the great majority of Muslims want to become the victims either of terrorists or excessively fundamentalist religious zealots.

But there are enormous, intractable schisms within the Muslim world: Sunni vs. Shia, between hundreds of religious sects and subgroups and schools of thought, between believers and non-believers, between men and women, young vs. old, conflicts between ancient tribes and clans, conflicts involving unfair and inequitable divisions of wealth, cities vs. rural areas, between political ins and outs, and always, the tyrannies of some power elite imposed on average citizens. These schisms mean interminable conflicts throughout all of Muslim society, and they tend to carry forward into the roles of government such as education. In truth, there are hundreds of millions of Muslims who live quite successfully in very mixed cultures, and as minorities in many countries. Divisiveness is often exacerbated by bad governments seeking to hold on to power.

But the education systems have serious problems all their own. Despite their traditional respect for learning, almost every Muslim country underfunds it elementary and secondary education systems. National political leadership tends to say the right things about the values of education, but priorities for the allocation of scarce funds will inevitably favor economic development in any form, and very high expenditures on the military establishment. It is a common pattern for elementary and secondary education to be delegated to provincial and town levels of government with the full recognition that they seldom have the funds to support them properly. As a consequence, this long term neglect has resulted in entire national systems that are wretched: the physical plant tends to be poorly built, old, shabby, often filthy, ill maintained and repaired, and often lacking water, sanitation, and even heat or running water. Teachers lack adequate training, decent books, black boards or maps. Ane seldom can they hope for anything as astonishing as a classroom computer.

The teachers themselves may be marginally educated, and most school systems seem never to have the money for the training, balanced distribution, economic wellbeing, in-service development and social wellbeing of this vital human resource. The reality often is small one room schools, and double shift education.

And what is taught is all too often marginal. Textbooks, when available, tend to be obsolete and poorly written. The curricula are usually regarded as simplistic, out of date, and irrelevant. Far too much teaching is in the form of older patterns of recitation and memorization. Educators all seem to mouth the more modern concepts for the stimulation of independent student thinking, but there is constant frustration that these ideas never actually penetrate the classroom. And yet, these systems seem to reward themselves. Administrative costs are usually very high, overhead costs are excessive, too many people are sitting in offices and too few are teaching in classrooms. Teacher salaries and benefits are seen as very generous (teachers vote!), and at the same time, classroom performance is heavily condemned as seriously inferior. There are usually very high drop out rates that school administrators and government officials do not want to acknowledge. About 15 percent of students do not complete even primary education, and 70 percent of those who fail to attend are girls. In some rural areas, more than 50 percent of girls never even enter school. While some countries such as Jordan and Syria have 95 percent student enrollments, half of the children in Sudan are not in school, and in parts of Egypt the enrollment is as low as 10 percent. Given this reality, it sad to see how educators surround themselves with a halo of virtue, setting noble objectives for school systems that are never realized. For example, here are the criteria for drafting of a new law in Iran: (1)

* Religious education to be provided for all to develop noble character.
* A teaching and learning process, pedagogical, as well as participative.
* A competency based curriculum.
* Educational evaluation, accreditation and certification
* The enhancement of qualifications and competence of educational personnel.
* Sufficient funding for education as a priority in national development.
* Making primary education compulsory and free.
* The autonomous management of education.
* Development of community centers and civil society participation.
* Monitoring the implementation and evaluation of activities in national education systems.

In Iran, the official objectives of the education system also include such values as kindness, respect, order, discipline, honesty, truthfulness, politeness, patience, optimism, helpfulness, cleanliness, hard work, courage, chastity, modesty, proper dress, obedience to one's parents, observance of the law—plus assuring the progress of the Nation, the security of the people and national unity!

In Turkey, the Ministry of Education has established the following general objectives: (2)

1. To develop scientific and technological activity programs that will provide the development of intelligence and bring forward research and creativity in all stages of education.
2. To equalize the education level in our country for males and females.
3. To provide equality of opportunity of all kinds and at all levels of education.

4. To reach the European Union indicators in all levels of education.
5. To increase the qualitative productivity of the education system.
6. To increase student's success at all levels of education.
7. To improve school libraries in all education institutions.
8. To increase efficiency of resource utilization.
9. To provide the employment of qualified personnel in all levels of the education system. In addition, there are must be objectives to increase the use of pre school preparation.

There is nothing wrong with these objectives, except they were dreamed up by a professional academic bureaucracy in a country with a historically weak and neglected education system.

The Education Systems of Muslim Countries

Education in Egypt

Since independence from the British in 1952 until the early 1990s, education in Egypt showed a history of massive neglect, even during the days of Nasserite socialism. Since then, the efforts of the government have been far more serious, but underpowered. The country has an exploding population and the school system has had trouble trying to keep pace. Growing demands have left the system underfunded, obsolete, and losing quality. Increasing numbers of graduates are unemployable for both economic and education reasons. The official curriculum is seen as largely irrelevant. Teachers are still underpaid, low in prestige, low in the quality of their teaching, and lacking contemporary professional and technical knowledge.

An over abundance of administrators created bad bureaucratic practices, and robbed classrooms of teachers. Facilities are old and in bad shape, classrooms are overcrowded, facilities and equipment are in constant shortage, and schools have often been forced to use two and even three shifts. There is a common pattern of having many students who are officially registered but never attend class. There are many complaints about rote learning, mechanistic learning, obsolete course content, obsolete knowledge bases by teachers, and lack of modern equipment, especially in information technologies.

There is a major disparity between perceived need and school offerings, which were said to create incompetent degree holders in unwanted subjects. In addition, financing is always scarce, and parents have to pay high fees (10% of annual income) for their "free" schooling. This includes exam fees, uniform charges, enrollment fees, and even private tutoring, often by the same teachers who are underpaid in their official jobs. The rigid centralized bureaucracy, clogged with excess seniority-promoted staff is cumbersome and slow moving, and the highly centralized educational planning and policy making tend to disenfranchise the very people at the local level who are entrusted with achieving its goals. In other words the central government, having officially delegated primary education to local governments, insists on keeping bureaucratic control at the center. And, as the usual common pattern, there is a vast difference between grandiose plans and actual accomplishment.

Like the country itself, the education system includes, and reflects several experiences: the British (exclusionary and elitist); Egyptian local culture; Islamic culture; and Western secularism. Muhammad Ali (1805-1849), with a succeeding dynasty lasting until independence in 1952), was regarded as the initiator of modern Egypt, and the first and greatest reformer of the education system because he introduced many modern secular and scientific courses, and a far more modernist education philosophy. This revised philosophy persists today, but much of the older Islamic school structure has remained.

In fact, it must be said that Egypt has a two track educational system that runs in parallel. In Egypt as elsewhere in the Muslim world, religious teaching is seen by its practitioners not as a second system, but as the only system. Thus, Egypt has a system of Mosque Quranic schools (*kuttabs*); religious schools (*madrassas*); and separate Sufi schools. This system is seen as not simply supplying education, but as defining and inculcating a whole concept of a culture—and in fact, two—that of Islam and of Arabs. It also seems to be true that Nasser's excursion into Pan-Arabism and state socialism has left at least a philosophical impact on education. But in total, Egypt has tried to keep the education as open as possible and as conflict free as possible.

Egypt has the usual kind of elementary and secondary structure; in their case, two years of pre-school, five years of primary school; then three years of prep school, all free and mandatory. Enrollment figures are impressive: "enrollment" stands at more than 90 percent (1991), but after dropouts, the numbers actually attending are said to be 84 percent, with unofficial estimates closer to 70 percent. But rural enrollments are far worse, as low as 10 percent in some regions. Gender enrollments are fairly good; there is even a law which prohibits girls from being married before age sixteen, but it is largely ignored. And, enrollment at the secondary level is far lower than at the primary school level. Students may now attend private schools or religious schools. Secondary schools may be either general preparation, or vocational education. Advancement is by examination, and after secondary school, they may be used to direct students to further education.

"The parallel Islamic educational system, also known as the Al-Azhar system, has a four year primary stage, a three year prep stage, and a four year secondary stage. Girls and boys attend separate schools. Classes are essentially the same as the public schools with the addition of study of the Quran and "Islamic sciences". The system has about 165,000 students in 57 secondary schools who automatically qualify for entry into Al-Azhar University. Both Arabic and English are official languages of instruction.

An interesting and successful idea has been creation of a number of rural welfare centers which offer limited health care and literacy education; there are almost 10 million illiterates between ages fifteen and thirty-five.

Education in Indonesia

Education policy, along with all else, is dictated by interpretations of what is deemed for the good of the State. Young people must be guarded by traditional and religious values. Students should acquire: "firmness, openness, tolerance, risk-taking, independence, self-confidence, sincerity, patience, self-discipline, and modern values guarded by faith and piety." But it is clear that most of this is a pompous, self-serving litany of virtue.

The Constitution says that one of the national goals should be to obtain an education, and that education is deeply rooted in the national culture, but early examples of education are, strikingly, about political education and not education in general. Many felt that Indonesia could not achieve independence without the people being educated, but that is exactly what happened. When the Dutch withdrew, less than 10 percent of the people could read and write, and less than 20 percent of children were in school.

Muslim schools were an early development, and the system remains dual track: one is religious, and the newer one is for teaching of science, technology and other forms of "secular" education. A Ministry of Religious Affairs administers Islamic education, which educates from 10 to 15 percent of students in the country. The shift away from the more conservative grip on education is in part because of the fact that there is a real split within the Muslim community itself; Indonesians are mostly moderates. The moderate view is that education is mainly for developing modern skills to deal with the economic, political and social world, and not for developing the perfect sense of the Muslim religion.

The system is generally divided into elementary, secondary and higher secondary, for both tracks. In addition to universities, there are theological seminaries, which are primarily, as elsewhere, designed to produce eminently qualified religious scholars. Secular education is divided into two tracks: school and non-school, which is more technical and practical. Education up to age seven is the sole responsibility of the State; education up to the ninth grade is mandatory. No real effort was put into school administration until after 1990, and this included the decentralization of responsibility for schooling generally and of school finances, but in a common pattern found in so many countries, the central government still insists on the authority to set the curriculum and about 80 percent of course content. This central authority extends to private schools.

Education in Iran

Iran has seen two waves of educational development. The first was under the regime of Shah Pahlavi from 1925 to 1979, in which the older traditional clerical based system was pursued in local primary schools and religious colleges. The Pahlavi regime set its main objectives as the training of Iranians for modern occupations in administration, management, science, technology and economics, with a new and more highly educated teacher corps. The Shah envisioned a more European secular middle class.

The second wave occurred after the 1979 revolution when a total and swift "Islamization" of the system was undertaken. Universities were closed down between 1979 and 1982 while major changes were mandated. All students were segregated by gender. The Cultural Revolution Committee was formed to revamp the curriculum to reflect Islamic values, and this revamp was extended to the university system where several thousand new textbooks of varying quality were produced within the first few years of the conversion. Professors who were not considered sufficiently "Islamic" were removed; the student body itself shrunk by as much as 75 percent between 1979 and 1983 in part because those who were not Muslim were often no longer admitted. Another victim was the Literacy Corps, established by the Shah in 1963 to send educated conscripts to the villages and towns. During its existence, the Corps helped 2.2 million children and 600,000 adults become literate. But it was shut down shortly after the Islamic Revolution.

And yet, again in May of 2011, Iran's Supreme Leader, Ayatollah Ali Khamenei once more denounced the national education system as "imported" and argued once again that it needed to become more Iranian and Islamic. **(4)** To this end, the authorities have launched about 10,000 new Quran Schools (toward an ultimate goal of 50,000 such schools) to act as cultural bases for student indoctrination. These schools will largely offer classes after regular school. But this is an extraordinary confession of some kind of failure. It says that, after more than 30 years, an education system designed heavily to produce the New Islamic Citizen, especially one who is also properly educated and useful, has failed to deliver. In fact, the serious debate within the country makes it clear that the regime has still not really figured out what such a citizen should be like, or how to teach both revolutionary ideology and modern knowledge to its children. Meanwhile, teachers struggle along, teaching to the text, because that is the only safe course of action.

Education in Iran is remains highly centralized. The Ministry of Education is in charge of educational planning, financing, administration and textbooks for the primary system, along with teacher training and evaluation. At the university level, supervision is also through the Ministry of Science and Technology. In an unusual provision, every university student is required to commit to serve the government for a number of years, and much of this service for men is in the military.

Despite the gender separation, women have done particularly well in the last fifteen to twenty years. It is now estimated that they make up more than 50 percent of university students, with some fields of science and engineering, and Iran is said to have the highest female to male ratio in primary schools among world countries at 1.2: 1. Today, 77 percent of the population is literate. After 1989, private universities have been permitted. Secondary education at state institutions is free but there may be heavy fees borne by students. At the level of grades nine through eleven, two tracks are offered. One is the General/Academic track which offers areas of study in the literature and arts, natural sciences, physics and mathematics, and social sciences and economics. The other track is the Technical/ Vocational track which aims to train for service occupations, technician skills, and agriculture.

The reconstruction of the university system has permitted some emphasis on science, technology and management, and if there is a new trend, it is to provide more training at all levels in the skills that are needed by a modern economy.

But many people and groups in Iran still persistently argue that the school system has obligations more than religious education, and in these other roles, the system is failing. As one observer put it "The debate that our schools are not Islamic enough, or include western culture is irrelevant. Students must learn today's science and life skills, like elsewhere in the world, taking cultural difference into consideration. In general, rankings in international student comparisons place them in the bottom half. Instructors tend to give lessons to students as passive listeners, and spend too much time rote cramming students for the all-important, and feared university entrance exam." (5)

Private schools have been permitted since 1989, but their record is mixed. They are expensive, they often use the same teachers that were trained for the public system, and they often use the same textbooks. They are often suspected of padding their results to attract customers. But it seems that, whatever their reputation they are still seen as better than most public schools and their enrollments are still growing.

Education in Jordan

Starting with almost nothing in the early 1920s, Jordan has built a comprehensive high quality education system with 2787 public schools, 1500 private schools 48 community colleges and 19 universities. Education is free, and there is about 95 percent enrollment. Women are educated, and they are now two thirds of community college enrollment and 45 percent of university enrollment. The system is trying to upgrade the curriculum to teach more "thinking". In total, Jordan has the third lowest illiteracy rate in the Muslim world. Jordan ranks 90th out of 177 nations in the Human Development Index—the best in the Arab world, and its graduates can usually be accepted in the best universities around the world. Its education policies are secular: to meet the needs of a knowledge-based economy; to upgrade the physical plant; and to promote early childhood education. In a next step, targets will shift to upgrading teacher qualifications and performance, curriculum modernization and better means for evaluating student performance.

Basic education is two years of pre-school, ten years of compulsory basic education, and a final two years of preparation for either academic or vocational education. The Jordanian population is very young, and almost one third of them are in some form of school. Schools have also enjoyed great success in dealing with gender equality, and in bringing rural education almost up to the level of urban education. At the secondary school level, Islamic studies are mandatory for all students except Christians. There has been some decline in vocational education, in part because the academic track is more popular, but vocational education is highly prized as an attractive pathway to good jobs, and the government wants to make this track stronger. The United Nations Relief and Works Agency (UNRWA) operates a region-wide school system for Palestinian refugees—one of the biggest such systems in the region.

Jordan shares a common pattern with other Muslim countries in that the education bureaucracy is seen as too narrow and self-aggrandizing, and does not recognize the fact that most education takes place outside of the formal state administered schools system. Over and above formal technical training organizations, most companies teach new employees how to do their jobs, including formal On the Job Training (OJT) programs, or just by coaching of new employees. In most Muslim countries, a large proportion of the economy is in the informal sector where jobs are largely self-taught. Much of what is taught in formal schools is intellectually correct, but of little relevance in the real world, but almost nobody in government thinks this way.

Meanwhile, the Jordanian government is supposedly pursuing an agenda of reform, including financial reforms, judiciary reforms, modernizing of administrative and service delivery systems, economic liberalization, attempts to shift the economy to higher value added products and services, and the development of more sophisticated legal bases. Part of this is the supposed modernization of the formal education system, whose advocates claim that education is the keystone to all else. But like most Muslim countries, Jordan's population is more than half under the age of 18, and each year, more young people enter the job market than the economy can accommodate.

Education in Morocco

Morocco has the usual type of pattern: two years of pre-school (voluntary) plus five years of primary school and four years of secondary school. This is then followed by three years of general secondary school or technical education. In the primary schools, the language of instruction is Arabic, but French is used in the universities. This language requirement is seen as a real barrier to enrollment which Morocco can ill afford.

There is a Supreme Council for Education, linked with a Supreme Council for National Development and Planning under the King. At the time of Independence (1956) only 10 percent of children were enrolled in school, and only fifteen thousand boys were enrolled in secondary level—no girls allowed. Less than four hundred students were enrolled in any university.

Morocco is a strange and frustrating story of continued, earnest efforts to improve the education system with disappointing results. In 2000, 50 percent of the population was still illiterate; only 30 percent of women could read or write. King Mohammad V and the government had to fight their way through a debilitating war with the religious establishment, centered at the ancient and prestigious Karaouine University and educational establishment to force it to offer such classes as mathematics, chemistry, physics, foreign languages, and especially, the education of women. According to a Time report of 1960, "Karaouine's hidebound ulemas protested that the King's education would spread license, debauchery and degeneracy. But the King refused to give way and, as the "Commander of the Faithful' for all Muslims insisted on his right to decide. Facing the collapse of their powers, the white-gowned ulemas abandoned their plans to boycott the independence anniversary ceremonies and glumly turned out to hear Muhammad extoll the university's renaissance". **(6)**

The same conflict marked the whole education system. In 1959, education was largely Koranic, but a pitiful 10 percent of children actually attended elementary schools, and fewer than 5 percent made it to any secondary school. And these students were only boys. Now, more than 50 years later, school systems remain marginal, despite all of the plans and committees and high sounding rhetoric. Literacy rates remain very low (52 percent), access to schools is still limited, especially in rural areas, many students never make it to school, and for those who do, drop-out rates remain high (22 percent), and girls still are badly under served. In addition, schools have been generally underfunded, there is a congenital lack of decent facilities and equipment, teacher training is weak, and the children themselves seem to hate the whole thing. There seems, still, to be too much rote memorization, too much junk work, too much emphasis on cramming for the university exam, and little recognition in schools of the realities of life outside of schools. There are widespread feelings that students will never actually learn anything that will get them a job, or prepare them to deal with life's uncertainties. The Human Development Index ranks Morocco at one hundred thirtieth place.

Official policies aim at full integration of all school systems (public, Koranic, private). Private schools are usually independent, and are growing in numbers, mainly because many public schools are not very good and private schools are seen as preferred by those who can afford them. Almost 40% of vocational schools are privately run. At the university level, Morocco has 14 public universities and many private universities, but they are small and represent less than 3.5% of the university population. The University Al-Karaouine in Fez was founded in 859, and makes the claim to be the oldest university in the world, and it has (often reluctantly) done much to restore its reputation after the debacle of 1960. At the university level, the language of instruction generally shifts from Arabic to French (and English) in large part because of the huge quantity and quality of available material compared to that in Arabic.

Education in Pakistan

Education in Pakistan is under the general supervision of the Ministry of Education, but its role is largely policy formulation and the issuance of uniform educational objectives and standards for evaluation. The government has devolved responsibility for schools down to provinces and municipalities. Education is not mandatory; it is divided into primary (5 grades), middle stage (3 grades); lower secondary (2 grades); and upper secondary (2 grades). A program of vocational/technical instruction is offered after the middle stage for boys, and the primary stage for girls. This kind of technical education extends into the university level.

But the government proposals for education devolution have long been stalled by a legal case before the Supreme Court. Strong opposition to devolution has been led by academics, teachers, opposition political parties and even students. The general case is that provinces will not maintain curriculum uniformity, but perhaps the more compelling argument is that provinces do not have enough skills or the infrastructure to run schools, and that they don't have the money either. In addition, the government has sent thousands of students abroad to study, and students fear the death of that system. Further, if the provinces try to raise more money by higher school fees (rather than general taxation), it is suspected that parents can't afford such fees, and student attendance will suffer. In Islamabad, an increase in fees of 700 percent has just been enacted at a time when one fourth of the population is living under the $2 per day poverty line.

So what is the consequence of all of this? Pakistan's education system is one of the worst in the world. Even the government is forced to admit that the country is in the midst of an educational emergency because the current system has produced a disastrous human and economic result. A government study, reported on the BBC in March, 2011 **(7)** stated that funding for schools had been cut from about 2.5 percent of GDP to less than 1.5 percent in the last 7 years. Few of Pakistan's twenty-five million children will ever receive an adequate education. Three million will never ever attend classes in schools. Of those children who do attend school, a third will stay there for less than two years. Of those who attend, half of them are incapable of reading even the simplest of materials.

School system physical plant, never very good, has been allowed to deteriorate from prolonged neglect. Only about two thirds of schools have proper rest rooms or even drinking water. More than 20,000 schools do not even have a building. Overall, lack of funds, poor curricula, poor and limited teaching materials, inadequately trained teachers, high rates of absenteeism, and poor facilities all seem eternal and governments seem totally incapable of doing anything about them. Parents who can afford it will send their children to private schools, especially if they have any intention of sending them on to a university.

Private education is available at all levels, with little or no government assistance. Currently, the government spends just under 2 percent of GDP on education, and plans to increase this to 7 percent simply sound ludicrous. Expenditure has remained stagnant for most of the last thirty-seven years.

Most of the private schools must follow government defined curricula. But that curriculum is very much under fire. The Sustainable Development Policy Institute reported in 2008 that "for over two decades, the curricula and official textbooks in subjects such as English, social studies, civics and Urdu have contained religious propaganda. The chairman of the Islamabad based Quaid-i-Azam University wrote in Foreign Affairs: "Pakistani schools—and not just madrassas—are churning out fiery zealots, fueled with a passion for jihad and martyrdom." **(8)**

And the general view is that the government bears a lot of the blame. Even the official National Education Policy 2009 said that "the weak education sector results from a lack of commitment to education and a poor implementation of policies." It urges increased spending, a wider range of subjects taught in *madrassa* schools, better teacher training, curriculum reform, public-private sector partnerships, and even food based incentives to increase enrollment and retention. But figures show that Pakistanis fifty-five years or older have a literacy rate of less than 30 percent, the consequence of old sins. Only 63 percent of Pakistani children make it as far as finishing the fifth grade, and just 6.3 percent make it through college (8.9 percent for men; 3.5 percent for women). In truth, the system has been making progress in narrowing the gender gap, with a lot of public acceptance. But to quote the newspaper *THE NEWS (Jan. 21, 2009)*, the Taliban "imposed enforcement of a complete ban on female education in the Swat district. Some four hundred private schools enrolling forty thousand girls have been shut down. At least ten schools that tried to open after the January 15, 2009 deadline were blown up by the militants in the town of Mingora. More than one hundred and seventy schools have been bombed or torched, along with other government buildings."**(9)**

A further serious impediment is the culture of many tribes and clans, especially in the Federally Administered Tribal Areas where male literacy is just 29.5 percent and female literacy is a miserable 3 percent. There is some research evidence based on citizen polls indicating that the public believes that illiteracy is a cause of religious extremism. Registered *madrassas* number somewhere between ten and twenty thousand, but there are many more that are unregistered. The consequence of this appears to be that a significant number of children get a very inferior education, especially in coping with the real world. And it should be recognized that much of the extremism that may be learned in these *madrassas* is not aimed just against the West, but emphasizes conflicts within the Muslim world itself. The government has set out to reform *madrassas* but their programs have shown little success—less than five hundred out of ten thousand have accepted any kind of reform. It also does not seem that this is an area where the U. S. or any outside interest can be influential.

Education in Saudi Arabia

Saudi Arabia is highly conservative in both religious and governance terms. It believes in education, both for religious purposes and for economic development needs—and this is a constant balancing act. Until 2003, Saudi Arabia maintained three separate school systems: a general system for all through primary education; a secondary system which offers tracks for either religious or secular training; and a separate system for girls. It was not until 2003 that these systems were consolidated into a Ministry of Education, and girls may now attend all classes except those designated as agricultural or commercial. There are now nursery schools and kindergartens. Primary schools are "lower"—three grades; and "upper"—four, five and six grades. Intermediate schools are where the divisions begin. They are for three years and may be religious, general, or technical. Again, girls may attend only the general and religious schools. Secondary education is for students age fifteen to seventeen. Here, there are general, religious, technical, vocational, commercial and agricultural tracks. The numbers of students in these schools is very low.

As for the schools themselves, they are competent but lack a strong edge; teachers are capable but lack really good in-service training. The physical plant is acceptable, but could well be improved, especially in rural areas. The one major concern is a common pattern throughout the region, and in most developing countries. Students may be lucky enough to learn knowledge, but they do not learn how to THINK. They are said to lack a competitive edge, and not to understand the concepts of creativity, or such other ideas as excellence as a desirable human quality, or initiative, or productivity, or "agility".

That said, Saudi Arabia is moving, slowly and often reluctantly toward a more versatile and productive education system, pushing through what is often adamant resistance from the more conservative elements of society. Some of this is religious, but some is simply the long term conservative nature of a rural and Bedouin society. Indeed, it is a common pattern. All of these Muslim countries are having trouble coping with the pace of change, or even the very idea of change. It is hard to decide how much of this lag is attributed to conservative Islamic influences, but it is clear that nowhere is religion solely at fault. Most Arabic societies are still rooted in rural conservatism, and cities are relatively rough and unsophisticated.

Education in Sudan

Education is supposedly free and compulsory, with eight years of primary, and three years of secondary classes. But in fact, schools are really available only in the urban areas of the North: in the South and in Darfur, little education is really available. There never seems to have been much, but most have been destroyed by years of civil war in the south, and government sponsored terrorism in Darfur. Rural/village schools are pathetic; about 45 percent consist of a flip chart under a tree. Enrollment is about 45 percent at the primary level and 20 percent at secondary: meaning that more than one half of Sudanese children (a total of about 2 million) are not in school. Male graduates of secondary or university programs are required to perform military service. The system since its earliest days has been elitist; in the south, it was mostly provided by missionary schools, but whoever provided it, it was seriously inferior, and then the government ejected all foreign missionaries in 1964 at the start of the civil war.

The government began reform in its core Muslim areas in the North as early as 1969, but the system continues to be limited. It is structured in the usual pattern aimed at sorting out academic and technical streams. It has failed to offer courses that are real world in the sense that they prepare students for actual jobs. Post-secondary education now includes universities, higher technical schools, and teacher training for secondary and upper secondary schools.

Literacy, which was 23 percent had risen only to 30 percent by 1990, and is not much higher today because a whole generation of students were deprived of an adequate education. The system remains highly elitist. University costs are borne by the government for selected students. There is a small Islamic University of Omdurman to train religious judges and scholars.

Traditionally, girl's education was rudimentary at best, by intent, and was frequently provided by a religious school teaching girls right and proper thoughts from the Quran. When girls did begin to get educated in the sixties, they were confined to primary education and seldom got up to secondary, vocational or university education—again by government design. Even parents often were suspicious of schooling for girls, worrying about corruption of their morals.

The regime in Khartoum remains ultra conservative, drawing support from S. Arabia and Wahhabist support from elsewhere. Education reform has really meant a deepening of Islamist influence and a heavy Muslim curriculum. Membership in the Popular Defense Forces, a paramilitary body allied with the National Islamic Front, became a requirement for university admission.

Government schools are poor. They suffer from huge classes, lack of teacher qualifications, run-down facilities, neglect of education in most of the country (south, Darfur, rural areas), and lack of professional and technical training. Mission schools have been nationalized, new Christian schools have been banned, there is constant harassment of non-government or non-Muslim schools, and many schools of all kinds were destroyed in the civil war. Often, young men were conscripted into military service off the streets or right out of classes, and lost years of education as a result. In 2000, less than 20% of eligible students were enrolled. And, in the usual pattern, "free" education has proved to be quite expensive. Most teachers are inadequately trained and educated; many have not even completed primary school themselves. As a result, Sudan has the second lowest access to primary education of any country in the world after Afghanistan. In South Sudan, just 16 percent of children

180

can read. Less than 3 percent of children make it through primary school. Less than one half of schools have running water, and only one third have latrines. Illiteracy is high, especially for older people. Even when parents have children in school, 76 percent of them cannot read their child's report card.

"Arabization" was forced on the south which is largely Christian or Animist. This oppression heavily contributed to the revolt and subsequent independence of the south and the creation of a new country of South Sudan. One very positive note is that, since independence in 2005, S. Sudan has made remarkable strides in school upgrading. The number of children in school has tripled; hundreds of new classrooms have been built or adapted; many new teachers have been recruited. As of yet, this reform has not come close to being adequate, but it continues. It simply proves the horrible degree of neglect that existed in the hands of the Arab regime in Khartoum.

Education in Syria

Syria has had a relatively good education system, providing almost universal government furnished primary education, and the last decade has seen a pattern of gradually growing expenditures on education. Literacy levels are high, exceeding 82 percent; women have full access to the system, and the percentage of students enrolled is high, exceeding 95 percent. By law, all students receive free education through nine grades. If there are problems to work on, they relate to regional disparities and the usual rural vs. urban gap. The system gives strong emphasis to a program of Technical and Vocational Education and Training and almost 40 percent of students choose this path, with more than a third of them women.

Higher education is under the supervision of the usual Ministry of Education. Most of the system is public, but since 2001, private universities have been permitted. In general, fees are modest for those students who maintain satisfactory levels of attainment. There is an understandable emphasis on engineering and medicine, but less development in law or business. The government appears to recognize that the system has suffered from a low reputation for both quality and relevance, and it has been criticized as contributing to the low productivity of the workforce. Youth unemployment has been high for a long time because their education seemed unable to provide them with the skills and competencies demanded in the labor market, but the basic fact is that the economy itself is weak and largely obsolete. The government now has a specific goal to support the modernization of the economy, and part of this strategy is to use the education system to make computer literacy mandatory at the high school level, and to make English and French language instruction compulsory in the elementary schools

Syria, however, is subject to another form of stress and strain in the system through the strong but declining presence of the older Islamic schools which are seen as traditional, rigid, overwhelmingly Sunni in outlook, and often strongly intolerant of others. The current president, Bashar al-Assad, has expressed the intent to moderate these problems, but religious instruction and text books seem little changed. Children are required to receive religious instruction several hours a week, all the way up to the twelfth grade. And to some degree, the real emphasis is on Arab and not Islamic education. Educators in general have tried to stay out of the line of fire and hope that there is enough elbow room to promote the urgent needs within the system for modernization and some degree of increasing liberalism in human terms.

In a sense, this is not "Syrian" education but "Sunni/Arab" education, which often believes that it is their duty to save the world and to save humanity and human values. There seems to be little interest in reality, which, in the Muslim world has led to harsh wars and vicious dictators in Iran, Iraq, Syria, Egypt, Sudan, S. Arabia, Libya, Morocco, Afghanistan, Pakistan, Indonesia, Somalia, etc. The great Sunni/Arab vision seems to cause struggle and confusion in Syria. The alliance of Syria with Iran, Hezbollah, and Hamas looks increasingly like a loser, and Syria's leadership has come under severe internal insurrection and may not survive. Even before the unbelievable destruction of the raging civil war, the fear was that a much beleaguered education system was on the verge of collapse.

Education in Turkey

A background report issued by the Turkish Department of Education (10) is full of earnest statements of objectives and intent. As of 2005, there were about 10.5 million students in the mandatory eight year primary education; taught in 35,581 schools by 400,000 teachers. Secondary education is for four years, with three million students in 6861 schools with 168,000 teachers. In addition, there are general high schools (three years) and many technical high schools. Religious education is offered, but is optional, and is really comparative religion rather than Islamic training. At present, the national literacy rate is 82 percent, with 89 percent for males but only 69 percent for females. Almost one half of the national population is under the age of twenty-five, and the population, while 98 percent Muslim, is still 75 percent rural. Education is free except for private schools, but there are often high fees for parents for uniforms, books, pencils, and building maintenance.

This report lists the following main problems in education:

1. Crowded classrooms
2. Unsatisfactory school fees and rates
3. Waste of resources and time caused by failure or repetition of a grade
4. Double shift education
5. Integrated classrooms, especially in rural areas.
6. Lack of equipment
7. Lack of finance
8. Problems related to the training, balanced distribution, economic conditions, social status and in-service training of teachers.
9. Review need of the curricula, and the educational material according to the changing and varying educational needs of society.

Three others should be added: the high costs of teacher salaries and benefits, especially in the light of poor performance; the high cost of administrative overhead; and very high dropout rates which the government does not want to acknowledge. About 15 percent of students do not complete even primary education, and 70 percent of these are girls. In some rural areas, half of the girls never even enter school!

To deal with these problems, the Ministry has established the following general objectives:

1. To develop scientific and technological activity programs that will provide the development of intelligence and bring forward research and creativity in all stages of education.
2. To equalize the education level in our country for males and females.
3. To provide equality of opportunity of all kinds and at all levels of education.
4. To reach the EU indicators in all levels of education.
5. To increase the qualitative productivity of the education system.
6. To increase student's success at all levels of education.
7. To improve school libraries in all education institutions.
8. To increase efficiency of resource utilization.
9. To provide the employment of qualified personnel in all levels of the education system. In addition, there are objectives to increase the use of pre school preparation.

In general, the national government is responsible for the funding of basic education, but with some local money, largely for construction and maintenance. The national budget allocation is at 22 percent for education, but as in many other countries, the national government wants to keep policy control but to transfer the financing and operation of schools to local governments—or even NGOs. Actually, "Turkey's spending on education is very high as a share of GDP (seven percent)—among the highest in the world." But this is not because of public spending, which is somewhat below other EU and OECD countries. The main reason why Turkey spends so much on education is because of the large share of private out-of-pocket expenditures. Families are mostly providing these funds to pay for cramming and exam preparation courses, for additional subsidies for their children's primary and secondary schooling, or for fees for universities. "Compared with Europe and most of the world, Turkey's public schools have the least autonomy over resources, staff deployment in schools, textbook selections, allocation of instruction time, and selection of programs offered."(11) In effect, government funding for education is very confused; as many as sixty different fund sources are used, all with different ground rules and high degrees of uncertainty. University education is not free and usually costs $200 to $350 per year. Private universities are in the range of $4000 or more per year. Universities are under the supervision of a separate Council of Higher Education.

Perhaps the most interesting type of reform being undertaken is a shift from fixed often rote learning to teaching intended to get children to "think". Teaching techniques are being changed; more interaction and questioning is allowed in both directions; games and role playing are more often used; textbooks are being upgraded; and there are more classes for creative writing or art. But these are complex changes, and are difficult to achieve. Part of the slow pace of change is this, and part is plain inertia, and Turkey continues to lag far behind EU countries in the levels of learning competency.

There is a separate Turkish/European Union (EU) program to design a curriculum for teaching religion. Teaching religion is mandatory, but it has been a more general assessment of religion rather than religious instruction of any faith. Most of Turkish society is satisfied with the secular nature of the country and society, but the Muslim faith runs deep and 25 percent of the population is Alevi which is a moderate form of Islam, neither Sunni nor Shia. The Alevi are especially worried that any kind of religious education will end up being solely Sunni and much too fundamentalist in nature.

Another complication is the fact that the Turkish economy itself is changing, away from routine manual labor and machine tending toward more sophisticated manufacturing and the growth of service industries which demand higher levels of education. But the education system has trouble keeping up, and it still has real trouble giving students more relevant education for the market pace. More than 1.1 million of Turkey's 3 million secondary education students are in the technical/vocational track, but it is felt that their training is really not yet attuned to actual employment needs.

The Turks are trying to educate girls, but there is the usual pattern or parental or religious resistance, and a gap between registration and actual attendance, especially beyond primary. And the current trend is for students to seek to get into the general academic track rather than the vocational track because it seems to lead to better pay and more prestige. The system quite rightly wants to make sure that students in the vocational track still get a good grounding of general education. Meanwhile, the training of teachers progresses, apparently slowly, in part because—as almost everywhere else—pay is low, and many potential teachers opt for better paying jobs elsewhere. There are still small efforts to upgrade what teaching students learn—not just pedagogy, but better substance education.

What to Do

Some greater leadership must be taken by social leaders. This leadership can be within the government if possible, but it must also come from outside sources. The best hope for new leadership is from women, linked with a devout capable merchant class, plus lots of outside world help. The outside help cannot just be the professional academic community, which worships words and has trouble with action. Outside help is now primarily from technical or management sources, but this kind of talent should be brought to bear earlier to deal with school systems design and effectiveness of operations.

Some form of coalition is needed in most countries to solve the financial problems. Outside organizations can't really fund national school systems. Parliaments should try to create internal coalitions to block out adequate funds through a matching fund arrangement with local governments similar to the U. S. highway funding.

There is no issue more worthy of the attention of Muslim women than elementary and secondary education, but again, this cannot be solely in the hands of the professional academics. More effort must come from cause leaders, managers, technical experts and coalition builders. This is a mighty cause that could link and unite women's groups and interests like no other. It is useless to whine about Islam vs. the West; this whole issue is entirely within the power of Muslims themselves.

SCORE CARD FOR MUSLIM EDUCATION

Egypt: Education was badly neglected under Nasser. It is much better since, but underpowered and cannot keep up with an exploding population. The economy is incapable of providing enough serious jobs for the educated.

Indonesia: The education system is steadily broadening beyond its narrow religious history, but it is still dual track; religious and secular. Muslims here tend to be moderate, and most people strongly support the teaching of more modern subjects, and the government appears to be really trying.

Iran: The country has a decent system that was very good, then got very bad for a time after the Revolution, and is now good again. The improvement for female students at all levels has been remarkable.

Jordan: One of the best school systems and programs in the Muslim world. Education is free, there is about 95 percent enrollment, most women are educated, and the illiteracy rate is the third lowest in the Muslim world.

Morocco: A very bad system, even after liberation, when only 10 percent of students were enrolled in secondary schools. The country is still 50 percent illiterate and only 30 percent of rural women can read or write.

Pakistan: Pakistan's education system is widely viewed as one of the worst in the world, leaving the country with what even the government admits is a national educational emergency—a human and economic disaster.

Saudi Arabia: A good system, but not very good. Everything is OK, but never first rate. That said, Saudi Arabia is moving slowly and often reluctantly toward a more versatile and productive education system, but often in conflict with the more conservative elements of society.

Sudan: A horrible system which has produced horrible results. Sudan has the second lowest access to primary education of any country in the world, after only Afghanistan. More than 90 percent of teachers are considered inadequately trained. The long neglect of the Christian/Animist south of the country has left the new South Sudan country with only 16 percent of its students capable of reading or writing.

Syria: Syria has had a relatively good education system, especially in technical and vocational programs. It still suffers from resistance from older Islamic schools, and from a bias favoring "Sunni/Arab" education rather than "Syrian" education. It is certain that education will suffer greatly, and may take decades to recover from the current heavy civil conflict.

Turkey: A weak system, suffering from all of the usual main problems of education in developing countries. Elementary education is free, but in fact is largely financed by large fees paid by parents. Turkey is trying—to teach girls, to teach more relevant subject matter, and to teach students to think.

SOURCES

http:/education.stateuniversity.com, "Egypt: Educational System Overview, 2011.

http:/education.stateuniversity.com, "Egypt: Summary", 2011.

http:/education.stateuniversity.com, "Morocco: Education System Overview, 2011.

www.kinghussein.gov.jo, "Education in Jordan: A Commitment to Excellence", Office of the King, 2012.

Wikipedia, "Education in Jordan", March 2011.

World Education Services—Canada, "Saudi Arabia: Education Overview", May, 2004.

Wikipedia, "Education in Saudi Arabia", June, 2011.

Enjoyturkey.com, Turkey Ministry of National Education, "The Turkish Education System", 2011.

Ministry of National Education, government of Turkey, "Basic Education in Turkey: Background Report", June, 2005.

UNICEF, Division of Policy and Practice, Statistics and Monitoring Section, "Education Statistics: Turkey", May, 2008.

Vorkink, Andrew, "Education Reform in Turkey", The World Bank, December, 2005.

Jones, Dorian L., "Turkey: A Revolution Long in the Making", Open Society Foundations, Education Support Program, 2006.

Demir, Cennet Engin, and Paykoc, Fersun, "Challenges of Primary Education in Turkey: Priorities of Parents and Professionals",

International Journal of Educational Development, Vol. 26, Issue 6, November, 2006.

Yoicu, Huseyin, and Kurul, Nijia, "Evaluating the Finance of Primary Education in Turkey Within the Context of Neo-Liberal Policies", International Journal of Educational Development, Vol. 3, No. 2, 2009.

Sudan Tribune, "South Sudan Calls for More Financial Support for Education", June 22, 2011.

Wikipedia, "Education in Sudan", February, 2011.

U. S. Congress, Library of Congress, Country Studies: "Sudan—Education", 1991.

Liliir Education Project, "Sudanese Education", 2011.

Morse, David, "Hope for Ariang: What Challenges are Facing Education in Sudan?", 2010.

http://education.stateuniversity.com, "Sudan—Secondary Education", 2011.

British Council Learning, "Education System: Skills Around the world: Libya", 2011.

Cardinal, Monique C., "Religious Education in Syria: Unity and Difference", British Journal of Religious Education, Vol. 31, March, 2009.

Clark, Nick, "Education in Libya", World Education News and Reviews, July/August 2004.

Clark, David, and Hough, James et al, "Financing of Education in Indonesia", Asian Development Bank and Asian Comparative Education Research Center, U. of Hong Kong, 1998.

Wikipedia, "Education in Indonesia", July, 2011.

Arze del Granado, Franscisco Javier, et al, "Investing in Indonesia's Education: Allocation, Equity and Efficiency of Public Expenditures", EconPapers, 2011.

UNICEF, Fact Sheet "Girl's Education in Indonesia", 2002.

Word Bank World Development Indicators, "Education Outcomes", and "Participation in Education", 2012.

Heritage Foundation, Information on Economic Freedom: Sudan, 2012.

Abeywickrama, Kenneth, (blog site), "Foreign Aid and Economic Transformation: :The Case of Sudan", March 3, 2011.

Business Anti-corruption Portal, "Sudan Country Profile", 2011.

English Shared, "Indonesia Education System", 2010.

Landzettel, Marianne, "Pakistan Faces Educational Emergency, says Government", BBC News South Asia, March, 9, 2011.

http://www.marcopolis.net, "Education in Morocco: Analysis of Morocco Education Sector", March 16, 2011.

Wickipedia, "Education in Morocco", January, 2012.

Bekkioui, Nauoal, "Quality Education in the Case Study of Morocco", American Language Center, Rabat, June, 2010.

Almiraat, Hisham, "The World is Talking, Are You Listening?", Global Voices, October 23, 2009.

Kjeilen, Tore, "Morocco/Education", Looklex Encycolpaedia, 2012.

http://countrystudies.us/Iran, (Library of Congress), 2011.

Slavin, Ted, "What is the Iranian Government So Afraid Of?", The St. Catharines Standard, June 11, 2011.

Sedgewick, Robert, Ed., "Education in Post-Revolutionary Iran", World Education News an Reviews, May/June, 2000.

Wickipedia, "Education in Iran", June, 2011.

Landis, Joshua M., "Islamic Education in Syria: Undoing Secularism", Brown University Watson Institute for International Studies, November, 2003.

Encylopedia of the Nations, "Syria: Education", 2012.

Wickipedia, "Education in Syria", June, 2011.

Wickipedia, "Education in Pakistan", July, 2011.

Bajoria, Jayshree, "Pakistan's Education System and Links to Extemism", Council on Foreign Relations, October, 2009.

Khan, Saad, "The Great Rot in Pakistani Education", Huffington Post World, April, 2011.

Middle East Institute Viewpoints Special Edition, "The Iranian Revolution at 30. Iran: Poverty and Inequality Since the Revolution", January, 2009.

NationMaster.com, "Education Stats: Canada vs. Iran", 2012.

Khalaj, Monavar, "Critics Give Iranian Education Low Marks", Financial Times, July11, 2011.

World Education Profiles, "Pakistan: Education Overview" May, 2004.

CHAPTER V

HEALTH CARE IN MUSLIM COUNTRIES

Health Care Common Patterns

Muslim countries as used in this book are identified as those countries where a majority of the population of the country is Muslim and the government is declared or de facto Muslim. This listing shows these countries, their current population, and their ranking of health care systems in 190 countries by the World Health Organization: **(1)**

1. Afghanistan (30 million), (139th)
2. Bahrain (< 1 million), (42nd)
3. Bangladesh (148 million), (139th)
4. Egypt (80 million), (111th)
5. Indonesia (213 million), (111th)
6. Iraq (25 million), (176th)
7. Iran (70 million), (168th)
8. Jordan (5 million), (49th)
9. Kuwait (4 million), (45th)
10. Libya (6 million), (130th)
11. Lebanon (4 million), (91st)
12. Morocco (30 million), (89th)
13. Oman (2 million), (8th)
14. Pakistan (162 million), (139th)
15. Qatar (2 million), (44th)
16. Saudi Arabia (26 million), (63rd)
17. Sudan (26 million), (176th)
18. Syria (20 million), (126th)

19. Tunisia (10 million), (65th)
20. Turkey (75 million), (61st)
21. United Arab Emirates (8 million), (27th)
22. Yemen (21 million), (154th)

The total population of these countries is 964 million, or 72 percent of the total estimated population of Muslims in the world. All Muslim countries have a combination of secular and Sharia law, but only in four is Sharia law seen as the primary system: Afghanistan, Iran, Saudi Arabia, and Sudan, now having lost the southern provinces of the country to the new nation of South Sudan.

Health care in Muslim countries has passed through several phases. Historically, provision of health care was mainly by religious organizations—by mosques either directly or through voluntary associations under the supervision of the Imams in one or more mosque institutions. This provision stemmed directly from interpretation of the Quran and Sunnah, and is one of the fundamental core responsibilities placed on all Muslims—the support of charity. In many jurisdictions, a special tax called the Zakat is still levied on both individuals and businesses, to be employed solely to support health care and other charitable purposes.

Then, as governments in Muslim countries expanded and grew more significant, part at least of the health care responsibility shifted to them. This was especially true in those governments that adopted some form of Communism or state socialism, which usually made "cradle to grave" provision of social services a key element of their political philosophy.

But this wave of government assumption has often failed or has been poorly implemented. Where the government provides health care, it is almost always judged to be inferior, suffering from a whole litany of problems. Whatever may be promised in Constitutions or laws, the tendency of Muslim governments is to dodge the health care costs by delegating the problem down to local governments.

The recourse of governments was not to return health care to the mosques. Instead, two other tides began to run. The first was to extend private sector involvement more extensively by pressing companies to provide health care benefits to their employees. Other companies are now much more active in providing health care insurance on a commercial basis, and in the direct business of operating hospitals and providing medical services.

A second wave has also occurred when international organizations began to involve themselves in the humanitarian role of supplemental health care providers or financiers. But industries try to reject their role because it is expensive and enormously uncertain and complex to administer. There is no guaranteed correlation between national wealth and the quality of health care. Private sector contributions are greatest in Bangladesh, Afghanistan, Indonesia, Iraq, Syria, Tunisia, and Yemen.

The current situation is approximately this: central governments deal primarily with health care for the ruling elite, mostly in cities. The private sector providers are also oriented to the urban elite because that is where the money is.

There are some public programs which attempt to provide health care at the very basic level in rural and village areas. These local clinics range from rudimentary but decent down to mere first aid stations. Where they have been most useful and successful has been in providing midwifes and pre-natal and post natal care for mothers and small children. In many countries available services are seldom covered by any form of health insurance, and medical care is <u>cash up front.</u> That is, no money, no care.

Health care organizations in both the public and private sectors tend to be built in layers. Layer one is the provision, as widely as can be financed, of basic services in thousands of rural and village areas. Layer two is at the regional or state or provincial level, where the first provision of more professional and comprehensive medical care is available. The government pattern seems to be that these facilities are too few, understaffed, underfunded, and short of everything. Whether public or private, they are dealing with people who are poor and have little or no heath insurance and thus care will usually be cash up front. The third level is in urban areas, especially the national capital, where the elites live. Here, full service hospitals, often of high quality, are available, and more people have been able to provide themselves with health insurance, either from the government or privately.

Must Muslim countries suffer from a shortage of doctors, nurses and medical technicians. Notable exceptions seem to be Saudi Arabia, Jordan, Tunisia and possibly Iran. Doctors are generally underpaid, and their portable skills allow them to practice more profitably elsewhere, and many of them leave for greener pastures. Those who remain have a "combination" practice, where they are resident in some government controlled hospital but they also develop a private practice which is usually more profitable.

Medical Issues

There are many medical/health problems that are common within most Muslim governments. These include:

1. The need to continue gradual reductions in the existing long term problems of infectious diseases.
2. Coping with the "new" problems of non communicable diseases and illnesses.
3. An almost universal lack of public sanitation.
4. The rapid growth of elderly populations; most governments have few pension plans or provisions, so most elderly are poor.
5. While most countries suffer from smoking and obesity, few have any concept of preventative medicine.
6. High levels of illiteracy reduce effectiveness, especially for preventative care education.

7. There continues to be serious cultural and government prejudice against women which impairs effectiveness of medical service for both women and children.
8. Increasing problems with drug addiction, AIDS.

Health System Issues

Similarly, there are many common characteristic problems with the health care system itself. These include:

1. Almost universal underfunding.
2. Poor selection of priorities; little emphasis on preventative medicine, great disparities between cities and rural areas, and between the rich elite and the general population.
3. Lack of adequate, proper facilities; health care systems are overwhelmed. Most small local facilities are limited and inferior.
4. Lack of trained staff in terms of both numbers and skills.
5. Much medical service is of low quality, with a lack of quality control.
6. Public health provision has been widely discredited.
7. The abandonment of the universal public service commitment, despite many commitments in Constitutions, in favor of a combined public/private service.
8. In fact, health care is fading as a purely public responsibility, and is fast becoming "the health care industry" with heavier private sector involvement.
9. Vast universal bribery and corruption.
10. Lack of regulation of services and financing.
11. The extensive general pattern of decentralization of health care to local governments. Health care is not now seen as a purely national government responsibility. But decentralization is partly cynical avoidance of national government financial responsibility.
12. Underdeveloped health insurance programs. Usually, only about 15 to 20 percent of people have any.
13. Too many programs are elitist: they take care of civil servants, workers in State Owned Enterprises, the military

and other elites. In some countries, there are programs for the very poor; it is the middle class that is most neglected.

14. Serious problems from wars, insurrections and terrorism which destroy health care facilities and disrupt service.
15. Internal conflicts (religion, tribalism, political affiliations, etc.) skew health care provision.

External Issues

Most of these Muslim countries experience a complex intervention of outside involvement from funding to actual provision to critiquing. This includes the United Nations, the World Health Organization, the European Union, the United States, and many non-government organizations (NGOs). It is less obvious that much of this aid comes from Muslim countries. In some countries (Turkey, Egypt, Jordan, Lebanon) there are masses of displaced persons who impose heavy demands on often overburdened systems. The World Health Organization is often used as a source of professional standards and advice, but is suspected by some governments, largely because they make expensive recommendations which governments can't afford. There is little information about help coming from inside of the Muslim community, but much of this help is in fact directed to street level Mosques.

Disease patterns have become more complex. Non-communicable diseases are becoming more prevalent while infectious diseases remain high. Infectious and parasitic diseases account for 22 percent of deaths. Maternal and infant mortality rates are higher than other countries in the region. Communicable diseases include cholera, HIV, malaria, diphtheria, whooping cough, tetanus, measles, gastroenteritis, polio, diphtheria, and tuberculosis. The efficiency of public health services is said to be declining, and most people avoid public services because of high costs, front end demands for payment, and low reputations for quality of treatment. The poor tend to make much greater use of non-medical health staff and have lower hospital utilization rates. Health care financing is now overwhelmingly personal, with individuals providing 75 to

80 percent of all health care outlays, and most of this is front end and out-of-pocket. Insurance coverage is very limited, with only formal sector workers covered—about one third of the population. But even those covered receive only a low portion of actual costs, and have to make up the difference out-of-pocket.

Consequently, in the absence of adequate public services, the private sector has come on strong. In most areas of Indonesia, Afghanistan, Bangladesh, Libya, Syria, Tunisia or Yemen, the private sector is the dominant provider of health care and now accounts for more than two-thirds of ambulatory care, more than half of hospital contacts and 30 to 50 percent of all baby deliveries. The general pattern is the failure of government provided health care, the gradual "bottom up" shift to private provision, the government latching on to the growing private care wave to make private provision an official policy, and then, ultimately perhaps, to a policy of abandonment of health care as a central government responsibility beyond central planning and policy formulation. But in all countries, there seems to be a strong tendency for private sector health care involvement to become big business, with maximized profitability.

Where governments are involved it is almost always local government, and their share of total public spending has increased from an average of 10 percent to over 50 percent by 2001. So again, in what seems to be another common pattern, the health care system is designed to take good care of the elite, cater to the poor as a politically popular stance, and ignore the great mass of people in the middle. But help for the poor often turns out to be mostly talk and little action.

Health Care Levels in Muslim Countries

Health Care in Afghanistan

"Before the recent wars, the health situation in Afghanistan was among the worst in the world; the health infrastructure was grossly inadequate and mostly limited to urban centers. Infant mortality

(1993) was 163/1000 live births. Two hundred and fifty-seven out of every one thousand children born died before the age of five. Maternal mortality is one hundred and thirty times higher than the U. S. Life expectancy was 43.7 years. The Taliban, when in power, significantly worsened the plight of women, and the country is still trying to recover. Women suffer from malnutrition, vitamin deficiencies, anemia, and iodine deficiencies in addition to adequate pre and post natal care. Few have money for medical care, and can't find care even if they have the money. Most children die of preventable diseases including infectious and parasitic diseases, acute diarrhea, respiratory infections, tuberculosis, diphtheria, polio, malaria, measles and malnutrition—over and above the serious disorders associated with pregnancy and delivery. Eighty to 85 percent of these diseases can be avoided by preventative measures, by proper health care, or by relatively affordable cures."(2)

Currently, there is only one health care center for every 100,000 people, and 75 percent of physicians have fled the country, so that there is only one physician for 95,000 people. As a result, the population still relies much on midwives, herbalists, and barbers. Mullahs and others sell protective amulets.

Housing is scarce, old, deteriorating and often lacking sanitary facilities. There are perhaps 1.5 million people who are physically disabled by war injuries including amputations, blindness, and paralysis. There are still an estimated 10 million land mines and unexploded ordnance—the largest such concentration in the world, effecting residential areas, farm lands, roads, and urban streets. Despite many clean up teams, it will take perhaps another decade to clean up this mess.

Given the inability of the government to cope, more than sixty Non Government Organizations (NGOs) are at work, with special attention to the health of mothers and babies, mass immunizations, and the cleanup of water sources. The government maintains that it has opened hundreds of new health facilities, but new or refurbished facilities for health care are empty for lack of staff. Yet trained people cannot find work because nobody is organizing these facilities. Emergency health care is an acute lack. There is a huge shortage of medicines and equipment. In southern Afghanistan, only two public referral hospitals are functioning.

Health Care in Bangladesh

Bangladesh is one of the world's twenty least developed nations. As a result, it has drawn very large support from international organizations, especially the UN Children's Fund, the United States Agency for International Development, the International Center for Diarrheal Disease and Research, and many other private or semi-public NGOs. It maintains the usual three-level system: a first level in rural and village areas; a second more professional level in regions, districts and towns; and a more complete and modern level in bigger cities and government centers. But as usual, the public health care system is of low quality and very discredited, and the private sector is coming on strong. While the health care system is fairly well organized, it has the usual problems of underfunding and is generally overwhelmed by demands. Only 30% of the population uses the government system. The system does attempt to cater to rural areas, but in the process it neglects the majority of people, and especially the urban poor, where part of the gap has been filled by NGOs.

The Mary Stopes Factory Health Services is a recent innovative program that has focused on major cities, with a concentration on reproductive health. Its name suggests its approach: it deals with factories to set up a small clinic on the premises, and sells services to the employees and others for a modest fee charged the employer. Usually it recovers about 70% of expenses this way, and gets the rest from donors. (3) Here again, an NGO is substituting for a failed government program. Almost half of the country's population is living below the poverty line, often in makeshift homes and shelters with polluted water and inadequate sanitation. Flood-prone areas are sources of waterborne diseases. Home births are common, but the lack of prenatal care and treatment for complications increases risks for mothers and babies.

In Bangladesh, the primary service is called the Union Health and Family Centre" largely built around services for mothers and children, and family planning work. This includes scheduled home visits and birth assistance service. There are then District hospitals (100-250 beds) and medical colleges with around 650 beds. Tertiary care is national. Somehow, the poor seem to make low use of the primary care facilities, while the upper level facilities are overcrowded. The whole system is suspect and expensive. The private sector includes many traditional healers and faith healers, plus the equivalent of drug store pharmacies which dispense everything from antibiotics to herbs and charms. They also may do some low level treatment. NGOs are widely used, and both the NGOs and the government facilities are trying to make greater use of volunteers who get a little training.

A formal Health and Population Sector Strategy was introduced by the government in 1998. It emphasized universal accessibility, equity and greater attention to rural populations. A major shift in policy is to reduce the home visit approach because it is inefficient, in favor of a stronger "package" of priority services in fixed facilities. Consideration is being given to allow private providers into the tertiary system of major hospitals.

The government is trying two new ideas: a health benefit card, and health equity funds. The health benefit cards are issued to poor people free and their value can be spent in any health facility. To date however, only about 16,000 patients are given such cards. The health equity fund is a single revolving fund shared by a group of NGOs, managed by the NGO Services Delivery Project funded by the USAID. About 20 percent of outlays are recovered from patient fees, and the money put back into the revolving fund. This system works well, but it is still dependent on external funding. In the long run, there may be slow increases in user fees, or substitution of government funding.

Currently, there is no legal provision for the management of emergency situations, which are local government responsibilities. There is a Ministry of Disaster Management and Relief which issues "directives" which are largely not mandates but guides. The whole system is totally inadequate in a country that experiences floods and other disasters at the rate of two or three a year.

Health Care in Egypt

After the 1952 Revolution, the government finally committed to real upgrading of the national health care system. Per capita spending went up 500% in the period 1952 to 1979. Life expectancy increased from about 39 years to about 59 years during this period. Child mortality went down from 193 per 1000 to 85 per 1000 now. But still, half of the premature deaths were children and this remains one of the worst records in the world. And as usual elsewhere, high percentages of mothers and children showed marked malnutrition and vitamin deficiencies.

The Egyptian Ministry of Health and Population is undertaking an ambitious Health Sector Reform Program (HSRP) seeking expansion of services, greater cost effectiveness and higher quality. It is initially a family based primary care program, in large part in recognition of the extremely high child mortality rates and continued evidence of inadequate nutrition. Built around neighborhoods and communities, it will provide a network of clinics and a few good hospitals. Each family will be assigned a doctor (a Family Practitioner) and a hospital. Now, Egypt does seem to be avoiding the high levels of mother and child malnutrition which plagues other Muslim countries. Service may be provided by the government, the Health Insurance Organization, NGOs or private clinics.

In general, the Ministry of Health (MOH) provides free basic care through hundreds of public medical facilities including 1,300 social service units and over 5,000 social care cooperatives, and it is thought that nearly all Egyptian have some access to health care. The Ministry remains the largest single provider of health care, and has 344 general hospitals, and 280 specialized care units. The social service units provide not only health education and family planning information, but instruction in adult literacy, and some vocational training. There are about 85,000 beds provided: 45,000 in government hospitals, and 40,000 in private health institutes. Another government agency called the Health Insurance Organization (HIO) has its own network of hospitals, and will also decide where to buy health services.

Ultimately, the government wants a universal health insurance scheme in which every Egyptian is a beneficiary, but the program is not too far along. In fact, the private sector now provides over 56 percent of health care, compared to 36 percent by the MOH. But where care is inpatient, the government controls most of the beds. A good deal of less complicated care is provided by Mosque clinics. There is one physician per 715 people, which is high for developing countries. But as usual, medical care is primarily in cities, and not in rural and small town areas, and also as usual, government facilities are seen as inferior (shortages of doctors, nurses, testing facilities and modern equipment) to the degree that people avoid them if possible and favor private facilities. Also as usual in developing countries, public health, clean water, sanitation facilities, and indoor plumbing all are scarce. NGOs, both domestic and foreign are active in Egypt. And in general, Egypt compares well with other Muslim countries, but is below most international standards, and it also suffers from biases against women: low attention, female mutilation, unsafe abortions and other treatments, unwillingness for male doctors to treat female patients, and even violence against women.

Egypt is experiencing the typical evolution of health problems from communicable to non-communicable diseases, and in some ways, the Egyptian program is falling farther behind. It has the highest rate of Hepatitis C in the world, and other serious communicable diseases include tuberculosis, trachoma, hookworm, dysentery, beriberi, typhus, schistosomiasis and malaria.

Egypt does have a social security program to provide pensions, but in typical pattern is it patronized by civil servants and employees of state owned enterprises, and it has reached less than half of the workforce. The program also covers children in school, but that is just 57 percent of school age children. More than 57 percent of health care expenditures are paid out of pocket by patients, and more extensive treatment is usually available only for the wealthy.

Health Care in Indonesia

Indonesia has made significant progress in heath outcomes over the last decades, but new challenges have emerged. Non-communicable diseases such as heart and diabetic problems have become increasingly important concerns. Infectious and parasitic diseases account for 22 percent of deaths, and maternal and infant mortality rates are higher than for comparable countries in the region. The poor suffer disproportionately, with low levels of attended births and immunizations. Performance and utilization of public health services is declining and the private sector is now the major source of health care.

Government health care spending is declining, and health care funding is now overwhelmingly private, with individuals providing 75 to 80 percent of all health care outlays, and most of this is out-of-pocket at the time of service (compare this to the fact that the U. S. government funds 47 percent of health care costs in the U. S.). Insurance coverage is very limited, with only formal sector workers and their families covered, or about one third of the population. But even for those covered, their benefit payments cover only a part of their actual costs. 50 percent of public health care costs are provided by local governments. HIV/AIDS transmission rates are increasing, but problems are still mostly limited and localized.

As usual, government utterances are mostly propaganda and little action. The system needs enlargement, greater financing, focus on priority problems and new challenges, and more productivity and quality control. In effect, government policy focuses now on the populist theme of helping the poor, and the rich take care of themselves. This leaves the great bulk of the population in the middle with little or no care. The country needs a national health care insurance program, but legislating in this arena has been all but useless for 30 years. The government is now emphasizing decentralization of health care responsibility, but this is like China: that is, dumping an expensive and insoluble problem on local governments. There is the usual blather about the need for greater accountability, the need for cooperation and coordination, a better information system, etc., etc.

Health Care in Iraq

Iraq under the monarchy and the early years of the Baathist Party regime had built up a good health care system, available to almost all urban residents and about 80 percent of rural and village residents. But the system was severely damaged through a series of catastrophic events: the ascent of the Hussein regime which neglected the system (in 2001, his government spent just $16 million on health care, and much of the system was controlled by ignorant party hacks); serious internal conflicts with Shia and Kurdish populations; the ten year war with Iran; the invasion of Kuwait leading to serious sanctions by the UN, starting in 1990; the American invasion and the collapse of the Hussein regime; and now, the bumbling and corrupt current regime.

As a result, the system is now a shambles, but in fact, it had been declining for about 35 years. Many facilities have been destroyed or have ceased to function. Doctors, nurses, technicians have fled the country in large numbers and are reluctant to return. There is an almost universal shortage of equipment, supplies, pharmaceuticals and almost everything else. Also, former programs against communicable diseases have been abandoned, and there is a resurgence of malaria, diphtheria, whooping cough, tetanus, measles, gastroenteritis, and polio. Thugs and thieves steal, kidnap, extort both money and drugs.

The UN had administered a program of "Oil for Food and Drugs", allowing the government to sell oil and import these needs despite the general sanctions, but much of this money was diverted by Hussein, and the whole pipeline for medial imports shriveled up. In addition, public infrastructure such as transport, clean water supplies, sanitary facilities, all deteriorated and in turn hurt health care. It has been estimated that almost 4.8 million people were displaced during these many disasters. While public systems are in bad shape, many people have turned to private sources, but they are expensive: costs have inflated, price gouging is common, and it is all cash up front.

Health Care in Iran

Seventy-three percent of all Iranians have health care coverage and 94 percent have adequate access to health care facilities and this includes 86 percent in rural areas, which is one of the best levels in the region and among Muslim nations. The World Health Organization (WHO) ranks Iran's overall health care performance ninety-third among world nations. Improvements in the last 40 years have been very substantial.

The Constitution entitles Iranians to basic health care, which includes subsidized prescription drugs and vaccination programs. Since 2009, a new government plan called "the comprehensive insurance plan" provides basic coverage to all Iranians. The professional workforce has been extensively retrained and is now seen as adequate for national needs. The largest health care network is operated by the Ministry of Health and Medical Education, providing education, care, and insurance. There is also a Medical Services Insurance Organization, which also provides emergency relief response. Iran has 730 medical establishments with 111,000 beds, of which 77,300 are provided by the Ministry.

Iran experiences most of the common problems that plague Muslim countries: the emergence of newer non-communicable diseases which must be responded to; an aging population; a widespread problem with obesity, where 60 percent of the population is overweight; lack of sanitary facilities and the treatment of waste water; high levels of smoking (ironically, tobacco products are a state monopoly through the state owned Iranian Tobacco Company, which controls tobacco imports). Iran is experiencing a growing rate of HIV infection, and it has the highest rate of opiate addition in the world, serviced by smugglers out of Afghanistan.

By government policy, Iran produces about 96 percent of its pharmaceuticals locally, and in fact, has become an exporter. There are 92 pharmaceutical companies in the domestic industry, largely because of a long term import substitution policy and heavy government subsidies. The Ministry of Health and Medical Education is the main stakeholder of pharmaceutical affairs in the country. The Social Security Investment Co. is Iran's largest holding company, is affiliated with the Ministry of Welfare, and owns and controls 22 pharmaceutical companies, representing 40 percent of total national production. In other words, this is really a State owned and operated system. But 50 percent of the raw materials and chemicals used in the drug manufacturing sector are imported. In a similar vein, Iran has attempted to develop a medical equipment manufacturing base, although much of this trade is handled by the private sector, although heavily subsidized by the government.

Health Care in Jordan

The Hashemite Kingdom of Jordan was established in 1946, and the original king, Abdullah, ruled until 1952. He was succeeded by his son Hussein who ruled from 1952 until his death in 1999 when he was succeeded by his son, Abdullah II who is still on the throne. This is a reign of 65 years! On the whole, the people of Jordan have been satisfied with this leadership, in part because of the very high level of medical care in the country

As usual, city dwellers do relatively well, but rural and village populations are underserved. For a change, both drinking water and sanitation facilities are almost universally available for everybody, and electricity has been widely extended into rural areas. There are many good quality facilities—health centers, village clinics, maternal/child care centers, tuberculosis centers and school services—but they are scattered and not uniformly available. These facilities and services have allowed Jordan to upgrade its health care system quite a bit. All of the usual communicable diseases such as polio, diphtheria and cholera have been drastically reduced and even eliminated. More deaths however are occurring from a growth of non-communicable diseases such as heart, respiratory and gastrointestinal problems. Child birth care is still a problem, in part because of a cultural reliance on "folk" medicine that prevents some women from seeking more modern treatment. Gender prejudice continues, while somewhat reduced. Nursing homes for the elderly—or anybody—are virtually unknown. The Social Security Act of 1978 mandates health care provision by employers of more than 10 persons, and now covers 465,000 workers.

Jordan has been ranked by the World Bank as the number one healthcare provider in the region, and among the top five in the world, and as such, it has become the most popular health care "tourist" destinations in the region. The Ministry of Health operates 1,245 primary health care facilities and 27 hospitals, accounting for 37 percent of all beds. The private sector provides 36 percent of care, and the military provides 24 percent.

Jordan experiences the usual pattern of health care problems including a large but declining percentage of problems with communicable diseases and a rise in the incidence of non-communicable diseases. Life expectancy is 78 years—one of the highest in the world. There is little alcohol use, largely for religious reasons. Non-communicable diseases are increasing, including cancer and cardiovascular diseases (41 percent) which are the nation's number one killers. Other leading killers are drug addiction, road accidents, and depression.

Health Care in Libya

The government is widely accused of lying about the state of health care in the country in order to look good. The country is said to have 97 hospitals with more than 20,000 beds. According to a rights activist group "The health condition in Libya is awful, as shown by citizens selling their cars and homes in order to afford treatment—and that in foreign countries." **(4)** A single hospital in Benghazi serves all of eastern Libya. Critics say that neither the government nor the medical profession is stepping up to their responsibilities by facing up to the need for reform and expansion. Too many facilities are concentrated in the capital and too few elsewhere. Public transportation is bad. The system is both good in spots and bad in general. The annual budget for health care is now $2 billion, but much money is said to be stolen or misappropriated. Some hospitals are operating at very low standards: lack of facilities or staff, missing equipment, dirty and dangerous. A few years ago, 393 children were infected with AIDS in a children's hospital!

The report of a more recent USAID health team in 2004 **(5)** showed better results. It found a mixed public/private system through which health care was said to be good. Libyans receive free health care, and their health status is reported to be good compared to other Middle Eastern countries. Child immunization is nearly universal; infant mortality is just 20 per 1,000 births. Water and sanitation are improving. But this health team did a lot of talking to local officials; it is not clear how many facilities were actually visited. Widespread diseases include typhoid, venereal diseases, infectious hepatitis and tuberculosis, but at least, malaria has been virtually eliminated.

Health Care in Morocco

Morocco's health care system is at best marginal. It shares the common patterns of too few doctors, too few nurses, too few hospitals, poor access to clean water, poor sanitation, and the system is considered too small, underfunded, badly maintained and not very effective.

The principal causes of mortality are circulatory system diseases, perinatal diseases, cancer, endrocrinological, nutritional, metabolic, respiratory, infectious and parasitic diseases. Infant mortality rates have been slowly declining. AIDs affect less than 0.1% of the population.

Social/economic inequalities are serious, and the country ranks a miserable 125th place ranking in the World Human Development Index. There is a general lack of access to social services stemming largely from long term social inequalities, health care inequities, illiteracy, poor education, and long term health care neglect. At least, there has been improving performance in problems related to child health care.

In general, the health care system has three sectors:

1. Public health care: 85 percent of hospital beds and health care workers are provided by the government, and this is the part of the overall system supposedly aimed at the poor and rural population.
2. Private sector: for those who have money or health insurance.
3. Non-profit sector: Available primarily in big cities and serving about 16 percent of the population.

The growth of the economy is stagnant, and personal income is low and not growing much. About 19 percent of the population lives below the official poverty line, but far more people are "near poor". The income of women is low in general and as compared to men. 50 percent of the population remains illiterate. Illiteracy rates in the Arab world remain higher that the international average, and is higher even than in developing countries. And Moroccan school performance is low by Muslim country or developing country standards, and they are not catching up. The availability of doctors, nurses, hospital beds, and technical services is very poor by any standard, and too few doctors, nurses and other health care workers are being trained. Health insurance is possessed by about 16% of the population, almost exclusively in cities. The government passed a Compulsory Health Insurance law in 2006, and its target is to cover 32 percent of the population, and this seems like mission impossible. Even where the government attempts to provide health care for the poor, somehow it ends up benefitting the relatively well off.

As in so many other countries, an increasing percentage of health problems are from non-communicable diseases: heart attacks, respiratory diseases, diabetes, hypertension, and overweight. Cancer is increasing along with breast, lung, cervical, colorectal and stomach problems. The country also suffers from the usual range of communicable diseases such as tuberculosis, typhoid, viral hepatitis, schistosomiasis, and these are not declining in frequency. These diseases are preventable, but as usual, Morocco lacks the infrastructure, staff, and governmental will or management ability.

Health Care in Pakistan

Pakistan is almost the complete exhibit of all of the ills that plague the countries of the Muslim world. Health care for the poor is neglected; the better off go to private providers. Public health services are of low quality; so low that even the poor seek out private care. Public sector facilities are marginally effective, with low pay, low productivity and efficiency, lack of facilities and high staff absentee rates. There has been some attempt to provide service in rural and village areas through rural and basic health care units. Full service hospitals are almost all in larger towns and cities. Maternal/child care has been seriously neglected, but has become slightly better than average in the basic health units. There is however, a shortage of doctors and especially nurses.

The health care system that has emerged is one in which the private sector now provides 77 percent of all health care. Public sector provision is down to 23 percent and is widely regarded as inadequate, inefficient and expensive. Yet, private health care is also seen as expensive and not that great. Only about 70 percent of women receive pre or post natal care, 57 percent are anemic, and some form of malnutrition is common for both mothers and babies.

In general, things were getting better slowly until the clashes in Afghanistan and with India. The government is now in decline and funds are getting scarcer. Health care is the responsibility of the provinces, some of which have been very hard hit by the fighting.

Health care planning has been going on for 50 years, but still, in 1992 there was one physician per 2100 people, one nurse for 6,600, one hospital for 131,000 and one dentist for 67,000 people. These are significantly bad numbers. Some people still turn to "prophetic medicine": honey, herbs, and prayer, despite the point made by Mohammad that Allah created medicines for people to use. 25 percent of the people smoke, and there are now more opium users; the country still transports opium and produces heroin.

There is no widespread social security system. Traditionally, most people rely on a family, and on a church based system of voluntary charitable taxation called the Zakat, of about 2.5 to 5 percent of income, with payments and eligibility set by local Zakat committees. A more recent approach has been for the government to contract with NGOs to provide health care services—largely successfully. Part of this success results from restructuring of basic health units, eliminating wasteful bureaucratic regulations and pushing up productivity. But of 40 million low income people, both rural and urban, 99.3 percent are uninsured, and they pay 97 percent of health care costs themselves, out of pocket and up front. In urban areas, the government hopes to leverage employers and other enterprises to broaden existing health insurance programs. But for almost everybody, there is no protection against catastrophe with plenty of catastrophe happening. The concept of HMOs is only now being developed, having been ignored by insurance companies.

Health Care in Saudi Arabia

Saudi Arabia has one of the best health care systems in the Muslim world, and it offers this system not only to its residents, but to millions of pilgrims each year visiting the holy sites in the country.

The older forms of communicable diseases such as malaria and smallpox have been virtually eliminated, and the Saudis have extended the health care system to cover the newer non-communicative diseases such as heart attacks and pulmonary diseases. Saudi ratio of 1 bed per 411 people is among the lowest in the world, infant mortality has been drastically reduced, and life expectancy has climbed.

The government has implemented a two tier system: first is a network of primary health care centers and clinics throughout the country run by local administrative units. These centers concentrate on primary care, basic health care services, preventative medicine, pre and post natal care, and handling of health emergencies. This system is backed by a network of advanced hospitals and specialized treatment facilities such as obstetrics, respiratory ailments, contagious diseases, eye diseases, psychiatric care and convalescent facilities. Many of these specialized facilities are the largest and most efficient in the whole Middle East.

The Ministry of Health operates 62 percent of the country's hospitals and 53 percent of its clinics; most of the rest are operated in the private sector. Separate systems are operated by the Ministry of Defense, the National Guard, the Ministry of Education and the Public Security Administration. The Red Crescent Society operates more than 140 medical centers plus 500 ambulances and evacuation helicopters, and plays a key role in providing health care for the millions of pilgrims. There are also rehabilitation center for the handicapped run by the Ministry of Labor and Social Affairs.

Health Care in Sudan

The health care system in Sudan was never much good, and it has been turned into a shambles over the last twenty years of heavy conflict. The protracted civil war destroyed virtually all southern medical facilities except those that were maintained to treat victims of the war, and even these facilities suffered from a lack of staff, equipment, facilities, nurses, technicians, and everything else. The government could not or would not provide funds for even the most basic of needs. The private sector facilities continued to function, but there was a uniform lack of even basic medications. The government was not only viciously neglectful, but tended to punish medical practitioners, sending many to jail.

Famine has been a recurring problem, culminating in the great famine of 1991 during which an estimated 7 million Sudanese died. In all, some 4 million people in the South had been displaced, and more than 2 million had died or been killed as a result of 20 years of civil war. A further 1.6 million had been displaced, and 70,000 killed in Darfur. In general, the new country of South Sudan is one of the least developed places on earth, with more than 90 percent of the population living in abject poverty as defined by UN standards.

The most common illnesses are the usual communicable problems: malaria, dysentery, other intestinal diseases, tuberculosis, schistosomiasis, sleeping sickness, plus lesser levels of meningitis, measles, whooping cough, infectious hepatitis, syphilis, and gonorrhea. Malnutrition is widespread, especially among children, and half of the population under 15, or one quarter of the total population, suffers. In fact, South Sudan has one of the world's worst rates of infant mortality and maternal deaths in child birth—the highest anywhere in the world. And child immunization is said to be less than 13%—again the worst in the world. AIDS has reached epidemic proportions in the South, where there are just 50 physicians to serve a population of more than 5 million. In theory, medical consultation and drugs are free, but the limitations of the system make this a bitter joke. Often, drugs prescribed simply were never available.

In the usual manner, the basic element of the system is a network of primary health care centers, most of them in rural and village areas, and most of them of very low capability. More general capability hospitals are supposed to be available in cities, but few exist. The war has also had the effect of terminating promising health care still depends heavily on programs initiated and maintained by foreign assistance through 66 Non Government Organizations (NGOs). Problems are compounded by the fact that as much as 70 percent of the population lacks safe drinking water or adequate sanitation facilities. Life expectancy is a discouraging 57 years; infant mortality is high; spending on health care is very low at less than 1 percent of GDP.

Health Care in Syria

Prior to the current civil war, the health system in Syria looked like this: the Syrian government offered free health care for all citizens through a system run by the Ministry of Health. In addition, there has been a well developed private sector for health care provision, with a number of health insurance programs available for both public and private employees, and in sum, the coverage has been very high at better than 90 percent. Special programs have been offered through ministries such as defense, education, social affairs and labor. Health care programs have been available for civil servants, employees of SOEs, employees of professional associations, and many private businesses, but there is a recognized need to expand insurance to a larger range of people. Much improvement has been achieved in those areas dealing with women's and children's health care, but there is a serious concern that women are not yet fully educated, and what is needed is more community outreach and education efforts.

The health care system is based on the provision of primary health care at the lowest level of the village. There is a second level at the district level and a third at the provincial level. Each district has had several health centers, usually with a staff of about 10 people, plus at least one general hospital. At the provincial level there are urban health centers and a fuller range of doctors dealing with family planning, prevention of communicable diseases, environmental control, preventative medicine and health education. The national government apparently has been providing a network of ambulance, blood bank and drug distribution services. In recent years, the government has attempted to upgrade the quality of health care through more oversight and accreditation.

Problems center around the facts that salaries are generally low, equipment is scarce, service is still slim in some rural areas, and many people find that private practice is better. In general however, the Syrian health care system had been in very good shape. Most health indicators are very presentable, although obesity, smoking and hypertension have been growing. In general, malaria has been virtually eliminated and more than 80% of the population has access to clean water and sanitary facilities. But intestinal and respiratory diseases are still common especially in rural areas. The health care insurance system is seen as pretty ineffective and in need of reform. In addition, it is felt that a greater emphasis on preventative medicine rather than just curative medicine would be far more effective.

Syria has had two additional special problems in the sense that there are more than 300,000 persons of Kurdish origin who were rendered stateless by political decree in 1962, and this has become a large underserved population. Some Kurds who are employed and have official work documents are entitled to a limited amount of health care, but others without work documents get nothing. And in addition, there are, or have been as many as 1.5 million Iraqi refugees who have had to be assisted, but there seems to be a growing flow of these people back to Iraq.

Finally, and most tragically, it seems certain that the civil war now raging in Syria will inevitably change everything described above, all but destroy the health care system, nullify its advances, and leave the country with huge problems of reconstruction and revitalization.

Health Care in Tunisia

Tunisia is a relatively modern and stable country. After gaining independence from France in 1956, the government under Habib Bourguiba set out to modernize, reduce the Socialist control of the economy, allow the emergence of the private sector, and the reduce the numbers of State Owned Enterprises. The country also moved toward a more open society, and a remarkable abandonment of prejudices against women. As a result, Tunisia has the reputation of giving women a greater role in society (and government) than any other Muslim country in the world.

As usual, a Ministry of Public Health is the main health provider, along with the Tunisian National Social Security Fund which deals largely with health care for students, the self employed, and retired persons by offering them both health insurance and pension plans. The private sector represents about 12 percent of total care, but this includes almost 70 percent of the higher end and more sophisticated treatment facilities, 50 percent of the doctors (some of whom practice in both sectors), 73 percent of dentists and 88 percent of pharmacists.

In total, Tunisia is seen as having one of the most advanced systems in Africa, well up to European standards, and now covering over 80 percent of the population. Infant mortality is the second best in Africa, and many of the usual communicable diseases have been largely eradicated.

But the tide that is running is that public facilities are falling behind, and are increasingly inadequate to deal with the needs, especially because of the usual growth of non-communicable health problems found everywhere. Public facilities are increasingly overcrowded, understaffed, short of funds, and growing technologically obsolete, and as usual, the cities are better served than the countryside. Many services are free of charge if available, but even the poor people are forced to spend front end money to get care. Patients in the Social Security program now have to pay 20% of their costs up front, in addition to the regular fees for examination, x-rays, and other medical procedures. 79 percent of expenses are for medications and outpatient service; few can afford major in-hospital surgery. Still, Tunisia's health care system has in many ways risen to the standards of European countries. It has lowered the infant mortality rates, increased life expectancy, and expanded coverage to most of the population.

The Constitution of Tunisia states that each citizen has a right to health protection, and more than 70 percent of the population is in fact eligible under some system. A major policy was formulated after 1990 involving continuous upgrading of the primary health care system, upgrading of professional and hospital performance, and encouraging private sector participation. As a result, the private sector has flourished, and much of it is top end, especially in the provision of surgery and inpatient care. But this has forced individuals to spend more or their own money in place of free government care. Regional Directorates of Public Health are used, under the supervision of the Ministry of Health (MoH). There is the usual pattern of three levels of care. In addition, the Ministry of Defense and the interior security forces have their own health care facilities. So the public sector remains the major provider, with more than 80 percent of the beds.

Financing is provided through the state budget which funds capital investment, professional wages, and subsidies for public facility operating costs. In addition, there is major funding through the Social Security National Fund, created in 2004, and some of the medical services by those covered by the system is provided by contract with the MoH. Patients may receive free care as a social service; may share costs through employer plans or reduced official charges; or may pay almost all of their costs themselves. In summary, there is a real and increasing intent to sharpen the oversight of the system, including regulation of private sector providers, and to encourage system effectiveness upgrades.

Health Care in Turkey

The Constitution states that "—every individual is entitled to social security. The State must take the necessary measures—". Therefore, the Ministry of Health is responsible to provide health care for the people, organize preventative health services, build and operate state hospitals, supervise private hospitals, train medical personnel, regulate the price of medical drugs nationwide, control drub production and all pharmacies. Health service has gradually improved but is still less than good, although 80 to 90 percent of the population is covered. The problem is outside of cities because less than 1 percent of agricultural workers are covered. Private providers are advancing quality of service better than public providers. Facilities and staff tend to be more and better in cities than elsewhere. The Ministry of Defense has its own system, and some universities run hospitals. Major sources of funds for state hospitals are allocations from the government, fees paid by insurers or individuals, and some dedicated taxes on fuel and cigarettes.

The Social Security System has three parts:

1. The Social Insurance Institution (SSK) for private sector and blue collar public sector employees, available to all employees in these groups. Payment of old age pensions is also included.

2. The Pension Fund for Civil Servants, which includes health insurance which covers all costs beyond a 10 percent co-payment obligation. Oddly, current civil servants are not charged premiums, so this is a big drag on the current budget.

3. The Social Security Institution for Self Employed. This includes crafts and trades people, technical and professional people, small businessmen, shareholders of some companies, and agricultural self employed. Each patient chooses his/her financial participation level which covers both inpatient and outpatient diagnosis and treatment.

There is also a Green Card System; a special card entitling the holder to free medical services except outpatient drugs. The Ministry of Health issues the cards, but there are so many (11 million) that this has created a big dent in the budget.

Employer's plans include coverage for illness, disability, retirement and death benefits, and both employers and employees contribute to these plans. Employers pay to cover work related injuries or illnesses, and for maternity leave.

Private health insurance is well developed, and many join a private plan but also pay for state insurance, hoping to get upgrading choices. There are many pharmacies, mostly private, in neighborhoods, and the government tries to control only certain dangerous drugs.

In 2003, the new Justice and Development Party was elected to run the country, and it promised a sweeping health care reform program, aimed at increasing the ratio of private to state health provision, and making health care more generally available. This policy is largely driven by the poor quality and level of service of the traditional public services. Private provision through private insurance programs is the most expensive, but still, less than 2% of the population have private plans, largely because most of the cost is out-of-pocket and up front. This remains a government goal, and a "work in progress".

Advances have also been made in cleaning up the water supply, and providing more public sanitation. Diseases such as measles, pertussis, typhoid fever, and diphtheria have decreased sharply, the infant mortality rate is much reduced, but infectious and parasitic diseases are still the most frequent causes of death. As in other developing countries, heart, lung and cancer diseases are on the upswing. Infant mortality which was at 120 per 1,000 in 1980, among the highest rates in the world, had been cut to 55 per 1,000 by 1992, and government sources state that the rate has dropped to about 14 per 1,000 by 2009.

Health Care in Yemen

Hospitals are as usual divided between public and private, but in both sectors, there is a further split between top quality hospitals and run-of-the-mill hospitals. Thus, this has become a system designed to serve the elite and not the general public, and certainly not the poor. The whole government seems strangely disconnected from reality.

"The Ministry of Health and Population and the Ministry of Legal Affairs are busy supposedly drafting the legal framework required to establish health insurance schemes (2007). Where have these people been for 50 years? This planning supposedly emphasizes "facilitating" health care for the largest segments of the population, including building and equipping 800 clinics in rural Yemen. The government has spent seven or eight years supposedly drafting a new universal health care program, which has yet to be issued, much less enacted. Recently, the Health Minister stated "there are *probably* millions of people who don't have real access to health care", but he appeared not to know for sure. The private sector however, has recently initiated a number of health insurance programs, some of them linked with employers or hospitals.

But meanwhile, the whole system remains seriously underdeveloped, per capita expenditure remains very low, and such things as emergency services, ambulance service, blood banks, health care education and sanitary services are virtually non-existent. One valuable program has been the creation involving new nutrition education centers at local levels, dealing with the management of diarrhea, malnutrition, vitamin supplements especially for mothers and children. There are now 80,000 baby weighing/treatment posts in 41,000 villages. Many of these posts are staffed by volunteers plus a few professionals to supervise. These posts also deal with immunizations against major diseases, and coverage is now estimated at 80 percent.

A SCORE CARD OF HEALTH CARE IN MUSLIM COUNTRIES

1. Afghanistan: Among the worst in the world.
2. Bangladesh: Simply overwhelmed.
3. Egypt: Good in cities; less good in rural areas.
4. Indonesia: A mostly public system with declining performance from modest levels.
5. Iran: Surprisingly good—a "B—", but poor public sanitation.
6. Jordan: The best in the Muslim world, along with S. Arabia.
7. Lebanon: very devastated by long term fighting and destruction. 25% of health care facilities are not operating, and the rest suffer from serious shortages of everything and everybody.
8. Libya: Awful, and irresponsible
9. Morocco: Marginal: too little of everything and everybody.
10. Pakistan: Mostly a low functioning public sector, which satisfactorily serves only the elite.
11. Saudi Arabia: one of the best, and serves everybody.
12. Sudan and South Sudan: A shambles for more than 20 years; everything is lacking.
13. Syria: Quite good; attention paid to those on the lower end of the economy, but the civil war is enormously distructive.
14. Tunisia: One of the most stable and advanced systems in Africa and the Muslim world.
15. Turkey: Skewed toward cities where health care is good, and aimed well to poor. Little health care is available in rural areas, and everything is underfunded.
16. Yemen: The whole system is bad and seriously underdeveloped.

SOURCES

UNICEF, "Community-based Health Care: Indonesia Sets the Pace", 1991.

UN Office for the Coordination of Humanitarian Affairs, IRIN News, "Indonesia: Health System Failing Millions", 2011.

The World Bank, Bank Dunia, "Improving Indonesia's Health Outcomes", Indonesia Policy Briefs, 2011.

Sansai, Burak, "All About Turkey: Health Care in Turkey", 2010.

Wikipedia, "Health Care in Turkey", June, 2010.

U. S. Library of Congress, http://countrystudies.us/turkey/51, 2011.

Kronfol, Nabil M., and Bashshur, Rashid, "Lebanon's Health Care Policy: A Case Study of a Health System Under Stress", Journal of Public Health Policy, 1989.

World Health Organization—Regional Office for the Eastern Mediterranean, "Syria: Health Systems Profile", 2004.

World Health Organization,—Regional Office for the Eastern Mediterranean, "Lebanon: Primary Health Care Development", 2002.

World Health Organization, "Lebanon Health Facilities Have Suffered Considerable Damage", 2006.

World Health Organization, "Health Performance Rank By Country", 2011.

Dean, Laura, "How Iraq's Health Care System Has Changed", Change.org, April, 2010.

Newsweek, "In Iraq: The Doctors Are Out", October, 2008.

Dentzer, Susan, "Health Care In Iraq", December 31, 2003.

UN Office for the Coordination of Humanitarian Affairs, IRIN, "Iraq: Health System Needs Years of Work", May, 2011.

Mohammed, Abeer, "Iraq's Crumbling, Corrupt Healthcare", Guardian.co.uk, March, 2010.

Levingston, Steven, "War Cripples Iraq's Health Care System", March, 2010.

UN Office of Operations in Cote d'Ivoire (UNOHCI), "Notes on the Health System in Iraq and the Oil for Food Program", March, 2003.

World Health Organization, "The World Health Organization's Ranking of the World's Health Systems", 2000.

Geographic.org, "Healthy Life Expectancy(Hale)",2000.

UN Office for the Coordination of Humanitarian Affairs, "Yemen: Making Health Care Accessible for Refugees in South Yemen", April, 2010.

YemenTimes, 'Yemen's Health Care Industry: Untapped Potential", 2007.

Medicins Sans Frontieres: MSF, (Doctors Without Borders), "MSF in Yemen", December, 2007.

MacDonald, David, "Zahrawi Medical Center: Service in Medicine", Yemen Today, 2010.

Medecins du Monde, "Yemen: Improving Medical Care for Rural Populations", February, 2008.

Middle East Online, "More Yemeni Women Benefitting from Antenatal Health Care", 2010.

World Health Organization, Eastern Mediterranean Region Office (EMRO), Yemen: Health Care Systems Profile, 2009.

World Health Organization, Eastern Mediterranean Region Office (EMRO), Health Systems Profile—Tunisia. 2009.

Arafoul, Jamel, "Libyan Critics Dispute Health Care Quality Reports", Magharebia, April, 2010.

Oxford Business Group, The Report: Syria 2010, 'Health, Education and Development", 2010., UN Special Rapporteur—"Stately Kurds Denied the Right to Health in Syria, (see jttp;// supportkurds.org/reports), November, 2010.

Spainexchange.com, "Health and Safety in Syrian Arab Republic", 2010.

Via Recta, "Health Care in Syria", 2007.

Encyclopedia of the Nations, "Syria—Health", 2011. Also, "Tunisia—Health".

Global Insurance News, "Tunisia: Health System Information and Insurance News", 2009.

CHUP!: Changing Up Pakistan, "Providing Health Care for Pakistan's Urban Poor—Q&A with Naya Jeevan founder Asher Hasan, February, 2010.

Rabbani, Babar Tasneem Shaikh Fauziah, Safi, Najibullah, and Dawar, Zia, "Contracting for Primary Health Care Services in Pakistan: Is Upscaling a Pragmatic Thinking?", Journal of Pakistan Medical Association, 2010.

U. S. Library of Congress, http://countrystudies.us.pakistan, "Pakistan—Health and Welfare", 1992.

U. S. Library of Congress, http://countrystudies.us.afghanistan, "Afghanistan—Health", 1997.

Medecins Sans Frontieres, "Afghanistan: Reinforcing Emergency Health Care in Helmland", July, 2010.

PBS Independent Lens, "Afghan Reproductive Health", 2005.

Ryan, James M. Dr., "Health Care in Afghanistan. SpringerLink, World Journal of Surgery, 2005.

U. S. Library of Congress, http://countrystudies.us.egypt, "Egypt: Health and Welfare", 1990.

British Council, "Health Sector Reform Programme, Egypt", 2011.

Wikipedia, "Health in Jordan", November, 2010.

U. S. Library of Congress, http://countrystudies.us/Jordan, "Jordan: Health and Welfare", 1989.

McConnell, Tristan, "South Sudan: Health Care is Badly Needed", Global Post, February, 2011.

Wikipedia, "Health in Sudan", April, 2010.

Sudan Tribune, "Health Care the Next Challenge for Sudan", 2012.

U. S. Library of Congress, http://countrystudies.us.sudan, "Sudan—Health", 1991.

Wikipedia, "Health Care in Iran", February, 2011.

World Health Organization, "Health System in Bangladesh", 2011. Also, "Country Health System Profile, Bangladesh", August, 2007.

Chaudhuri, Aadel, "Factory Health Services: An Innovative Method of Providing Health Care in Bangladesh", 2003.

Wikipedia, Health in Morocco", July, 2010.

ArabMedicare, "Saudi Arabia", 2011.

Wikipedia, "Healthcare in Saudi Arabia", December, 2010.

CHAPTER VI

THE ENVIRONMENT

There is almost universal neglect of environmental needs by governments in the Middle East and North Africa (MENA) region, and this is largely the result of how governments set funding allocations. First priority is given to the government's own bureaucracy and to its military establishment. The next priority is given to economic development, and much money is spent on subsidizing state owned enterprises. The next priority is given to public infrastructure, especially that which supports economic activity. All of these activities carry an additional heavy overburden of corruption. If there is any money left, it is allocated to social services, but most of these funds are actually provided by local governments. Environmental problems are conveniently seen as future problems and thus can be put off, even where the urgency of problems is compelling.

Further, despite continuing claims to the contrary, national economies throughout the Arab world are not even equal to the task of maintaining current levels of economic wellbeing. Over almost two decades, there has been negative GDP growth, and studies from the World Bank and other studies show that development efforts over the past two decades have actually increased the gap between population growth and economic expansion. (1) Over the last decade and a half, the per capita GDP of the entire Arab region declined by 22 percent.

In addition, most of these governments seem to lack the managerial and technical skills to undertake a program of easier, cheaper, and the simplest of environmental improvement projects, but in truth, these skills could be obtained if they were really wanted. Another real problem is that, ironically, most governments have created a complex multiagency bureaucracy in which dozens of public agencies are involved, none of which seem capable of having any real impact. Very few of these agencies are willing to exercise any real enforcement authority because it is almost always politically risky to do so. It is totally frustrating to recognize the hundreds of organizations, assessments, analyses, plans, papers, studies, conferences, working groups, coordination committees, test programs, pilot studies, experiments, national and international meetings and grand sounding policy pronouncements, most of which are about **getting ready** to do something—only to see that little or nothing is actually achieved.

It is also deeply disturbing to realize how conflict ridden the Middle East and North Africa has been during the most recent decades when some greater willingness to deal with environmental problems has begun to emerge. Conflict has meant wars, insurrections, terrorism, tribal and clan conflicts, and hundreds of thousands of people who have been killed, injured or driven from their homes and jobs. These conflicts have wreaked havoc with almost every constructive program in the area. The same kinds of conflict plague the Muslim nations in the Far East, including Pakistan, Bangladesh and Indonesia. In addition, the Muslim world still experiences a deeper set of conflicts centering about the schism between the Sunni and the Shia, which has gone on for almost 1400 years, and shows no sign of ever being reconciled.

Almost none of the elements of these developing economies have ever been seriously forced to operate in an environmentally safe manner. There is unchecked industrial pollution, and deep suspicion that corruption lets private companies and state owned enterprises buy their way out of the need for regulatory compliance. Almost no city seems ready to deal with the increasing crises of air pollution, water pollution, lack of water availability, or the provision of safe sewage treatment or adequate trash removal. Most cities are now clogged with auto traffic and remarkably, most cars run on leaded gasoline, dumping lead into the air. Really, almost nobody seems to understand the concept of clean sustainable development.

In most of the Muslim world, the physical environment is very fragile, with large areas of desert, semi-desert experiencing high temperatures, low levels of rainfall and ominously low levels of surface and underground water sources. And yet, almost all of the Muslim countries of the Middle East and the south coast of the Mediterranean Sea suffer from remarkably incompetent environmental and water management. Most Muslim countries have historically been heavily rural, although they are almost all now moving rapidly toward overwhelming urbanization. However, they cannot abandon the ancient agricultural sector of their economies, and most are attempting various forms of development of agricultural production. But expansion of land under cultivation, and efforts to intensify agricultural productivity inevitably create further environmental threats.

Most Muslim countries have an economic development program, but most are relatively weak and unsuccessful. These development programs include the agricultural sector, but in truth, the real hope is that the industrial, commercial, and government/military sectors will develop sufficiently to absorb the flow of people into cities throughout the Muslim world, so that, in the long run, the agricultural sector could contract rather than expand. Then the average income of individuals would increase, and the many threats posed to the environment would be mitigated. For now, that is not possible. What then are the environmental threats posed by agriculture?

Too much land is used for agriculture; marginal land is forced into use, wooded land is cleared, and land with inadequate water availability is put into irrigated production. Too much water must then be committed to agricultural uses which can never achieve more than marginal productivity. Agriculture typically uses up from 50 to 85 percent of available water in each country. Productivity is low because farming techniques are obsolete, most land must be irrigated, and irrigation systems are expensive to construct and are extremely difficult to maintain and repair. The poor quality of the land and natural threats to crops have led to almost universal overuse of pesticides, insecticides, herbicides and soil enrichment chemicals. These are not only expensive and labor intensive, but they represent ominous sources of water pollution.

And still, there are almost universal problems of desertification, deforestation, soil depletion, soil erosion, siltification, declining crop production, and reduced rural incomes. In other words, real enhancement is the agricultural sector, while it may be politically necessary, is probably a failing economic experience. It would be cheaper for many countries to buy food elsewhere, reduce low value low productivity agriculture, and devote the water—and the people—to support growing cities and industries with greater value added potential.

The average annual rainfall in the Middle East and North Africa is less than 9.8 inches per year. It is better on the Mediterranean coast and in upland areas of Lebanon, Syria and Iraq, but only Turkey and Iran have a relative water surplus. **But overall, per capita water availability in the Middle East has become the worst in the world**. It is just one third of the availability in Asia, and 15 percent of African levels. The Palestinian Gaza Strip is the most water starved political unit on earth—relying on underground aquifers, which are rapidly being dissipated. (Efforts to join Israel in water desalination projects have foundered.) The densely packed Palestinian enclave, a narrow coastal strip between Israel and Egypt is running out of drinkable water today. Kuwait and the United Arab Republics are almost as bad off.

Agriculture accounts for from 60 to 85 percent of national water usage, but still, most countries suffer from wasteful and poorly maintained irrigation systems, uncontrolled pollution from runoffs of chemicals such as fertilizers and insecticides, and from too heavy a concentration on water intensive crops like wheat and cotton. In general, Muslim nations are still very rural, and the well-being of the agriculture sector of the economy is very important—and usually politically important as well. But if the water supply simply cannot support a large or growing agriculture sector, it would be wise to level it off, let populations continue to move to cities, and pay to import food. Desalinization seems very expensive and can't really generate enough water to make a crucial difference. Water desalination, especially in Israel, Jordan, Syria, Egypt and Morocco is widely used but expensive, and can satisfy only a small portion of total demand. According to the Institute for Advanced Strategic and Political Studies (IASPS), "Desalination is a dangerous and ultimately futile mechanism for change in the region." **(2)**

It is true that there is a growing number of organizations in the Muslim countries to attack environmental issues, and there is a substantial alliance between these governments and foreign sources for support. These sources may be both official and private, but their common denominators are that they exist to deal with environmental problems, and they have money to dispense. Often, at the same time that some government condemns and blames foreign intervention, it may be accepting foreign money and technical assistance to help fill the gap of things the government itself cannot or will not do.

These Muslim/Arab countries do not seem able to compromise. There are long standing disputes involving Israel, Jordan, Syria and the Palestinian Authority; Turkey and Syria; Egypt, Sudan and Ethiopia; Saudi Arabia, Qatar, and Bahrain; and Turkey, Saudi Arabia and Kuwait, over a pipeline from Turkey. Lebanon is another case in point. It has enough water so that it could share with Israel and Syria, both of which have shortages. But all are too busy fighting each other to work out sharing. Muslim countries are doing many constructive things but there continues to be more plans and paperwork than accomplishments. Serious environmental problems in this region are deepening and they cry out for government leadership—but do not get it.

The Middle East and Northern Africa are bordered by the Atlantic Ocean and the Mediterranean Sea, but it also includes six major marine basins of critical importance: the Levant Basin in the Eastern Mediterranean; the Red Sea; the Gulf of Eden; the

Arabian Sea; the Gulf of Oman and the Persian Gulf. These marine environments are under constant threat because of the heavy ship traffic, especially in the Suez Canal, and the Straits of Hormuz. The main issues of the Middle East marine environment are pollution (municipal, industrial and agricultural), coastal erosion, fishery threats, oil spills and shipping disruption.

Finally, anything that can be done can and will also be done illegally. Consider secret water poisoning, water theft, illegal air and soil pollution, food poisoning, illegal fisheries, untreated chemical disposal, oil spills, excessive use of insecticides, pesticides and herbicides, heavy metals dumped into the water supply, and poisonous chemicals polluting air and water. Add illegal logging and fires; poaching and illegal hunting; uncontrolled handling of trash and garbage; poor sanitation, and trash full of toxic wastes, especially medical. Bribery and other forms of corruption accompany all of these things. Almost all developing countries in the Muslim world are riddled with corruption. Estimates suggest that as much as 40% of scarce funds destined for water management (or anything else) are dissipated in some form.

Water Management

Given the absolutely critical need for water, and the serious problems suffered by every Middle East/North African (MENA) country, it is really astonishing how Few Middle East countries have practiced real water management. The techniques are well known and relatively inexpensive, so the answer seems to be government incompetence. The main culprit for water usage is agriculture which uses from 60 to 85 percent of the water in the region. Irrigation is mandatory in most areas, but is very wasteful, with up to 50 percent of water lost through leakage and evaporation. Note that only 2.5 percent of the world's water can be used for drinking, sanitation and food production. 1.1 billion people lack access to clean water, and 2.6 billion people lack access to adequate sanitation.

Politics and armed conflict are highly destructive of water systems, as well as almost every other social service. Sudan is a particularly somber example. Almost from its independence in 1956, Sudan has suffered through a series of conflicts between the Muslim north, the Christian/Animist south, and the western province of Darfur. The results, after 50 years, is the universal deterioration of public facilities of all kind, an economy that has been seriously damaged, tens of thousands of people killed, injured or displaced from their homes and forced to live in shanty towns, refugee camps or crowded urban slums. The National Geographic (2007) stated that "Under the stress of civil war, the water infrastructure has crumbled. At least one third of existing waterworks, such as hand pumps, water yards, and "hafirs" (small ponds used for irrigation and to water livestock) in the region are broken. Water, potable and otherwise is in desperately short supply. Only 40 percent of the rural population has access to any clean water. Homes may be miles from the nearest remaining water source. Water distribution systems such as water pipelines and indoor plumbing are nearly nonexistent in places like the Nuba Mountains, where more than 600,000 people were displaced by fighting." (3)

It is clear that the basic solution to a whole range of water problems lies within the agricultural sector of the economy, and the villages and small towns that make up the rural environment. Even where the majority of Muslims are now urban dwellers, most Muslim countries still also have important rural populations that form the traditional base of support for most regimes. It is therefore politically important for these regimes to "take care of" their rural populations, and they are often heavily subsidized at considerable cost. But here is the quandary: agriculture, especially in the difficult climates of the MENA, is difficult, relatively expensive because of the costs of irrigation and chemical protections, and ultimately, relatively low in the value of its products. Governments, in order to cater to these populations, subsidize water, electricity, seeds, insecticides, pesticides, fertilizers, and almost anything else they can think of. Yet the agriculture sector is also a prime polluter of water resources. When rain occurs, some of it will go to replenish underground sources, but farmers have too few ways to catch surplus rainwater for near term use. But yet, some of the technical solutions for these shortcomings are so simple, and inexpensive and easy to use. Dams are expensive and have many disadvantages, and often, simpler catchment techniques are easier to achieve. There are endless opportunities for farmers to catch and store water from rain or from running streams.

In China for example, more than 2 million people get their domestic water almost entirely from cisterns dug into their basements and in cisterns dug into fields for irrigation. Some people simply set aside small fields as a catchment area, laying out plastic sheeting on the ground to hold the water. In other cases, small ponds are developed, often for the purpose of allowing the water to seep through the soil as replacement for underground aquifers. Indian farmers have grown skilled in different techniques to catch and store monsoon rains. In many cases, ponds or reservoirs can be stocked with fish. Also, silt accumulating in these catchments is dredged up and used to fertilize crops. Check dams slow water drain-off to allow more seepage into underground aquifers. All of these relatively simple and inexpensive techniques can be used by farmers in the MENA, and governments could become very popular by assisting and financing such ventures.

Irrigation systems can be made greatly more efficient through the use of drip irrigation technology. In some cases, it would be possible to shift from high water demand crops to those with lower needs such as fruits and vegetables. Countries drawing back from socialist collectives find that water discipline is magically better when individual ownership is permitted. Many collectives have been successfully converted into more successful farmer run cooperatives.

But in the end, and not too long from now, the leadership in Muslim countries will be facing a far more significant set of decisions. The population in the Middle East is increasing at a rate among the highest in the world, and has exceeded 415 million. Most of this increase has been in cities. As populations increase in urban areas, they will become increasingly more demanding competitors for water. At the same time, the agricultural resources of the region can never be expanded or modernized enough to meet growing food needs, and most countries will have to be buying food from outside of the country. The priority then becomes to expand the national economy, mostly in the cities, to generate the wealth to make these purchases, while at the same time protecting the farm population. But this is not mission impossible. If governments let nature take its course and stop subsidizing and attempting to expand agriculture beyond its reasonable limits, most marginal but expensive subsidies can be cut back or eliminated. The consequences for the environment of such a shift could be profound. More water could be freed up for urban and industrial use. The high costs of subsidized irrigation and chemicals could be avoided. Some land could be returned to wood and grass land and deforestation and desertification mitigated.

But all of these countries have a second and a third arena in which better environmental protection is urgently needed. The second arena is now the most critical, and that is about governments and especially city governments. Many Muslim governments in the area adopted some forms or elements of state socialism, and all of them were committed to highly centralized national governments with heavy involvement in the control of the economy. Most utilized state owned enterprises where the government owned and funded and supervised enterprises in both industry and services. But few of these governments found that such centrally controlled economies were very effective, and none proved to be capable of expanding and investing fast enough to keep up with demographic needs, much less improving existing conditions.

Now, these governments need several things to happen. First, more successful means must be found to expand the economy and make it more financially rewarding. This is already under way in most countries in the region even including Iran. Ineffective State owned enterprises (SOE) are being privatized or formed into joint ventures with private companies, or devolved onto local levels of government. This wave of devolution is still fairly new, and has been pursued in a spastic and timid fashion, but in other countries, it has resulted in substantial surges of investment and in notable improvements in operating efficiency and productivity.

In some cases, governments have started to undertake expensive public infrastructure projects, for example the construction and operation of a power generation facility, in some form of joint venture with the private sector. In this new pattern of development, it is increasingly important that both the government and the private companies accept the obligation to make such development as environmentally sustainable as possible.

The expansion of industry is the third major problem, and while it is highly desirable in economic terms, it is making it more difficult to allocate scarce water resources, and it is enormously polluting of water. The industries requiring the most water are petroleum refining, food processing, metals, chemical processing and pulp and paper. The industrial use of water creates toxic and hazardous pollutants that render waste water unfit for subsequent human consumption or even use in the agricultural sector. Other industrial problems include air pollution, heavy metals dumped into the water supply, the runoff of other chemicals; waste from oil wells and petrochemical processing plants, and heated brine from desalination plants returned to rivers or lakes. A lot of urbanization is on the coasts, but this then concentrates coastal pollution problems: industrial waste, dredging and filling, silt accumulations, garbage and trash disposal, mining and quarrying, salt penetrations of coastal aquifers. Problems are especially serious in Jordan, S. Arabia, Egypt, Sudan, Yemen.

Every city in the Muslim Middle East and North Africa suffers from lack of waste water treatment systems and this means that wastes are dumped into water sources needed for drinking water and household use. This creates the further danger of poisoning of these water sources leading to severe health problems. Some countries, most notably Yemen and Jordan already have severe water shortages, and have been rapidly depleting underground water aquifers which are almost impossible to replenish.

The State of Environmental Protection

Algeria

Algeria's biggest problem is desert encroachment into the fertile areas in the North, and there is now too much land in crops and cattle grazing. Next is water shortages and water pollution in most of the country. Another is air and water pollution from oil production, petrochemical manufacturing and other industries. Algeria does, however, have one of the largest desalination plants in the world, serving 1 million people.

Algeria has a protected area system, and 24 percent of the country is in it including national parks, nature preserves, special hunting areas, and protected forests—but no protected marine areas. Algeria, like most other countries, has signed on to dozens of international treaties, protocols, and agreements, but again, like most other countries, the problem is in lack of implementation. "Algeria is substantially involved in global warming and environment issues on the political and economic planning fronts. However, the actions taken to remedy the situation are almost non-existent." **(4)**

There is a very acute industrial pollution problem on the eastern coast. Oil pollution is very serious, and almost all other industrial and municipal waste water is simply dumped untreated into the sea. New oil and gas reserves have been discovered in recent years, and a sharp increase in exports is expected to begin soon. The government seems seriously concerned that the new production be environmentally clean. As usual, there is a national plan and a variety of international cooperative ventures.

Algeria seems to be having problems at the second and third levels of economic activity in ridding itself of its State Socialist past, and coming to understand a more market based economy. After gaining independence from France in 1962, Algeria adopted Arab-Socialist economic policies which led to the nationalization of Algerian companies and the emergence of a centrally planned and controlled economy which, as in many other countries, proved to be inefficient and unable or unwilling to deal with social concerns such as environmental protection. Progress toward a market based economy remains slow, and often poorly understood by Algerians used to state control. Even today, some 20 years after the abandonment of state socialism began, the overwhelming majority of Algerian companies are still state-owned, and the private sector is only slowly gaining in significance. There are no laws concerning the social responsibilities of private companies, either for the wellbeing of their workers beyond wage payment, or for social issues like environmental protection. Yet in the Muslim community, it is customary for companies to donate money into the Islamic Zakat charity system, based on the requirements spelled out in the Quran, and this can serve as a powerful argument for enhancement of corporate social obligations in general.

Egypt

The history of Egypt since ancient times has been the story of the Nile River basin, which extends more than 4100 miles from the highlands of Ethiopia and the great lakes of Burundi down to the Mediterranean Sea. Nine nations (Egypt, Sudan, South Sudan, Ethiopia, Uganda, Kenya, Burundi, Tanzania, Zaire) make up the Nile River basin, but its principal beneficiaries are Sudan—and now South Sudan—and Egypt. But for all of these countries, the Nile is critical for their agriculture, their economic development, and for the state of their environment. These countries, in varying degrees, face common problems: rapidly increasing populations; heavy movement from rural areas to cities seldom able to cope; emphasis on industrialization to diversify the economy and generate more national wealth; and frequent conflicts in the MENA regions which disrupt development, shatter human wellbeing, destroy social services, and waste huge and badly needed financial resources. All of this in turn has led to widespread inadequacies in dealing with pressing environmental problems, which tend to sink to the bottom of everybody's priority lists.

Eighty percent of Egypt's usable water resources come from the Nile, and this source is rapidly approaching maximum utilization. Everybody either faces real water shortages now, or foresee such shortages in the near term future. Egyptian coastal areas are heavily dependent on desalination, which is expensive and has negative consequences. Most coastal towns, industries and tourist centers have their own desalination plants, but they dump their brackish water back into the sea, killing fish life and damaging coral reefs and mangrove swamps.

Agriculture is still very important to Egypt both as the home of a large rural population and as the producer of economically valuable products. But agriculture is almost 100 percent irrigated and heavily dependent on the flow of the Nile. The locust control program reaching down into Sudan is the largest in Africa, but this means that there are extensive uses of pesticides, insecticides, herbicides and fertilizers for agricultural purposes, and much of this runs off into the Gulf, or into underground aquifers which are themselves rapidly being drawn down and eventually exhausted. It appears that nobody quite knows what is in these chemicals, and there are few efforts to find out.

The tourist trade is extensive and economically important, and tourism is booming. Large stretches of shore have been developed as beach resorts. Tourist traffic prior to the Arab Spring exceeded more than one million people per year. Neither the government nor private interests seem willing to deal with the environmental consequences of this expansion.

Everybody in Egypt, Sudan and the other countries in the Nile River basin is well aware of the growing problem, and some of the most extraordinary public works of the last century have been designed to tame the Nile and enhance its usable water output. The Aswan High Dam was begun in 1959 as the show piece of the State Socialist regime of President Anwar Nasser. It stretches more than four kilometers along the river, is over 100 meters high and more than one kilometer thick. It has created Lake Nasser reservoir—the second largest man made lake in the world, stretching more than

600 kilometers long, 50 kilometers wide, and is surely one of the great public works in history. It controls and regulates the flow of the river, spreads its steady flow over the full year and is used to generate more than one third of Egypt's electricity.

Beginning about 1980, Egypt and Sudan began to cooperate on a second huge water management project on the Nile: the Jonglei Canal. (5) This was a comprehensive engineering project to cut a canal through the Sudd swamps of the upper White Nile. By speeding the flow, the project was expected to get more water through the swamps, reduce the degree of evaporation in the very high heat of the region, drain parts of the swamp and allow the land to be used for crops and cattle. It is intended to reduce annual flooding and regulate and steady the flow of the river. It was hoped that the new agricultural land could be worked with modern mechanical farming techniques thus substantially enhancing productivity. The new wealth from farming and cattle raising would galvanize the economy in a poor and remote part of the country.

Unfortunately, only the first stage of the project ever got completed. Some 260 kilometers of the canal were dug, but the remaining 100 kilometers were prevented by the outbreak of the final stages of the Sudanese civil war starting in 1983. But in the first months of the existence of the new country of South Sudan, its leadership announced an intention to renew and complete the Jonglei Canal project, and there is hope that both Sudan and Egypt will share in such an initiative, since both will benefit greatly.

But there are several major concerns: is the government of South Sudan strong enough and stable enough to carry off such a major undertaking? Does anybody have enough money to finance it—perhaps with more help from the World Bank which was heavily involved in the earlier project funding? Can the nations involved come to agreement on parceling out the percentages of water flow that will be assigned to each? Can protests against the project by environmentalists and others be mitigated? Right now, the whole project seems to be caught up in the fate of the new country of

South Sudan which has a whole series of problems to face and cannot live forever on big noble statements of intent.

Iran

Iran has the eighteenth largest economy in the world, but it lives on its exports of oil and petrochemicals, half of which now go to countries in the Far East. The population has doubled in the period 1980 to 2000, to about 75 million. This despite the eight year war with Iraq which claimed at least 300,000 lives and injured another 500,000, along with huge displacements of people and destruction of facilities.

After the revolution of 1979, the government essentially seized the economy and converted the country into a political theocracy. State owned enterprises (SOE) control 70 percent of the economy including 30 public agencies owning 120 of the "commanding heights" enterprises, religious foundations created by the government controlling 30 percent, plus about 120,000 government sponsored cooperatives. About a third of that 70 percent is owned by the Iranian Revolutionary Guard Commission (IRGC), including about 100 companies of all kinds. The IRGC gets huge government contracts for oil production, infrastructure, construction and weapons manufacture. They also control most of the smuggling, including weapons in and out. SOEs, and especially the religious foundations, have bad reputations for inefficiency, low productivity, and corruption, despite government favoritism and subsidy. There has been a pattern of neglect of energy infrastructure, a decline in the production of older oil fields, and an unwillingness to invest in modern energy production and environmental protection technology.

In general, the economy is slow growing, over-concentrated, short of skilled labor, low in productivity, and needing lots of government subsidy. The country as a whole suffers from brain drain and high poverty levels. Thus, subsidies are politically important, and include not only fuel but electricity. There is a growing dissatisfaction with the government, and thus government subsidies of food, fuel, and housing, and inflated wage rates and redundant employment have become increasingly politically urgent.

Despite the sanctions imposed by the U. N. and western countries, Iran continues to reform its economy, bringing more of it under the direct control of the State, but also attempting to diversify it so that it is not so reliant on oil and energy intensive products. The government has also become very dependent, politically, on subsidies for Iranian citizens. Fuels under state controlled markets have maintained prices that are artificially low, ultimately unsustainable, and costing the government more than $100 billion per year.

This has resulted in unbelievable waste; despite its huge national reserves of both oil and gas, Iran still imports gas from Turkmenistan. Iran's energy intensity ratio has been more than four times the world average, so finally, in 2010, the Parliament announced the intent to slowly remove many of its subsidies, increase the efficiency of energy use, and make more energy products available for export, again despite sanctions.

In theory at least, funds saved from the reduction of energy subsidies would be reinvested by the government in social infrastructure, public transport, and water desalination. Increasingly, Iran is dependent in foreign investment from China, Russia and India, mostly in the production and refining of energy products that are then exported to these countries.

Jordan

The environmental management system in place is profoundly constrained by lack of funding, weak enforcement capacity and lack of technical and scientific knowledge. Jordan has one of the highest growth rates in the world, and 55 percent of people now live in the Amman area. The numbers of automobiles increased 200 percent by 1985, and another 100 percent by 1995, with 85 percent of these vehicles operating in and around Amman. Remarkably, almost all fuel is leaded!

Solid waste is a serious problem on beaches, in sea grass and reef areas and in the Gulf of Aqaba. This is in part because the principle industries of Jordan are located along this coastline, including a large thermal power station, fertilizer manufacturing facilities, a cement plant, storage and processing areas for potash, and numerous plants for chemicals and solvents, along with associated port facilities.

Jordan's Environment Protection Law of 1995 was considered a land mark, including the establishment of the Agency for Environmental Protection, (AEP) but the staff is small, the budget is inadequate, the authority is weak and political backing is low. Jordan has signed 23 international agreements, and the AEP actually is pushing 37 projects that it hopes foreigners will finance. There seems no sense of priority, nor the will to set them. Objectives for the office include such absurdities as "restricting population growth" and "enhancing the economy." In other words, the whole thing is a classic example of a lot of political posturing, resting on academic wishful thinking. The test of success however, is in the implementation, and it seems to be a common pattern in the Arab world, and probably the Muslim world, that the tough stuff is simply beyond the capabilities of weak and bumbling governments, running more on corruption than on skill.

Jordan produces about 50 percent of the water it needs, despite the Jordan River, because much of its is usurped by Israel. And the problem is expected to get very much worse very quickly. Already, Jordan has one of the lowest levels of water resources in the world. The nature of the crisis is made more clear by recognizing that Jordan is now drawing down ground water at about 25 percent above the level of sustainable yield, and much of the drawdown is irreplaceable.(6)

Agriculture is a major problem. Jordan, like many other Muslim countries, is trying to rise up out of its agricultural past, and maintaining the wellbeing of farmers is politically important. But in fact, it seems that the realistic potential for agriculture is low, expensive, and environmentally threatening. As with so many other countries in the MENA, it would seem wise to recognize that agriculture will continue to be a high cost—low return economic sector, and it demands about 80 percentage of water usage, a high proportion of which is lost through poor irrigation systems and evaporation. It would seem vital that national policy should be shifted from marginal farming to other elements of the economy, and that food be imported from elsewhere, probably more cheaply than it can be grown locally.

In summary, Jordan has not figured out how to enhance economic development without damaging the environment. Jordan acts like it knows what to do, but has no clue about how to do it, so it chips away at the problems.

Lebanon

Thirty-two percent of Lebanese are poor and they are heavily concentrated in urban areas, mostly Beirut and Tripoli, which now have 85 percent of the total population. This rapid growth has been unplanned, uncoordinated and chaotic. Many areas or individual users can't get what they need from the government and have had to develop their own sources of power, water, sewage, and even security.

The Lebanese fought a civil war started in 1975 and the Israelis invaded in 1978 and again in 1982. Syria meddled during this same period, and the conflicts between various elements of Lebanese society have continued to this day. In total, more than 250,000 people have been killed and between 800,000 and one million have been displaced. This constant disruption has resulted in drastic destruction of natural resources and an additional 30 years of neglect of environmental problems. The famed "cedars of Lebanon" have been reduced to small stands. Lebanon suffers from damage to public infrastructure, especially in water treatment and waste disposal; a decline in agricultural production; and failure to develop the economy. As elsewhere in the Middle East, agriculture is a main employer, but it is marginal in value and keeps a lot of people poor. The land cannot really support even the agriculture now practiced, and attempts to improve agriculture are environmentally threatening. The whole region needs to find a way to draw back from agriculture, presumably through economic development, which most do poorly. Even now, Lebanon must rely on food imports which are very costly for consumers, taking 70 percent of their incomes.

Water in Lebanon is relatively adequate (83 percent from internal sources), but it is poorly managed, and is tangled up with competition for water with Israel. Again, too much of available water must be committed to agriculture. Irrigation is required in most areas, but irrigation systems are inefficient to begin with, and have been allowed to deteriorate, causing losses of up to 40 percent of the water. Mining is extensive, with six hundred quarries, but most are poorly managed. Dust and conflicts with urban expansion have become problems. Water sources are often highly contaminated with dangerous bacteria, and there are problems from faulty cesspools, leaky pipes, and contamination of potable water sources. At times, one or more of the wastewater treatment plants are out of commission. Chlorination is scarcely known, and water treatment of any kind is disturbingly limited. Only 8 percent of wells are chlorine protected. In 1996, the government decided to use asbestos constructed water pipes in some rural areas. In sum, the government has been incredibly blundering and incompetent.

In general, the government has no laws dealing with these and other environmental problems, such as the whole arena of industrial pollution. Lebanon seems to be a serious case of overemphasizing economic development to the detriment of all else. Further, Lebanon has been the destination for waste materials from other countries, which are then put in uncontrolled dumps. The Ministry of Environment has "no plans" for industrial, construction or municipal waste management. As elsewhere in the region, ports are heavily contaminated with oil spillage, disposal of ballast waters, and dredged up dirt. Pollution has drastically reduced marine life.

Air pollution is now very serious because of the rather rapid increase in the number of cars, (1.5 million, the highest in the region) most of which operate in the two main urban areas. And almost all fuel is leaded! "Air pollution has not been the subject of any regulation, except a ban on the importation of diesel vehicles and some conditions for other vehicle engines. Neither of these regulations is enforced. There exists no authority in Lebanon which is directly responsible for air quality.

Morocco

Morocco is experiencing several important tides: the acceleration of economic development; the shift in population from rural to urban areas; growing industrialization; the emergence of export oriented agriculture; a growing crisis about the water supply; other accelerating environmental problems such as soil erosion and desertification, and urban air pollution. Still, Morocco is still seen as one of the fortunate Muslim countries in terms of resources and economic progress. Water is not a current problem for agriculture which uses an estimated 92 percent of all water resources, but water is an increasing problem for cities and industries, especially for the pollution caused by the failures of waste water treatment, which is the responsibility of cities.

The government has acted to establish regional environmental Councils which are extensions of the National Environmental Council. This body was created in 1980, and there is little tangible evidence that they have had much real impact on the ensuing 32 years. As one report puts it, "That policies formulated at the central level have failed to achieve positive effects at the local and regional level is certainly one of the major shortcomings of the environmental policy efforts currently under way in Morocco." And further, "no influence of the central environmental administration on the formulation of tasks in the environmental sector by municipalities was noted in any of the towns studied."(7) What appears to be the pattern is that all levels of government seem to concentrate on planning and objective setting and coordination (or the lack of it), and nobody is expected actually to do something!

The fate of Casablanca is a case in point. Casablanca has become a badly polluted city. It is important because it is the capitol and, with a population of more than 4 million, it represents more than 12 percent of the national population. The Economist magazine reports "the atmosphere is poisonous—major numbers of cases of bronchitis, asthma, eye/ear/nose/throat problems. The urban planning policy has not kept up with the demographic evolution and the growth of traffic." (8) The city now lacks green space, and many have become dumps for trash or the hangouts of tramps and drunks.

Some new efforts have been made to improve conditions. The government has instituted a program to plant one million new trees, and about 100,000 have in fact already been planted. But in total, the loss of green space is so serious that it may not be reparable, or can be reversed only through major and very expensive actions which the government does not want to afford. The usual conflict of development vs. the environment is relevant. Major problems occur because of rampant industrial development and overbuilding, and it seems as if it is always the poorest neighborhoods that suffer the most.

And meanwhile, industrial wastes keep being dumped into the water supply, municipalities pour raw sewage into vital surface and underground water sources, oil wells and refineries pollute both the air and the water, agricultural pesticides, herbicides and insecticides are dangerous sources of pollution, and little is done about defending against desertification and deforestation. But municipalities are poor, lack competent staff and equipment, and often lack the courage to press their responsibilities in the face of local resistance or indifference. These municipalities are heavily dependent on central government funding, much of which comes from a 30 percent sharing of the income from the value added tax, but up to now, the central government seems to have forgotten this commitment.

Another consistent failure is the expressed need for public participation about environmental concerns, but this is notably unreal. In a country where 30 percent of the population lives below the poverty, and another large percentage is "near poor", and in which education, health care and other social programs are marginal, people "participate" by damning the government for its failures in its more important social services obligations.

But it is increasingly important to recognize that functioning in the international economy now requires companies and even state owned enterprises to meet international environmental standards along with other standards dealing with contract relationships, quality and safety, truth in product information and customer service. Morocco and other Muslim nations find it difficult to meet these standards.

Oman

Oman has oil, but not enough. It therefore can't rely on oil income to resolve all fiscal problems, and it has been a deliberate policy for several decades to try and promote economic development and greater economic diversity. At the same time, the government seems to have assumed a serious responsibility for protecting the environment. Perhaps the most serious problem is the shortage of water, but the government has policies and plans for reducing air pollution and for disposal of non-toxic waste, industrial toxic wastes, and other hazardous materials. The main drive comes from the Sultan Qaboos bin Said, and a Ministry of Regional Municipalities and Environment.

The government actually has developed five fairly useful development plans which are noble statements, and are typical of governmental wish lists throughout the region. Oman's are as follows:

1. To develop new sources of national income to augment and, in time, to replace oil revenues.
2. To increase the ratio of national investments directed to income generating projects, particularly in manufacturing, mining, agriculture and fisheries.
3. To distribute national investments among geographical regions with a view of spreading prosperity and progress to all regions of the Sultanate.
4. To support the maintenance of existing population centers and communities, to safeguard those communities from potential emigration to densely populated urban centers, and to protect the environment.
5. To attach high priority to the development of natural water resources.
6. To attach high priority to the development of human resources, and to improve their capacity to contribute to the national economy.
7. To meet infrastructure requirements.
8. To support commercial activities by removing market deficiencies, particularly in the areas of transport, communications and storage, and other obstacles to competitive trading, with a view to enhancing the emergency of a competitive market.
9. To provide for the creation of a national economy based on private enterprise and free from monopolistic practices.
10. To enhance the efficiency of the government's administrative machinery.

The first Five Year Plan was initiated in 1976. In 1970, Oman boasted ten kilometers of paved roads, three primary schools for boys, and a single 12 bed American missionary clinic. The period 1976 to 1980 became one of astonishing advance, largely driven and financed by the government. The second Five Year Plan (1981 to1985) was driven by big increases in oil income, the continuation of development, and a new program to optimize water resources.

The Third Five Year Plan was a period of reduced oil revenues, and related slow downs in fiscal expenditures. The Fourth Five Year Plan began the search for a new balance in the economy. This included efforts to help the private sector to expand and to diversify. Efforts were made to substitute local workers for the heavy reliance on cheap foreign labor, and excessive reliance on income from expatriates. The industrial sector grew from $1.5 million in 1976 to $45 million in 1990, and surprisingly, agriculture and fisheries enjoyed an almost equal growth. The civil service grew from 1750 in 1970 to over 77,000 in 1992.

Pakistan

The British established a huge irrigation system in Sindh Province in the Punjab, around the city of Faisalabad, down a valley to the Arabian Sea. They eventually produced "the largest unbroken irrigated area on the planet." But then, they imported Indian farmers to grow only water thirsty cotton, to feed the new mills in Lancashire. After Independence, Pakistan continued this water development. It built a series of giant dams on the upper reaches of the river, including the Tarbela, which, when completed in 1974, was the largest in the world. "Without the Indus and its water engineering, Pakistan would be a desert."(9)

But the huge water diversion has inundated flat land with standing water which is salty and pollutes the soil. Farmers then have to use other water to "wash" the soil before they plant. But now, 10 percent of the land has been lost; 20 percent is badly waterlogged; and 25 percent now produces reduced outputs of crops. Expensive attempts have been made to install water drains to draw off the salt water with modest results.

The politicians want to involve more land and use more water in more irrigation systems. But the river itself is in big trouble. For many years, the river is now dry before it meets the sea. Meager water flows have killed mangrove swamps that used to be water reservoirs. Many of the fish in the river have vanished. Drinking quality water is scarce. The sea is advancing inland. Many farmers and villagers have abandoned the region, and the existing social structures are breaking down. Banditry and corruption are worse. Farmers who have fled have gone to the cities, which are ill equipped to deal with them.

Saudi Arabia

In theory, Saudi Arabia has developed as a thoroughly modern practitioner of sustainable development. Major achievements include the establishment of a Ministry of Environment in 2001, the establishment of a coordinating body, the Ministerial Committee on the Environment in 2010, the accompanying development of an elaborate ministry base of environmental management institutions, Saudi Arabian participation in most international organizations, and the drafting and promulgation of a whole array of laws and regulations covering the spectrum of environmental concerns. The objectives of the environmental law are as follows:

1. Preserve, protect and develop the environment and protect it from pollution
2. Protect public health from activities and acts that harm the environment
3. Conserve and develop natural resources
4. Include environmental planning as an integral part of overall development planning in all industrial, agricultural and architectural and other areas
5. Raise the awareness of environmental issues, strengthen individual and collective feelings of responsibility for preserving and improving the environment, and encourage national voluntary efforts.

This, along with a multitude of laws and regulations surely provides an adequate basis for action. Yet the actual record seems puzzling. There is a distinct reputation that all of these grand structures seem not to have produced much action. Enforcement has been at best limited and at worst nonexistent. In fact, the defined mission of the

Meteorology and Environmental Protection Agency (MEPA) is so very typical. It is officially stated as:

1. Review and evaluate the condition of the environment
2. Conduct environmental studies
3. Document and publish environmental information
4. Prepare environmental protection laws, standards and regulations
5. Promote environmental awareness.

All of this is soft "plans and studies" stuff. In fact, MEPA has substantial authority to issue cease and desist orders, take corrective actions, force compliance with regulations, and impose fines and demand imprisonment. Yet in the dozen years of its existence, not one single high profile case has been undertaken, and implementation of enforcement authority is seldom exercised. Saudi Arabia has the money, the laws, and the governmental infrastructure; why does it not have a better record of accomplishment? Yet, Saudi Arabia has developed more than 2.5 million acres of wheat production using desalinated water.

According to Fred Pearce **(10)** "Some of the most serious, indeed scandalous, groundwater disasters are being played out in the Middle East. Saudi Arabia has virtually no rain and no rivers or surface lakes of any kind. It has spent $10 billion on desalination works, and over $40 billion sinking pumps into the aquifer beneath the desert, marking out 2.5 million acres of desert for wheat farms. All of the water was provided to farmers free. Nobody cared how much water was wasted, and usually most of it evaporated in the sun. For every ton of wheat grown, the government supplied 2.5 acre-feet of water—three times the global norm.

Saudi Arabia is slowly waking up to reality. Finally, in 2004 it launched a water conservation drive, and the water vice minister made a radical statement: "We need to examine whether we need to produce the whole domestic consumption of wheat, or perhaps make do with half."

In general, Saudi business and military interests have outclassed the environmentalists and those who want more attention to social services provision. But there are increasing opinions that the long term movement toward sustainable development can be applied perfectly well in Saudi Arabia as it has been done elsewhere, and that this melding is consistent with Sharia law, and even with the more conservative Islamic attitudes that prevail in the country. Planning about the environment centers mostly around the future activities of the government, but as efforts are made to broaden the base of the economy, part of this effort is going into urging the private sector to develop more environmentally friendly goods and services, to increase the more prudent use of natural resources, to limit waste and wasteful practices, and to provide technical expertise and consulting services.

Sudan

Sudan is enjoying some new measures of prosperity using oil money, but after decades of neglect and the terrible destruction of the war with southern elements of the country and in Darfur, Sudan has been left with the largest population of displaced persons in the world today. An explosive growth in population is creating food demands that cannot be met. More intensive agriculture on land that is not suitable produces desertification, at a time when there is a period of extended drought. And it is ironic that, despite serious water shortages, floods are still common. It is inescapable: most of the problems are solvable but the government is unwilling or unable to cope. **(11)** They would rather fight.

Agriculture is poorly managed and programs for large scale mechanized farming assumed adequate rainfall became disasters leading to large scale forest clearance, severe land degradation, and loss of wildlife. Two thirds of the forest cover in north central and eastern Sudan disappeared since the early 70s. As in so many other Muslim countries, agriculture wastes huge amounts of water. An extremely low percentage of the population has access to safe water, but water shortage is not the real problem. It is a result of mismanagement and inadequate investment in treatment facilities and water provision infrastructure.

And here again, there is a good deal of bureaucratic posturing not culminating in results. The Comprehensive Peace Agreement and Interim Constitution completed with the new country of South Sudan contains the basis for a National Plan for Environmental Management. Its supposed objectives are to improve environmental governance and intergovernmental cooperation, supervised by Sudan's Higher Council for Environment and Natural Resources which was created by law in 2005. Environmental Impact Assessments are required, and many have been prepared, for major projects, but they have not been made public, and it is not clear whether they are effective or whether they are considered in the preparation of overall economic development plans for the country.

Sudan wants to build another 20 dams at Marowe despite the high likelihood of river bank disruption and silting behind the dams. All the pros and cons of dam construction apply. Even environmental issues are the victim of rampant and universal crime: illegal pollution (water, air, soil, food, fisheries), chemical dumping, oil spills, insecticides, herbicides, pesticides, metals, poisons, plus careless fires, illegal logging, game poaching and illegal hunting and massive poaching. Many of these crimes involve the additional shame of public officials practicing bribery and corruption.

Sewage treatment in the cities is totally inadequate and poorly managed. Garbage collection is slow and smelly, and usually culminates in undesirable burning. Industrial pollution is uncontrolled, but because of the low level of industry, it has yet to be a serious environmental problem. However, as the economy develops, lack of oversight and adequate treatment facilities for water and oil extraction waste will become a real threat.

Syria

Syria is a middle income country, with a fairly balanced economy. At the same time, it is mostly semiarid, largely desert, with its population concentrated on its narrow coastal plain. Oil continues to be its major source of wealth and exports. Syria has long had a developed sector of small scale businesses such as food processing, olive oil mills, textiles, and small scale metals working, but in recent years it has been attempting to diversify its economy, in such areas as chemicals, rubber and plastic, textiles and food/beverages. But now, the whole Syrian economy is badly battered by the vicious civil war, and it is difficult to know how much is left.

Syria suffers from all of the environmental concerns that plague Middle East and North African countries: water shortages and water pollution, untreated sewage in urban areas, industrial pollution of both water and air, wastes from petroleum refining, soil erosion, desertification and deforestation. As in other countries, most of the water—more than 90 percent—is used for agriculture. It also appears that this ominous situation is only going to get worse because of climate change. In the last five years, the average rainfall in the main agricultural areas has declined by as much as 45 percent or more, and the concern is that this decline is not merely cyclical, but may represent a permanent change in the national climate. Throughout the area, outputs of crops such as corn, rice and wheat has fallen significantly, but of course, the civil war has been adversely impacting life on farms and in villages.

The rapid increase in the general population ends up in greater urbanization and Syria is building up toward a genuine urban water crisis. But at the same time, nobody in the country wants to be seen as reducing water availability in the countryside or in the villages, and the rural population has long been a major source of support for the regime. There are many cities that dump sewage directly into surface water sources, and even where there are urban sewage systems, they tend to be old, in bad shape, and far too small for the expanding urban populations. Rural populations rely mostly on cesspools or discharge into surface waters. The government had instituted programs for construction of urban and industrial wastewater treatment plants, and low cost-effective treatment units in rural/small town areas, but progress has been slow, and the serious conflicts now taking place in the country makes it doubtful that such work is continuing. A comprehensive Ministry of Environment was not established until 2009, but it is not strong enough to compete for scarce funding against the demands for economic development and the military.

In a similar vein, municipalities have serious solid waste problems. Lack of properly designed landfills means that contaminated waste is leaking into rivers and the sea. Many of the limited number of waste disposal facilities are poorly located and poorly run. In addition there is a lot of illegal dumping both by cities and by industry. Construction companies seem to have a bad habit of dumping their waste along roadways, in ditches and in any unoccupied open country.

Air pollution is also a serious problem in Syria's highly populated urban areas. Industry and especially the growing number of automobiles are exacerbating this problem, and as elsewhere in the Muslim world, the government lacks the guts to do anything about it for fear of constraining economic development. As in most Muslim countries, even those that produce huge oil outputs, most local automobiles still use leaded gas. And agricultural land adjacent to industrial areas suffers from extensive soil pollution from lead, tannic acids, cadmium and arsenic deposits coming from cement plants, wastes from fertilizer manufacturers, power generation plants, and especially the oil industry. Few companies have up to date protection facilities, and few seem to care.

Here again, as in many other Middle East Muslim countries, the government is seen as heavy on paper plans, overly organized with dozens of environmental units, and full of talk about "coordination", but achieving little real action. The institutional structure of the government seems formidable but was seen as very weak even before the beginning of the civil war. There is a central government Council for Environmental Safety and Sustainable Development, chaired by the Prime Minister, which supposedly coordinates the work of the State Planning Commission plus 16 other government agencies, but the work of implementation has been delegated to a network of Environment Directorates and committees, the Ministry of Housing and Utilities, the Ministry of Agriculture and Agrarian Reform through field offices at local government levels.

Further, there is a separate group of agencies centered about water management: a Higher Water Committee, the Ministry of Irrigation, the Agriculture Ministry and a Syrian Environmental Association all of which are supposed to coordinate to develop a national strategy. But everywhere, environmental protections are usually ignored despite the existence of dozens of laws and hundreds of regulations. Most governments at all levels lack any enforcement capability, are universally underfunded, often deliberately, and lack staff expertise to pursue much of anything, even if they wanted to do so. And here again as in other MENA countries, much of the government's strategy centers around ways to get foreign donors to fund as many projects as possible, rather than the government of Syria.

And of course, now all of this messy façade, which seems not able to act in the best of times, has been intercepted, delayed or terminated by the civil war that now rages in the country and which is horribly destructive physically, financially and emotionally. Much of what has been accomplished in the last few years has gone down the drain. Even if and when the murderous civil strife is ended, it will take decades for Syria to crawl back even to the inferior position it achieved before the war.

Turkey

Turkey is experiencing a rapid rate of sustained growth in population, one of the highest in the world, and its current population is in excess of 65 million, up more than 50 percent since 1980. Almost 70 percent of the population now lives in urban areas, but like most Muslim countries, Turkey is still locked into its rural past. Rapid urbanization was obvious and recognized, but governments at all levels seem to have been locked in denial and almost every city has fallen far behind its needs, both physical and social. At the same time, Turkey, like most other Muslim countries, has been more or less willingly pursuing an intense process of privatization of its state owned enterprises, which have, as usual, proved inefficient. Most big private polluters do not see themselves as responsible for any level of environmental protection. Much of what little has been done about the environment has been done by the central government, but there is now a movement toward decentralization to the 81 provinces—with some of the usual cynical money motives. Provincial governors are appointed and report to the Minister of Interior Affairs, and the only really elected governments are in the municipalities and villages.

The Ministry of Environment was created in 1991, but there is a whole range of other ministries, including the Central Planning Commission, which have a piece of the environmental action. Turkey has the full set of laws and regulations, and it is a member of all of the relevant international organizations, but the track record is still lack of real action and enforcement. Even today, more than twenty years after its creation, the Ministry of Environment still does not have adequate enforcement capabilities.

There is a clear set of reasonable objectives: to implement environmental policies and strengthen enforcement; to invest in environmental infrastructure; to provide for public participation; to integrate environmental concerns into overall economic decisions; to conform to international standards, especially for industrial and natural resources exports. But there is also a depressing pattern of all of this planning culminating in projects which the Turkish government expects the World Bank or the IMF or some other international source to fund, again showing a massive reluctance to face up to its own responsibilities.

Air quality is bad, but this is one area in which the government has acted. Major changes have been made in the use of coal for energy—more foreign purchased coal with low sulphur content, replacing local high sulphur stuff. But it is doubtful whether the overall problem of air pollution will be mitigated until industries are forced to clean up their emissions. This is a huge, highly resisted change, weakened by a history of corruption.

As usual in Muslim Middle East countries, there is a serious and deepening crisis over water. Fifty-five percent of it is used for agricultural irrigation, and it is political dynamite trying to reduce this. The most serious problem is probably the huge lack of wastewater treatment, where only about 11 percent of the population has adequate service. Waste water treatment facilities for municipalities have been furnished by the central government, and have always been inadequate. Municipalities would like to get out from under central government control, but generally seem unable or unwilling to come up with the money themselves. For them, the ideal would be national money but local control.

The present process for industries seems to be to ignore the problems of water and solid waste disposal totally, or to dump waste in public facilities. It would be a major effort to get companies to provide proper treatment themselves. Of 2157 municipalities, more than 70 percent are unable to conform to their own solid waste regulations and standards. Almost 40 percent of solid waste in municipalities is hazardous in some form, but it seems to disappear into the overall waste dumps, and there is only one hazardous waste treatment facility in all of Turkey.

Forests cover 27 percent of the country and permanent crop land covers 35 percent, and most crops are irrigated. As usual, there are efforts to promote agriculture, but they seem more political than practical, and Turkey will increasingly be an importer of food. Major problems have emerged in the form of serious increases in erosion, effecting more than 80 percent of all agricultural land which is a big problem looming for the future. In addition, there are the usual problems of excessive use of chemicals, losses of water in obsolete irrigation systems, deforestation, and desertification.

The Path to Improvement

The demographics of the Muslim world in the MENA have been rapidly changing. The conflicts remain, but economies are slowly developing. More and more people are finding that rural life is not sufficiently rewarding and they are moving to the cities, ready or not. The development of more extensive and sophisticated economies creates the demand for a more educated workforce. People crammed into urban slums have found new sources of civic power and are demanding more social services from their governments.

It is therefore likely that part of this new tide running will be demands for more attention to the real neglected problems of the environment, and there are important things that any serious government might undertake:

1. It is perhaps time to rethink the real nature of the agricultural sector of these national economies. Ultimately, it does not make much sense to pour money into subsidizing agricultural economies that are low value added, cannot provide food self-sufficiency for the country and cannot provide more than a marginal living for farmers and villagers. It would likely prove to be far more satisfying and far less expensive for both government and private interests to import food from elsewhere, and let domestic agriculture settle down to a level that can be made practical. The world still has huge amounts of land where food can be grown effectively and cheaply. Use of this land should be substituted for the very poor land in places like the Middle East.

2. If this course of action is initiated, it would allow the government to all but terminate its expensive subsidies of water, energy, seeds and chemicals, with exceptions for the truly needy. It could also cut back on the hugely wasteful irrigation systems and use the saved water for both urban and industrial priorities.

3. Part of this reallocation would be to cities, and a top priority must be a long intensive upgrading of the ability of cities to manage their water systems. Clean water supplies must be available to all residents, even those in the slums. Water distribution piping systems should be made sound, and metering of water delivery to customers must be universal in order to eliminate the present situation of both leakage and theft. Waste water treatment needs to become standard, and while this is expensive, there will be collateral savings in the reduction of sickness and infection from poisonous untreated water. Industrial pollution sources must be regulated, and regulations enforced. Water recycling is a perfectly well understood technique and can be instituted place by place, where governments have the will to do so.

4. Desalination is now technically more feasible, but it is still expensive and few nations can afford enough of these systems to make a substantial difference in supply. So it is likely that its future will be limited to certain specific situations where is really does make sense, or is the only feasible option.

5. Perhaps most critically, governments in the region must wake up to the fact that they are allowing dangerous draw downs of their current sources of rivers, lakes and underground aquifers. Some of these draw downs result in permanent damage, as for example, cases where aquifers near the sea are drained, and sea water pours in instead, or where chemicals enter underground sources and can never be removed. In other situations mistakes can be stopped or fixed. No subsidy should be paid which permits or encourages the excessive use of water. No industry should be allowed to waste water supplied from a public source, or should they be allowed to escape payment for the water they use, and there seems to be a growing interest in the potentials of a pollution tax, although it is argued that the punitive nature of such a tax is bad public psychology. Water is easily stolen, but somehow, water theft must be controlled.

6. Another change which is emerging is the development of public interest groups who recognize the importance of an educated and supportive public, but see the failures of governments to generate such support. Most of these groups are being generated within each society but they have had a lot of support from the international environmental community, both officially and unofficially. In many countries where the land is owned by the government, there are ways to work out better ownership or land tenure agreements that give the occupants a sense of responsibility for water management. The results can be very gratifying.

7. Of course, it is still more than possible to discover new sources of underground water that could change the whole dynamic of water management in the Middle East. According to Fred Pearce, Libya has tapped into the giant Nubian sandstone aquifer under the Sahara Desert. **(12)** It is the largest freshwater source on earth, containing about 50 billion acre-feet of water in a series of basins. Libya's new "river" is a network of pipes, all of them large enough to drive a truck through, fed by hundreds of bore holes drilled in the Nubian aquifer. Quaddifi spent more than $27 billion of oil money to have the network developed by contractors and directed by Brown and Root, headquartered in London. Yet the outflow of this network is surprisingly low, far less than needed to provide irrigation for Libyan farms under their growth plan. "Irrigating the existing farm land at current standards of efficiency requires around four million acre-feet, more than twice the intended output of the man-made rivers. The vast capital costs and the growing bills for pumping water from increasing depths make wheat grown from the Saharan water some of the most expensive on earth. It is madness to use this water for agriculture" says Tony Allan, a British specialist on Middle Eastern water. **(13)**

SOURCES

"Environmental Issues in Egypt", Wikipedia, May, 2012.

Green Prophet, "Egypt is Middle East Region's Cleanest and Most Environmental Country", 2012.

Hussein I, Abdel-Shafy, and Raouf O, Aly, "Water Issue in Egypt: Resources, Pollution and Protection Endeavors", CEJOEM, 2002, Vol. 1.3.

Egypt Independent, "Government Report: Environmental Situation in Egypt Has Improved", November, 2012.

Mohammed Abdel-Ghani Sa'oudi, Dr., "The Jonglei Canel Project", Nile Buffalo Gazette, August, 2009.

New Sudan Vision, "Jonglei Canal Project May Hold Great Potential for South Sudan", August, 2011.

ICE Case Studies, Trade and Environment Database: "Nile River Dispute", 1997.

Encylopedia of the Nations, "Morocco—Environment", downloaded 2012.

El Ouali, Abderrahim, "How Green Was My City, IPS News, ipsnews.net, December, 2005.

National Diagnostic Analysis for Syria, UNDP/MASP, 2003.

Al Arabiya News, "Subsidies and Sanctions: Iran Gets High Marks in IMF Review", August, 2011.

Caritas Internationalis, "Climate Change in Algeria", July, 2011.

German Embassy, Algiers, csr-weltweit.de, "The Role of Corporate Social Responsibility (CSR) In Algeria", 2009.

Pacific Institute report: Clearing the Waters: A Focus on Water Quality Solutions", UNDP Environmental Program, 2011.

Fatani, Rafid, "Saudi Arabia Country Report", Global Information Society Watch, 2010.

Seha.alriyadh.gov.sa, "Development and Environment in Saudi Arabia", May, 2009.

United Nations Development Programme, Kingdom of Saudi Arabia, "Environment and Sustainable Development Forum", March 2012.

FANAK, Chronicle of the Middle East and North Africa, "Syria: Biodiversity and Natural Environment", 2012.

Syria Today, "Environment and Climate Change in the Middle East", January 26, 2012.

United Nations Development Programme, "Sudan: Post-Conflict Environmental Assessment", 2006.

Dahlberg, Emelie, and Slunge, Daniel, "Sudan Environmental Policy Brief", Goteborg, Sweden, Goteborg University, December, 2007.

Hamid, Abdel H., Mwiturubani, Donald A., and Ostro, Deborah, "The Nature and Extent of Environmental Crimes in Sudan", Institute for Security Studies, November, 2009.

Bitzer, Royce J., "Environmental Issues in the Middle East", World Regions Project, 2011.

Sanders, Edmund, "Another Disaster Brews in Darfur", Los Angeles Times, October 1, 2007.

Center for Middle Eastern Studies, Harvard University, "Water in the Middle East", Middle East Resources Newsletter, Dec. 1993, Vol. 15, No. 1.

Hadadin, Nidal A., and Tarawneh, Zeyad S., "Environmental Issues in Jordan, Solutions and Recommendations", American Journal of Environmental Sciences, 2007.

http://www.kinghussein.gov.jo/geo, "Jordan's Water Shortage", 1998.

Berman, Ilan, and Wihbey, Paul Michael, "The New Water Politics in the Middle East", Institute for Strategic and Advanced Political Studies, Tel Aviv and Washington, D. C., published in Strategic Review, Summer, 1999.

World Bank, News and Broadcast, "Coping With Scarce Water in the Middle East and North Africa", March, 2007.

Environmental Monitor, "Middle East: Environmental Issues", July, 2010.

Elgendy, Karim, "Sustainable Development and the Built Environment in the Middle East: Challenges and Opportunities", Middle East Institute, Washington, D. C., 2011.

Weidnitzer, Eva, "Environmental Policy in Morocco: Institutional Problems and the Role of Non-Governmental Organizations", The Middle Eastern Environment, St. Malo Press, 2002.

Al Haji, Zeina, "Mediterranean Blues: Facing Environmental Crises", Middle East Research and Information Project, #216, Washington, D. C., Fall, 2000.

Jarvis, Amy, "Environmental Problems in the Middle East", Incredibly Green, 2011.

Regional Environment Center, "Turkey's Environment: A Review and Evaluation of Turkey's Environment and its Stakeholders", Extension to Turkey Project, 2006.

GIZ: Deutsche Gesellchaft fur Internationale Zusammen: "Environmental Programme Morocco", 2011

United Nations Economic Programme, "Assessment of Land-based Sources and Activities Affecting the Marine Environment in the Red Sea and Gulf of Aden", UNEP Regional Seas Reports and Studies No. 166, 1997.

The Economist, "The Jordan Valley: A Dry Bone of Contention", Nov. 27, 2010.

The Knowers Ark Educational Foundation, The Global Education Project, "Water in the Middle East", 2000.

The Economist, "Asia and its Floods: Save Our Cities", March 17, 2012.

Islar, Mine, "Crisis of Water: Interrogating Neo-Liberal Water Discourses in Turkey", Lund University, 2009.

Middle East Web (www.mideastweb.org/water), "Water in the Middle East Conflict", 2002.

Watson, Robert T. Ed., "The Regional Impacts of Climate Change: Lebanon", International Panel on Climate Change, UNDP, 1997.

Nuba Water Project (http://nubawaterproject.org), "Bringing Water and Life to the Nuba Mountains of Sudan", 2010.

Jabbra, Joseph G., and Jabbra, Nancy W., "Challenging Environmental Issues: Middle Eastern Perspectives, Leiden, Brill Publishers, 1997.

Khan, Mohammad Hussain, "Dilapidated Irrigation Network in Sindh" Dawn.com, May, 2012.

Pearce, Fred, "When the Rivers Run Dry", Boston, Beacon Press, 2006.

CHAPTER VII

SOCIAL SERVICES

Attempts to deliver adequate social services in the Muslim world have proved remarkably difficult and frustrating. All of the Muslim countries in the world face the same set of horrendous problems, and progress since the mid 1980s has been meager. For the last several hundred years, after the glory days of the past, almost all of these nations have been relatively poor, despite the region's oil wealth, and all have been struggling to enlarge their economies enough to permit the reduction of widespread poverty—after, of course, financing the military and rewarding the elites. Many of these economies have been improving, but most at such a slow pace that they cannot even keep up with the great increases in their populations. Many are making significant improvements in key social indicator such as levels of literacy, numbers of children in school, reductions in many diseases, improved mother/child care and infant mortality, and extensions of social security. Muslims have a long and usually honorable history of private and Mosque charity and social service.

The substitution of social services provided by centrist governments has not always been very successful, and has hurt this voluntary tradition. Improvements result from a little more money and a little better service delivery, but they do not add up to any significant reduction in levels of poverty, and in general, little progress has been achieved above the levels found in 1980. It is also true that more help has come from foreign governments, international organizations and Non-government organizations (NGO) than in the earlier past.

A series of Arab Human Development Reports have been issued by the United Nations Development Programme, starting in 1990. The sum of these assessments about the social context of Arab nations is very disturbing, showing long term suffering from the following problems:

* Seemingly endless wars, insurrections, terrorist destructions.
* Widespread abject poverty and near poverty.
* A general condition of societal backwardness and obsolescence.
* Societies riddled by divisiveness, exclusion, and internal conflict.
* Weak and ineffective governments.
* Universal, cynical, rampant corruption, both public and private.
* Economies that are contracting and producing low total value, thus failing to generate the wealth needed to meet public needs.
* Widespread lack of women's empowerment
* A "knowledge deficit"—too few people possess high quality knowledge and skills.

While some countries such as Oman, Saudi Arabia, Tunisia, Algeria and Morocco are seen as better off over the last decade, most countries are seen as worse off: Afghanistan, Eritrea, Iraq, Iran, Sudan, South Sudan, Palestine, Pakistan, Nigeria, Mali, Somalia, Yemen, Lebanon. In summary, the Report of 2009 says "In the Arab region, with an estimated MENA population of about 318 million, human insecurity—pervasive, often intense and with consequences affecting large numbers of people—inhibits human development. It is revealed in the impacts of military occupation and armed conflict—. It is found in countries that enjoy relative stability where the authoritarian state, buttressed by flawed constitutions and unjust laws, often denies citizens of their rights. Human insecurity is heightened by swift climatic changes, which threaten the livelihoods, incomes and access to food and water of millions of

Arabs in future. It is reflected in the economic vulnerability of one fifth of the people in some Arab states, and more than half in others, whose lives are impoverished and cut short by hunger and want. Human insecurity is palpable and present in the alienation of the region's rising cohort of unemployed youth and in the predicaments of its subordinated women, and dispossessed refugees."

Note that the UN is now using a multi-dimensional Poverty Index which factors in education, health and living standards beyond merely looking at income. Thus, instead of 6.8 million poor, the Arab region has 39 million poor ranging from 7 percent in Tunisia to 81 percent in Somalia. (1)

Poverty is mainly a function of national economic development, and even in those countries where economies are improving, they remain too small, too low value and essentially non-competitive in international terms. Further, these economies tend to be unbalanced—strongest for the urban elite, weaker for the urban underclass, and worst of all for the old rural world. So poverty rates remain extremely high: Iran and Afghanistan at greater than 50 percent and among the worst in the world; the poverty rate in Azerbaijan is over 68 percent, Ethiopia is at 45 percent, Yemen at about 40 percent; Egypt and Turkey at over 20 percent.

In addition, standards set by the UN or the World Bank include two levels: "abject poverty" which means living on less than $1.25 equivalent per day; and "poverty" which means living on less than $2.00 per day. Many people who have moved out of "abject poverty" move not to wealth but to—"poverty". And for the slightly more fortunate, they may achieve "near poverty". Average per capita income grew by only 1 percent per year between 1985 and 2000, and during the same period, the total number of poor grew by 11.5 million up to a total of 52 million.

But beyond these more or less normal problems of money and the pace of economic growth, Muslim countries have experienced an absolutely horrible record of self inflicted wounds in the form of countless highly destructive armed conflicts, as detailed in Chapter One above. Time after time, slow painful progress in the provision of social services has been disrupted or destroyed by armed conflicts bringing only death, displacement and destruction. Schools and hospitals have been destroyed or closed down. Transportation is very bad, deteriorating, and highly dangerous. Water provision including wells reservoirs, pumping plants or agricultural irrigation systems are destroyed or never repaired. Huge environmental problems are neglected and go from bad to worse. Industrial plants close down and commercial businesses fail. Huge numbers of people are forced to abandon their homes and belongings to flee to somewhere less dangerous and insecure. Therefore, the state of social services in any country must be evaluated in the context of the total economy and society of the country, and statistics take on meaning only when the social service environment is understood. Here are the main characteristics of successful social service environments.

Economic Characteristics

1. A national economy large enough to provide jobs for everybody who wants/needs to work.
2. These jobs must be productive enough to earn the workers a decent wage or salary. "Decent" means enough income to cover all day-to-day ordinary expenses, plus enough to build personal assets for the long term such as a home, savings, education for children, health insurance and provision for old age.
3. The economy must be capable of competing against other economies, including an adequate level of efficiency, and adequate level of value produced to finance economic growth and improvement.
4. The economy must be relatively balanced, providing money for even the poorest, and for every area of the country. Most countries have both a formal and an informal sector, and both must be relatively productive.

5. The jobs available to the workforce must range from simple to highly sophisticated in order to provide work payoff for education and training.

6. Urbanization does, in general, contribute to the reduction of poverty. In many cases, the most important factor is the strengthening of the informal economy which absorbs many youths, women and people deserting farms and villages. The informal economy thus offers work for people who cannot be accommodated by the formal economy dominated by the government. The very act of migration from the farms to urban areas frees up people from obsolete low value conditions and lets them work out better opportunities for themselves, and to begin to build the safety nets of home ownership, savings and higher forms of education and training.

Political Characteristics

1. The political system must be very heavily committed to meeting the needs of the general public and not just a ruling elite.

2. This includes public infrastructure—at least schools, hospitals, modes of transportation, fresh water, electric power, waste removal, housing and security. These needs can and should be met by a combination of public and private provision, but government must provide what individuals and the private sector cannot.

3. Governments must also provide key elements of public services: education, health care, police and fire protection, public safety and wellbeing, and ultimate responsibility for the indigent, the helpless, and the unprotected elderly. But it is acceptable and necessary to expect people to provide for these needs themselves, with governments in a supportive or "last resort" role.

4. Politics is often the major way—sometimes the only way—in which decisions affecting a whole nation or region

can be resolved. Therefore, the citizens have every right to expect politicians who are capable of making decisions.

5. Constitutions all over the world establish the right of citizens to enjoy major benefits—liberty, justice, equality, opportunity, education/self advancement, peace, some degree of protection against the crises and threats that no society can avoid.
6. Since governments can impose laws on people and tax their resources, citizens have a right to expect that these authorities will be properly and honestly exercised.

Social Support

1. Citizens develop their own institutions to help protect themselves and develop their own abilities. These institutions include religious entities (churches, mosques, synagogues, church affiliated organizations, plus social services associations, advocacy groups, lobbying groups and charities. Public policy must and should act to support the effectiveness of such institutions, and avoid creating barriers to their accomplishment.
2. Within any country, there will be elements of society that are seen as in conflict: rich vs. poor, young vs. old, rural vs. urban, geographical regions against each other, religious differences, rivalries between clans and tribes, and the honest vs. the corrupt. Citizens themselves feed these differences, but it should be the fixed policy of governments not to use the authority and influence of the government itself to create or stimulate these conflicts, and but instead they should work to resolve or mitigate them. One of the most serious of these conflicts centers around the role of women in each Muslim society, and it should be the special responsibility of Muslim governments to move that relationship up to a higher level of success.

In almost every Muslim country, the trend has been for the national regime to get out from under direct responsibility for social services by "devolution" down to local governments, or by simply defaulting on these needs. But this devolution seldom involves the devolution of much money. Local governments are already net losers of funds to their central governments, and the recent 30 year tide of migration to cities has left most of them far behind the power curve, wholly unable to come anywhere close to meeting demands from their burgeoning populations for social services and public infrastructure. The World Bank, in its 2007 report "Sustaining Gains in Poverty Reduction and Human Development in MENA" stated "As a social cost of slow growth, an additional 11 million people were added to the ranks of the poor between 1987 and 2001 because the region's population continued to grow but its economies didn't." (3)

The Status of Women in the Muslim World

In order to understand what women in the Muslim world really experience, it is necessary to consider the broader world in which all Muslims, both women and men, are living. If women are oppressed, they live under repressive regimes. If women lack representation, most regimes refuse to permit it for anybody. If women can't find jobs, economies are weak and inadequate. If women lack education or health care, these services are notoriously inadequate almost everywhere. Bad politics and rejection of the rule of law harm everybody. Then, on top of this, women are the victims of further prejudice and neglect in addition to the broad failures of government and society in which Muslims live.

A classic example is the fact that all Muslim countries have formally committed to compliance with the United Nations Convention on the Elimination of All Forms of Discrimination Against Women (CEDAW), which seeks to become the world standard for these concerns. Many Muslim countries approve the Convention with certain specific exceptions from provisions which are seen as in unacceptable conflict with some important national law. But it has also become clear that acceptance of the U. N. Convention is merely voluntary and it is not often that any regime will ever really comply fully with its intent.

Further, there are serious elements in the culture of many Muslim countries that further inhibit the ability of women to improve their own situation. There are significant conflicts centering about religion, geography, clan and tribal conflicts, rural vs. urban attitudes, older and more conservative customs vs. new conceptions, and everywhere the "culture" of official corruption, criminal organizations, terrorist groups, threats and intimidation by thugs, and widespread armed insurrection. It is very difficult to find a government that is capable of pursuing women's reform agendas in the face of these major instabilities.

Even without the consequences of these convulsions, the ability or willingness of courts and government officials to address the need for the reforms sought by women is weak and reluctant. It is a universal common characteristic across the whole Muslim world that a regime's ability to enforce its own laws and regulations ranges from bad to nonexistent. Even if women succeed in securing the desirable reform of some law or regulation or administrative practice, there is no guarantee that the change will be implemented. Mostly, the courts are weak and not often independent, and they seldom have provisions for hearing complaints against the government. Even if some appeal is permitted, older conservative male attitudes still seem to shape judge's opinions.

At the next level of the structure of Muslim governments is the universal existence of some version of a Personal Status Law or Family Law or Civil Code which largely dictates the rights and status of women in a whole array of critical areas. These laws deal with marriage, divorce, family relationships, inheritance, rights to work, rights to travel, dress codes, standards for personal conduct, access to health care and education, and eligibility for a whole range of legal and public entitlements. There are separate laws dealing further with many of these personal status issues, but the key point to recognize is that the fundamental legal basis for these laws is some form of Muslim Sharia law.

In other words, Sharia law dominates most of the issues affecting women as persons, and thus most of the issues that women seek to reform. The overall legal system of a given country is probably some combination of ancient laws and customs, some older version of Sharia law, some updated Sharia law, then the addition of secular laws drawn largely from foreign, mostly European experience. But the real strength of Sharia law lies in this world of personal and family law, and this seems to have wide acceptability. But Sharia law is also the arena in which the religious leaders exert their own greatest influence. The adoption by governments means that they don't have to enter the thorny thicket of writing personal laws from secular sources. And indeed the people themselves are used to living under these Sharia laws and seem comfortable with them. But this general acceptability is now being challenged. It is challenged by women as individuals, or as advocates, or as participants in political and social civil rights groups. This challenge has, in many Muslim countries matured to the status of a <u>movement.</u>

The most important single aspect of Sharia law is the declaration that husbands are the guardians of the family and that wives have the obligation to obey their husbands in all things. This has been proven to be a very powerful factor, first in the interpretation of Muslim culture and then in the interpretation of Sharia law. One of the most frequent exceptions sought by Muslim governments under the U. N. Convention for the Elimination of All Forms of Discrimination Against Women (CEDAW), are those that relate to the stipulations for wifely obedience under Sharia law. Further, the husband's authority is so powerful that it has dominated the drafting of laws or regulations that might contradict it. In most court cases, judges seem to support this authority against almost everything else.

Muslim culture is very family oriented, and especially in more conservative rural areas, senior men and also older women become the enforcers of the husband's authority within the family. In a similar sense, the older cultural customs act to reduce women's capacity for self determination in such choices as when to marry and to whom, or women's right to participate in the distribution of family assets. Spousal abuse may well be regarded as righteous discipline. But there are countless reports of women who are accused of sexual promiscuity being killed by the family itself in supposed defense of "the family honor". Men may divorce their wives by simple declaration but a wife may obtain a divorce only through approval of some court, based on some substantial level of evidence, and in some countries, women have no basis for seeking divorce at all. In fact, women maintain that the Muslim courts are still relatively conservative in general and retain a bias in favor of men in almost any legal matter.

Sharia law itself dictates many inequalities. Almost universally, in matters of legal testimony, the testimony of a man is officially considered equal to the testimony of two women. Similarly, in matters of inheritance, male inheritors will receive twice the assets granted to females. Even where the national Constitution states that all citizens are equal under the law, there are countless Sharia based laws which simply violate that requirement and are written to deny female equality. In some places, women are not free to travel if they do not have the approval of their husbands. Women may not speak freely if they seem to speak out against their husbands or families or even the government. Governments and courts routinely dodge issues of spousal abuse or sexual harassment which is almost always declared to be a crime, but which is difficult to enforce, in part because the police are reluctant to investigate.

In many areas of the Muslim world, women now have the right to work at almost any job, and may now own assets, engage in businesses, enter into contracts, and engage in banking transactions. But here again, if a husband opposes any of these activities, the wife's legal position may be at serious risk. Women usually are legally entitled to equal pay for equal work, but employers and government regulators are notoriously willing to violate such laws.

A little recognized factor of these conflicts is that the death of many men in the region's endless conflicts often disrupts the application of Sharia family laws. When a husband is killed or abducted or simply disappears, the wife becomes the de facto head of the household, but still within the structure of the whole extended family. These women usually lack the capacity to earn a living, and the settlement of the disposition of family goods may take months or even years because of family squabbling or the slowness of an indifferent bureaucracy. Thus, the women may not have access to savings, title to property, or access to pension entitlements. Further, it appears to be tragically true that many hundreds of female survivors of abductions and rapes committed by armed groups are then rejected by their families and refused acceptance back into their homes, which may have been taken over by some male relative. A woman who has been assaulted sexually is somehow incredibly seen as having brought dishonor to the family. And many governments offer little or no assistance to these women because the whole situation is seen as a "family matter".

Women are now widely authorized in a legal sense to engage in politics, hold public office, and hold even senior positions in government. They are also usually given equal rights of entitlement for public benefits in such areas as education, public subsidies, social security, health care and pensions, but here again, the "husband" law, and the inertia of cultural change may deprive them of some of these valuables.

Social Services Conditions in Muslim Countries

In 2008 the United Nations Development Program published its Human Development Index which ranked 159 countries according to a system of key social indicators, computed in 2005, reflecting both social and economic development. With a top ranking of

1,000, Iceland led the rankings with a score of 968. For comparison, the United States scored 951, the United Kingdom scored 946, Germany scored 935, Poland scored 870, Mexico scored 829, Brazil scored 800, China scored 777, Bolivia scored 695 and India scored 619. In comparison, here are the scores of Muslim countries:

Kuwait: 891
Qatar: 875
U. A. R.: 868
Bahrain: 866
Libya: 818
Oman: 814
Saudi Arabia: 812
Turkey: 775
Jordan: 773
Lebanon: 772
Palestine: 771
Tunisia: 766
Iran: 759
Algeria: 733
Syria: 724
Egypt: 708
Tajikistan: 673
Morocco: 646
Pakistan: 551
Bangladesh: 547
Sudan: 526
Djibouti: 516
Yemen: 508
Nigeria: 470

The lowest score of 467 was "earned" by Tanzania. **(3)**

Life expectancy ranges from a low of 44 in Afghanistan to the mid sixties in Bangladesh, Iraq, Pakistan, Sudan and Yemen. But many other Muslim countries are closer to world averages of the low to mid 70s: Indonesia, Egypt, Iran, Libya, Morocco, Saudi Arabia, Syria, Tunisia and Turkey. In fact, a report issued by the

UNDP in 2010 was considerably more upbeat. It reported that "life expectancy in the Arab countries generally increased from 51 years in 1970 to almost 70 today, the greatest gain of any region in the world, while infant mortality rates plummeted from 98 deaths per 1,000 live births in 1970 to 38 in 2008, which is below the current world average of 44 per 1,000. School enrollment has nearly doubled over the last four decades, rising from 34% in 1970 to 64% today." It adds however that "<u>The Report's 40 year trend analysis reflects the adverse effects of military conflicts on human development; the Arab region has suffered almost three times as much as any other region in the world in terms of years of conflict from 1990 to 2008.</u> And what statistics seldom reveal is the sense that the whole region is being crippled by a lack of political freedom, of real justice, an excess of repression, especially of women, self isolation from the broad world of new ideas, new technologies and opportunities." **(4)**

Social Services in Afghanistan

An estimated 36 percent of the population lives in what is described officially as "abject poverty." Using UN standards, this means that they must attempt to live on the equivalent of less than $1.25 per day. But the UN has a second standard measure of "poverty", which means living on the equivalent of $2.00 of less, and using this standard, Afghanistan has almost 50 percent of its population living in poverty. Social realities are horrible. Wars have seriously destroyed public services. Despite a large public food security program run by the government, food is a major problem, and an estimated 54% of children are seriously malnourished—one of the highest levels anywhere in the world. Child mortality is very high, mothers lack pre and post natal medical care, education has been seriously disrupted, and on and on. And Afghanistan has now become the largest producer of opium in the world.

Social Services in Egypt

Rgypy id ranked in the Global Competitiveness Report (GCR) **(5)** at 81st, but youth unemployment is horrible, women's employment remains low, and the labor market is heavily burdened by bureaucratic overregulation. The government is a crushing bureaucracy, and workers lack modern technical skills. Inflation is high at 16.2 percent, which ranks at 135th. Poverty reflects the broader problems of lack of education and modern training, lack of opportunity, poor nutrition and health care, and heavy handed government inefficiency. These problems are clearly being addressed by the government, but the recent Arab Spring revolution has upset almost everything, and it is not yet clear how well the new government will address social problems. It is generally thought that their motivations are positive.

Social Services in Gaza and the West Bank

The economies of these areas are in deep crisis, made worse by the eternal conflicts with Israel. Official unemployment is above 30 percent, but much of the economic activity is in the low value informal economy. Large numbers of people are still heavily reliant on support from international organizations.

Social Services in Iran

The record of the Iranian government is surprisingly good in many ways. The country's health and education indicators are among the best in the region. Health outcomes have improved over the last 20 years and now generally exceed regional averages. The government's policy has been to give priority to primary health care and curative and preventative service rather than sophisticated, hospital based care. Government education reform efforts over 15 years have resulted in increased enrollment ratios, educational opportunities extended to women and into rural regions, and youth literacy rates increased from 86 to 94 percent. Health outcomes have improved greatly over the past 20 years, enabled by a strong commitment to basic health care, both preventative and curative. Social protection has been enhanced: 28 social insurance, social assistance and disaster relief programs benefiting large segments of the population. These include job search programs, health and unemployment insurance, disability, old age and survivorship pensions, and large subsidies for housing, food and energy. Employment has improved with a shift in policy encouraging the private sector, particularly in the non-oil and export sectors. Efforts are being made to make the education system more relevant to employer needs.

But the government still suffers from a whole series of problems. An overly generous and untargeted series of subsidies, especially in energy, is extremely expensive amounting to more than 10 percent of nationala Gross Domestic Product (GDP). Cities are slum ridden and poverty levels remain high. There are large disparities between the official class and the general population, especially in rural areas. It is almost as if the substantial middle class is slowly declining. Yet, much of the social service network lumbers along despite government preoccupation with political conflict. The civil service does its job while the politicians quarrel.

Inflation is high and rising; price subsidies and controls are inefficient and meddlesome. The real poor benefit from these subsidies (even for medicine and bread) far less than the better off people. And Iran has become one of the most corrupt governments in the Muslim world, and the corruption is heavily tied to associations run by the religious establishment, and enterprises controlled by the military Revolutionary Guard.

The country faces major environmental challenges, about which the government does little. Air pollution in Tehran and elsewhere is poisonous and creates many health problems. The Kyoto Treaty, which largely ignored developing countries, is seen as a toy of European politicians. **(6)**

Despite a heavy anti-drug campaign, Iran has become the principal transit country for drugs from Afghanistan, and in 2002, it accounted for one fourth of world opiate seizures. (7) Iran itself suffers from high levels of addiction, added crime, and high costs for treatment and prevention. Opium production was prohibited by law in 1955; now the government has to run an opium maintenance program. After the Revolution, drug controls on the growth of opium poppies became ineffectual, in part because the regime was fixated by worries about alcohol, which is prohibited in the Quran. After the Revolution, health services facilities were closed in favor of compulsory "rehabilitation" camps, and the main policy was one of severe punishments. During the 80's, courts sent thousands of people to these centers or to prisons—a total of 1.7 million. But in the last analysis, this heavy enforcement approach is considered a failure, and more and more, thinking has turned toward social rehabilitation and health prevention and treatment measures. Some of the outpatient clinics than had been closed down have been reopened, but not a lot of progress is evident. HID/AIDS treatment and prevention is still "a drop in the ocean".

But there seems to have been a fall in opium production in Iran itself, in favor of transshipping it from Afghanistan, which is now the largest producer of opium in the world. Iran serves markets in the Gulf, Russia, Turkey and Europe. Sixty-five percent of all drug seizures are in Asia, and 25 percent of the world total is in Iran. Ten percent of the population in large cities are said to be addicted, despite mandatory drug screening before marriage, on application for government jobs, and even when applying for driving licenses. Official figures list about 1.2 million addicts, but other sources say the number is closer to 3.3 million.

The justice system processed about 270,000 offenders in 2000, with 80,000 prisoners already in jail, and more than 140 officers and 900 offenders have been killed. 94 percent of offenders are men. Many young men who can't find work are still living with their families. There is a high rate of HIV/AIDS infection among injecting drug users, with widespread needle contamination.

In general, the United Nations Office of Drug Control reports that more than half of the world's opiate users are in Asia (7.8

million), primarily in countries surrounding Afghanistan and Myanmar, especially in Iran, Kyrgyzstan and Laos, with new worries about Iraq. Addiction is linked with economic decline, high unemployment, high medical and enforcement costs, and social dislocation. It appears that this problem has little or nothing to do with religion, and while Imams are not really part of the problem, they are also not part of the solution, preferring to rely on traditional theological opposition to alcohol carrying over into drugs.

Social Services in Jordan

Jordan has one of the best social services environments in the Middle East, and it tends to get better as the economy gets better. Per capita private consumption has grown to about 3.5 percent per year, and many of the poor have been part of this growth. If there is a most serious concern, it is whether successful anti-poverty measures can and will be sustained, and whether corrupt leakages from these programs can be controlled.

Social Services in Morocco

The success of the Islamist Justice and Development Party (PJD) in the elections of 2011 does not represent any real change in the Monarchy structure of the government and the status of what are called the "red lines" of Moroccan politics: the sanctity of Islam, the supremacy of the monarchy, and the claims for possession of the Western Sahara. (8) But Morocco was ranked 123rd in the UNDP Human Development Report (2006), showing that the relative wealth of the country had yet to produce adequate social services and citizen wellbeing.

The forces that brought the PJD to power want serious change: democratic practices, a stronger economy and more equitable economic opportunities, lower food prices, better public facilities, a freer media, and much more in the way of vital social services.

In addition, there is pressure for release of Islamist prisoners, and greater rights for Berber native populations. And there are other voices that do question the powers of the monarchy, the secretive royal court elite, the lack of an independent judiciary and the need for some greater degree of separation of powers. These views were vindicated on July 1, 2011, when these and other reform measures were incorporated in a new amended Constitution put to the vote. It passed overwhelmingly with and unbelievable 98.7 percent approval from a 72 percent voter turnout. But as ever, the real test has yet to come when implementation of the new Constitution must be undertaken.

Social Services in Pakistan

More than one-third of Pakistan's citizens or some 50 million people live in abject poverty, but this statistical number is not a true reflection of the almost desperate social conditions in the country. To begin with, this number deals only with "abject" poverty as defined by the UN. If the next level of officially defined poverty is included (living on less than $2.00 per day), this number reached more than 65 percent. It is more revealing to speak of the lack of vital safety nets for the poor, and their vulnerability to the great number of crises and risks that the country has experienced. According to a World Bank report on safety nets, "Managing Household Risks and Vulnerability", **(9)** nearly two thirds of all respondents suffered from one or more major shocks in three years before the survey. More than half of all shocks were caused by individual factors: health, sickness, disability. Other shocks were more systemic: unemployment, low wages, droughts, earthquakes or other natural disasters, local conflicts or economic shortcomings. These shocks have often imposed huge costs on people—often up to 50 percent or more of their annual consumption resources. It is true that the government has provided several safety net programs, but reality seems to be that such programs have very limited coverage, are fragmented and poorly targeted, very poorly administered, and gutted by government corruption. As a consequence, Pakistan ranks among the fifty worst off countries in the world.

What are the causes of this deplorable record? Perhaps the most important is the fact that the general population is growing very fast: one of the highest rates of growth in the world. The ability of the economy to grow is far too weak to absorb this growth and the increasing numbers of people trying to enter the workforce each year, and in fact, the national economy has been on a declining path for the last 20 years. This lack of adequate economic growth is a pattern common to the MENA region (and elsewhere); also a common pattern is successive governments which have been in the hands of a narrow elite who have maintained a consistent indifference to the needs of the broad public, and a marked unwillingness to finance adequate social services.

Pakistan's government finds itself in a fiscal trap. Too much of its scarce resources are tied up in servicing the huge public debt, and in financing the military establishment and this has almost permanently starved out funds for social programs. Expenditure on defense and interest payments accounted for more than 90 percent of total tax revenues. The economy remains too simple and obsolete, and the public sector, including most of the State Owned Enterprises (SOE), has not been competitive and has had to be heavily subsidized. Even where young people obtain a university degree, when they try to enter the workforce, they cannot find jobs that allow them to use their skills and knowledge. Pakistan is facing an increasing brain drain of doctors, nurses, engineers, teachers, and other educated people. Too many people can find work only in the huge informal economy, but there the wages are low, benefits nil, and there is constant hassling from the government bureaucracy.

But the education system produces far too few well educated people. Government run schools are of poor quality both in terms of classroom quality and in the lack of adequate physical facilities and student transport. While private sector education seems to be better, it is not designed for the poor and few families outside of the central elite can afford private education. Less than 47 percent of males and 34 percent of females complete primary education, and the illiteracy rate in the country is still over 56 percent. In a pattern common in MENA, much of the teaching content is out of date, obsolete, irrelevant, and simplistic, and fails to teach the skills really needed in a modern society.

Increasingly, it is feared that the deterioration of the uncontrolled political situation, and the inability of the government to solve any of its many conflicts, has led to a loss of control over national security. The military has constantly dominated the public debate by emphasizing doubtful military threats, and has succeeded in escalating defense expenditure at the expense of social service needs. But in the end, the country is now very insecure because of the uncontrolled emergence of terrorist and insurgent groups, many of which were earlier sponsored by the military establishment.

In addition to the heavy conflicts, both with India and with terrorist groups in the country, there seems to have been a deterioration of law and order as well. Terrorist attacks, suicide bombings, killings and kidnappings, robbery, extortion and other crimes have been on the increase, and the government seems less and less able to deal with these problems. These problems disrupt the delivery of social services and they discourage business activities and potential foreign investment in the country.

Corruption has become a major threat to Pakistani society, destroying confidence in all governments, driving off business ventures, draining off funds from badly needed social activities, and increasing the power of the worst elements in the country. What is corrupt? The UN reports lists the police, the whole power sector of the economy, land use and allocation, communications, local government, education, the health care system, the tax system, the customs service, and even the judicial system itself. What is not corrupt? Apparently nothing. In 1996, Amnesty International rated Pakistan as the second most corrupt country in the world, and most observers would argue that the situation is now far worse.

Social Services in Saudi Arabia

Health and education systems generally do not match the capabilities of other countries of similar incomes. Per the Global Competitiveness Report, health is ranked 74th, primary education is 74th; higher education and training is 51st.

Social Services in Tunisia

Two thirds of the population still lives in rural and village areas, characterized by conservative attitudes, government neglect, large families but few earners, and low formal education. Agricultural is marginal, suffering from small holdings, low production and productivity, and high costs for irrigation. Economies are weak and unproductive and even job holders earn little. Income distribution is very bad, creating stubborn pockets of urban poverty. Half of the children drop out of school after the fifth grade, especially girls. The government is really trying, with programs of food subsidy, direct cash payments, public works for poverty areas, temporary job programs, and development of more electricity and water facilities for urban slums, and even during crises, the government has managed to maintain the funds committed to social services, and especially aid for the poor. Access to health care is available to most of the population, but actual care seems lower in rural areas, and social indicators there are not up to urban levels.

Social Services in Turkey

In 2008 the United Nations Development Program published its Human Development Index which ranked 159 countries according to a system of key social indicators, computed in 2005, reflecting both social and economic development. Turkey scored a 775, which is about the middle of the pack, and fairly close to European standards. But the education system is weak, suffering from all of the usual main problems of education in developing countries. Elementary education is free, but in fact is largely financed by heavy fees paid by parents. Turkey is trying—to teach girls, to teach more relevant subject matter, and to teach students to think. Health service has gradually improved but is still less than good, although 80 to 90 percent of the population is covered. The problem is outside of cities because less than 1 percent of agricultural workers are covered. Private providers are advancing quality of service better than public providers. Facilities and staff tend to be more and better in cities than elsewhere.

Social Services in Yemen

42 percent of the population lives in serious poverty—one of the worst records in the world. Even when social indicators improve, there does not seem to be any impact on the nature of the poverty in the country. Rural areas are medieval; cities are slums. The social safety net is weak or nonexistent and somehow does not seem to reach the truly needy. Education for a large youth population is failing to keep up with population growth and the technical demands of a more complex world. The government seems to be adrift. And now, extremists have created debilitating conflicts throughout the country, threatening much that has been accomplished.

TIDES RUNNING
IN THE MUSLIM WORLD

Six Great Needs That Muslim Governments Must Meet

The world is learning that Islam is a growing force, but that it is endlessly varied and complex. Almost everywhere, the Islamic religion is of vital importance, reaching into every facet of Muslim culture, politics, national economies, and the relationships of Muslim countries with the rest of the world. While religion constitutes a strong common bond for Muslims around the world, it is, tragically, also a major contributor to endless violent clashes between Muslims themselves and with others in more than thirty-five countries involving hundreds of millions of victims. These countries include such shattering conflicts as those in Iraq, Afghanistan, Sudan and Somalia, along with wars, revolutions, insurgencies, terrorist attacks and armed conflicts in countries around the globe. The destruction caused by these conflicts kills the innocent, destroys personal and public assets, creates massive numbers of refugees forced to flee their homes, and seriously disrupts the provision of vital social services. Muslim governments are failures; they will continue to be failures until these horrible conflicts can somehow be mitigated, and five other extremely important areas of neglect and failure can be corrected. These areas are:

1. The need to expand and revitalize weak and obsolete economies throughout the Muslim world.
2. The need for a breakthrough in the role of women in all facets of Muslim society.
3. The need to upgrade education of all kinds from elementary/secondary programs to university education

and for a far broader range of professional, technical and managerial training.

4. Somehow, to find ways to extend the seriously inadequate health care service for upwards of 800 million people.

5. Dealing with growing problems of worsening environmental and water management neglect.

The future of the Muslim world does not lie with the West; it lies almost entirely within the Muslim world itself. Initially, one can expect to see a broader range of interests and organizations pushing their way into the elitist power base, usually over the resistance of the old establishment. Even in "Muslim countries" not all citizens are Muslim, nor are all Muslims the same. How can a Muslim citizen and family lead a devout Muslim life while still getting all of the advantages of a modern society and economy? State Socialism failed this test; most current dictatorships are failing this test; fundamentalist Islam is more of a threat than an opportunity.

Increasingly there is the growing desire by the majority of Muslims for major change for the better. Hopefully, there will be a gradual emergence of a more people oriented agenda—better elementary and secondary education, real health care widely available and affordable, rational measures to expand and enrich the economy in each country while avoiding the old patterns of the thieving rich keeping the rest of the population in poverty. Bottom up facilities such as food distribution centers, "store front" health clinics, vocational training centers, better sanitation, youth programs, and genuine anti-corruption attacks are relatively cheap and can be developed rapidly. There is a lot of potential help from the international community through government assistance, non-government organizations, and private sector investment. In fact, the U. S. and European nations could start up a new idea: a "war on social neglect" the equal of the current "war on terror."

The greatest need for governments in the Muslim world is to find ways to resist the grip of centrist power elites and to broaden the base of power sharing. This diffusion of power involves the structure of governments: the role of the chief executive, the legislative bodies, the courts, and the military, and the powers of government agencies. Yet most Muslim governments have a full array of such apparatus, ostensibly designed to balance power and restrain excess, but it is obvious that the mere existence of this apparatus is not enough, nor is the rule of law really alive and well. All too often centrist power simply overwhelms everything and everybody else. A new philosophy of government must be designed, adopted and implemented. It must emerge from and be largely defined by Islam's holy documents: the Quran, Sunnah and Hadith. This new philosophy cannot be provided either by centrist power holders or by narrow religious interpretation. It cannot be a mere imitation of the political philosophies of the West, nor can Western influences insist on any preferred pattern. The new philosophy must arise from within the Muslim community—and in fact, from many Muslim communities. The idea of a single political philosophy for all Muslims around the world is unreal and would be dysfunctional.

A serious failure stems from leadership policies that deliberately stir up and exacerbate any disparities between segments of the population, whether it is ethnic or religious or clan, or geography: plus rich vs. poor, young vs. old, urban vs. rural, or native vs. foreign. The one conflict that is peculiar to the Muslim world is "SUNNI VS. SHIA". There is an unwillingness to speak frankly about this most serious schism in the Muslim world. There are few admissions about its corrosive consequences, and certainly no admissions about the fact that nobody has any idea of what to do about it—or even whether to try.

Huge energy and vigor seems to be eagerly invested in the pursuit of Sunni/Shia conflict. Nearly all Arab leaders express a sense of unity with other Arabs, and yet historically Arabs have been among the most persistent antagonists among themselves of any segment of humanity in the world. The Arab world is broken up into hundreds of quarrelling sects and schisms, based on religion, religious aberrations, geography, history, culture and the competition for political power. The idea of a broader Pan-Arabism has been around for a long time, but has never really taken hold, in no small part because Arab nations have so often been ruled by egotistical tyrants. Note that this Arab agony seldom reaches Muslims in the Far East: Indonesia (230 million), Pakistan (162 million), India (134 million), Bangladesh (130 million) and China (20 million) in total have just about half of the Muslims in the world.

It is difficult to overstate how serious this conflict remains. It is greatly inhibiting progress in the Middle East and North Africa (MENA) and the rest of Africa. Yet nobody seems to know what to do about it. Nobody. There seems to be increasing public rejection or questioning of the false justifications offered by terrorist organizations, and the recognition that they stand for nothing positive and deliver nothing but pain. It must be recognized that most Muslim countries have suffered from severe and protracted conflict, from terrorist attacks, and they have been forced to suppress them—often harshly. But this is an endless loser cycle: government oppression breeds or justifies these attacks; the attacks are so vicious and menacing that the government must respond; the response is so harsh that it breeds further attacks.

Perceptions about the Arab world are increasingly grim. The Middle East is largely an Arab world and it is seen as stagnant and obsolete politically, and has failed with respect to the needs of youth or for general social welfare. Arrogant Arab aggression is now seen increasingly as obsolete, along with restrictive religious practices. Arabism has strong elements of longing for lost glory, the urge for new glory, a sense of oppression and fatalism, and a lot of guilt about "failure". But there is increasing disenchantment by other countries in dealing with governments that are so bad and discredited, and many of these foreign governments have jumped to support the Arab Spring. So now what?

Governments have seriously mishandled economic development. Foreign direct investment (FDI) is limited because investors do not trust the political leadership, or the environment for business. They see too much corruption, and too many bad laws. Muslim economies are seen as "old fashioned"—not bad, but not keeping pace with the modern world. There continues to be heavy government ownership of economic elements but far too many of the State Owned Enterprises (SOE) proved inefficient and ended up operating at a deficit. The governments tend to extract too much money out of the economy, and too much of it is wasted. Many countries continued to pursue import substitution policies long after it became clear that, beyond a certain point, they did not work. Banking systems tend to be state dominated and are forced into perverse lending policies. Private enterprise is heavily taxed and regulated and is secondary to state enterprises which are heavily subsidized.

There is a growing trend in which the public is rejecting religious, or religiously justified extremism. This is not just a rejection of Islamism as a justification for terrorism. It is also a rejection of the idea of theocratic governance a la Iran. But the most urgent concern about the economy is contained in the study by the World Bank of the economies of the Middle East and North Africa (MENA); the region needs to create <u>fifty million new jobs by 2020 to absorb its young graduates.</u> Right now, 30 percent of MENA citizens are between the ages of fifteen and twenty-nine, and 25 percent of them are unemployed.

In a sense then, economic development in the Muslim world faces such great and intractable impediments that rapid and sustained economic development often seems like mission impossible. Muslim economies, for economic, social, and religious reasons, are obsolete and mired in the past. Even bright, sensible efforts at development are really seen as puny compared to the magnitude of the problems. Fifty million new jobs? Not very likely unless, somehow, the leadership is radically changed, away from the tyrants and the war makers and thugs and the thieves, toward new leadership that really wants to practice cooperation, manage the country and put the efforts and funds of the government to work "bottom up" on the real life needs of their countries. But it simply boggles the mind to think about the enormous changes that would be required to result in the creation of fifty million new jobs. Does anybody really think that the narrow and corrupt elites that now rule are capable of such enormous and sophisticated efforts?

These conflicts have caused serious disruptions of social services and destruction of assets including medical facilities, schools, public offices and public infrastructure. Many educated professionals who have movable skills have been driven away. On the other side, few Muslim governments are entitled to claim that they have met even the basic social services needs of their citizens. While civil servants continue to try to teach school or run hospitals or put out fires, the political leaders seem far too preoccupied with fighting each other, and nobody really runs many of these countries. These policy and management failures also lead to huge misallocations of funds; mainly the fact that too much money is spent for war and too little for social services.

In most of the Muslim world, the physical environment is very fragile, with large areas of desert, semi-desert experiencing high temperatures, low levels of rainfall and ominously lowering levels of surface and underground water sources. And yet, almost all of the Muslim countries of the Middle East and the south coast of the Mediterranean Sea suffer from remarkably incompetent environmental and water management. Most Muslim countries have historically been heavily rural, although they are almost all now moving rapidly toward overwhelming urbanization. However, they cannot abandon the ancient agricultural sector of their economies, and most are attempting various ways to enhance agricultural production. But expansion of land under cultivation or efforts to intensify agricultural productivity inevitably create further environmental threats. Most Muslim countries have an economic development programs that include the agricultural sector, but in truth, the real hope is that the industrial, commercial, and government/military sectors will develop sufficiently to absorb the flow of people into cities throughout the Muslim world, so that, in the long run, the agricultural sector could contract rather than expand. Then the average income of individuals would increase, and the many threats posed to the environment would in part be mitigated.

Almost none of the elements of these developing economies have ever been seriously forced to operate in an environmentally safe manner. There is unchecked industrial pollution, and deep suspicion that corruption lets private companies and state owned enterprises buy their way out of the need for regulatory compliance. Almost no city seems ready to deal with the increasing crises of air pollution, water pollution, lack of water availability, or the provision of safe sewage treatment or adequate trash removal. Most cities are now clogged with auto traffic and remarkably, most cars run on leaded gasoline, dumping lead into the air. Really, almost nobody seems to understand the concept of clean sustainable development.

The other great schism in the Muslim world is that involving the role of women, where official positions are blatantly different from reality. In order to understand what women in the Muslim world really experience, it is necessary to consider the broader world in which all Muslims, both women and men, are living. If women are oppressed, they live under repressive regimes. If women lack representation, most regimes refuse to permit it for anybody. If women can't find jobs, economies are weak and inadequate. If women lack education or health care, these services are notoriously inadequate almost everywhere. Bad politics and rejection of the rule of law harm everybody. Then, on top of this, women are the victims of further prejudice and neglect in addition to the broad failures of government and society in which Muslims are required to live.

Most government attitudes are hopelessly hypocritical. With perhaps two exceptions, all Muslim governments function under Constitutions which clearly state that all citizens are equal and they may not be discriminated against for any reason. Then, in case after case, specific laws in almost every Muslim country authorize unequal treatment of women and legalize dozens of forms of discrimination against them that further inhibit the ability of women to improve their own situation. There are significant conflicts centering about religion, geography, clan and tribal conflicts, rural vs. urban attitudes, older and more conservative customs vs. new conceptions. And everywhere the people suffer from the culture of official corruption, criminal organizations, terrorist groups, threats and intimidation by thugs, and widespread armed insurrection. It is very difficult to find a government that is capable of pursuing women's reform agendas in the face of these major instabilities, even when they try to do so.

Even without the consequences of these convulsions, the ability or willingness of courts and government officials to address the need for the reforms sought by women is weak and reluctant. It is a universal common characteristic across the whole Muslim world that a regime's ability to enforce its own laws and regulations ranges from bad to nonexistent. Even if women succeed in securing the desirable reform of some law, regulation or administrative practice, there is no guarantee that the change will be implemented. Mostly, the courts are weak and they are subject to the standard authority from the top, and usually are not authorized to hear complaints against the government, or to resist political pressure.

At the next level of the structure of Muslim governments is the universal existence of some version of a Personal Status Law or Family Law or Civil Code which largely dictates the rights and status of women in a whole array of critical areas. These laws deal with marriage, divorce, family relationships, inheritance, rights to work, rights to travel, dress codes, standards for personal conduct, access to health care and education, and eligibility for a whole range of legal and public entitlements. There are separate laws dealing further with many of these personal status issues, but the key point to recognize is that the fundamental legal basis for these laws is some form of Muslim Sharia law. In other words, Sharia law dominates most of the issues affecting women as persons, and thus most of the issues that women seek to reform. But Sharia law itself enshrines many provisions that limit and restrain the rights and the treatment of women. In short, Islam has failed the crucial human test of bringing women forward to a higher and more modern level of freedom and accomplishment. It is important to note that most women's movements are <u>Muslim</u>, even when aided or assisted by external forces. But it seems to be the case that reform is weak and slow and only achieved with great difficulty.

Another telling failure of leadership in Muslim countries has been the lack of adequate social services—in primary and higher education, health care and health insurance, old age and retirement protection, assistance for the poor, and an overwhelming neglect of the region's fragile environments. Often, public infrastructure, especially in cities overwhelmed by skyrocketing populations is pitifully inadequate. These conditions make it very hard to attract foreign investors or really talented people, and it has produced a badly divided social structure of a small, powerful and wealthy elite, lording it over the general population that is poor, undereducated, with little future and little hope.

Governments need to recognize that corruption is far more than the old fashioned sins of bribery and theft. It has become far more sophisticated, attacking the workings of government in much more sophisticated ways, and it is practiced not only by thugs and crooks, but by very bright and able people who are clever, organized and innovative. It is tragic indeed that the greatest of skills in the region are the skills of the corrupt. No nation escapes this curse. <u>Corruption is not a characteristic of the political/economic system—**it is the system.**</u> Even where governments try to provide social services or build public works or let valuable contracts, or stimulate elements of their economies, these efforts are all too often beggared and crippled by thieves and crooks and cheats who divert scarce money and make it disappear.

And the legal systems of all Muslim countries are in constant flux. Court systems may be unitary or there may be two parallel and identifiable court structures for secular and religiously based Sharia law. There is a widespread pattern of conflict between these two legal frameworks, as well as a mutual overlapping third range of older traditional and local common laws and customs. But it has also been shown in many countries and in many ways that the purposes and intentions of these three legal frameworks prove to have much in common, and can be made to coexist, and in fact, be reinforcing. In fact, it is usually not the role or the meaning of Islam as a religion that is debated, but rather how it is interpreted and by whom. Islamic clerics cling to a tradition of legal interpretation going back centuries but they are being replaced by the political leadership of each country.

Ultimately, it would seem that there is nothing in Sharia law that fatally impedes reconciliation with the kinds of secular laws that many Muslim countries have absorbed, mostly from European sources. Recent trends have been for increasingly powerful elites to lock in ultimate authority over the courts and the laws, despite the powerful resistance of the slowly retreating religious fraternity and network. In fact, it appears that even relatively conservative Muslim scholars believe that most Western laws are, or can be made consistent with the broad principles of the Sharia. Put another way, where Sharia laws are mandated, they can easily accommodate a wide range of laws dealing with more secular dimensions of governance with little or no moral or ethical conflict as long as they are judged to be "consistent with" the Sharia. Mutually held concepts include the idea of government accountability; the responsibility of the State to help the needy; some form of the concept of checks and balances; the desirability of an independent judiciary; the concept of equal justice before the law.

These six huge gaps in Muslim society are like six huge mountains to climb, and it appears that few people anywhere have any confidence that the current leadership in Muslim countries have either the will or the skill to solve any of them. A new hope may be growing from the events of the Arab Spring, which is the most hopeful and significant factor in modern Islamic history. Perhaps the surge of Islam from the bottom up will galvanize hundreds of millions of Muslims who want both a devout life, and one of peace and prosperity.

SOURCES

The World Bank, "Morocco Fights Poverty Through 'Human Development' Approach", August, 2010.

The World Bank, "Development Program Touches the Lives of Morocco's Poorest Millions", November, 2010.

Ayboga, Ercan, 'Turkey's GAP and its Impact in the Region", Kurdish Herald, September, 2009.

Entelis, John P., "Morocco's 'New' Political Face: Plus ca change, plus c'est la meme chose", POMED Policy Brief, December, 2011.

The World Bank, citing the Kingdom of Morocco Poverty Report: Strengthening Policy by Indentifying the Geographic Dimension of Poverty", 2009.

Nissaramanesh, Bijan, Trace, Mike, and Roberts, Marcus, "The Rise of Harm Reduction in the Islamic Republic of Iran", The Beckley Foundation Drug Policy Programme, July, 2005.

The Human Development Report, 2010, "Inequality-adjusted Human Development Index", 2010.

World Economic Forum, The Global Competitiveness Report, 2010-2011, Middle East and North Africa, 2011.

The World Factbook, "HDI—Human Development Index, Country Rankings, 1975-2005, updated October, 2008.

Islamic Republic of Afghanistan, Ministry of Economy, "Poverty Status in Afghanistan, A Profile Based on National Risk and Vulnerability Assessment, 2007/2008.

The World Bank, "Sustaining Gains in Poverty Reduction and Human Development in the Middle East and North Africa", 2012.

The World Bank, "Yemen: Poverty Update", 2011.

The World Bank, "West Bank and Gaza: Deep Palestinian Poverty in the Midst of Economic Crisis", 2012.

The World Bank, 'Tunisia: Poverty Alleviation: Preserving Progress While Preparing for the Future", 2011.

The World Bank: "Jordan: Poverty Assessment", 2012.

Frost, Martin, "Frosts Meditations: The Strategies Behind the Poverty Reduction in Iran and the Middle East", October, 2007.

Lynch, Marc, "The 2009 Arab Human Development Report", July, 2009.

WFAFI 2005, "Official Laws Against Women in Iran", 2005.

The World Bank Group, "Middle East and North Africa (MENA)—Iran, September, 2006.

Williams, Ian, "Arab Human Development Report Takes an Honest Look at Region", Washington Report on Middle East Affairs, October, 2002.

The New York Times, "Study Warns of Stagnation in Arab Societies", July, 2002.

World Development Indicators, "Poverty, 2004.

Rihani, Samir, Dr., "Arab Human Development Reports: Part of a Bigger Jigsaw", 2005.

United Nations Development Programme (UNDP), "2010 UNDP Report Shows 40 Year Progress Driven by Dramatic Increase in Life Expectancy and the Reduction in Child Deaths", 2010.

Islamic Republic of Afghanistan, Ministry of Economy, "Working for a World Free of Poverty", March 2012.

Asian Development Bank, "Governance: Sound Development Management Policy: III—Causes of Poverty", 1995.

Sleek Articles, "Poverty in Pakistan", 2012.

The World Bank, "Social Protection in Pakistan: Overview", 2012.

Attachment A

Countries with more than 50% Muslim Population

**(Muslim Educational Trust;
UNDP Human Development Report, 2002)**

AFRICA
1. Algeria
2. Egypt 2.
3. Libya
4. Morocco
5. Sudan
6. Tunisia
7. W. Sahara
8. Ivory Coast
9. Gambia
10. Guinea
11. Mali
12. Mauritania
13. Niger
14. Senegal
15. Sierra Leone
16. Comoros
17. Dijbouti
18. Ethiopia
19. Eritria

EUROPE
1. Albania
Bosnia Herzegovina
3. Turkey

ASIA

1. Azerbaijan
2. Bahrain
3. Iraq
4. Jordan
5. Kuwait
6. Lebanon
7. Oman
8. Palestinian Authority
9. Qatar
10. Saudi Arabia
11. Syria
12. United Arab Emirates
13. North Yemen

307

20. Mayotti
21. Somalia
22. Tanzania
23. Chad
24. Camaroon
24. Central African Republic
25. Dohomey
26 Guinea-Bissau
27. Togo
28. Nigeria
29. Burkina Faso
24. Malaysia
25. South Yemen

ASIA
1. Azerbaijan
2. Bahrain
3. Iraq
4. Jordan
5. Kuwait
6. Lebanon
7. Oman
8. Palestinian Authority
9. Qatar
10. Saudi Arabia
11. Syria
12. United Arab Emirates
13. N. Yemen
14. Afghanistan
15. Bangladesh
16. Iran
17. Kyrgyzstan
18. Maldives
19. Pakistan
20. Tajikistan

14. Afghanistan
15. Bangladesh
16. Iran
17. Kyrgyzstan
18. Maldives
19. Pakistan
20. Tajikisan
21. Turkmenistan
22. Uzbekistan
23. Brunei
24. Indonesia

21. Turkmenistan
22. Uzbekistan
23. Brunei
24. Indonesia
25. Malaysia
26. S. Yemen

(58)

ATTACHMENT B

GLOSSARY

Al-Arabia: An Arab media service; seen as the voice of Saudi Arabia and the Gulf Cooperation Council.

Al-Aram: A major Middle East newspaper.

Alawite: A form of Shia Islam: the rulers of Syria are almost entirely of the Alawite sect.

Alevi: A moderate form of Islam.

Arab League: Officially the League of Arab States, it is a voluntary association of Arab speaking countries which seeks to advance Arab interests. Its members are Algeria, Bahrain, Comoros, Djibouti, Egypt, Iraq, Jordan, Kuwait, Lebanon, Libya, Mauritania, Morocco, Oman, Palestine, Qatar, Saudi Arabia, Somalia, Sudan, Syria, Tunisia, United Arab Emirates and Yemen.

Da'wa: A call to Islam. It is a classic approach for rallying the population behind some cause. Da'wa is seen as the personal responsibility of Muslims.

Death of Muhammad: 632

Egypt: recent presidents: Gamel Abdul Nasser, 1956-1970; Anwar Sadat, 1970-1981; Hosni Mubarak, 1981-2011; Muhammad Morsi, 2011—.

Fatwas: Legalistic statements issued by governments or by religious scholars and Imams. They may be issued as opinions relating to actual legal cases, or they may be general statements purporting to define Sharia law on some subject. Thousands of Imams feel entitled to issue fatwas, and other Imams issue fatwas on behalf of the government.

Gulf Cooperation Council (GCC): A group consisting of Saudi Arabia, the United Arab Emirates, Qatar, Bahrain, Kuwait and Oman.

Hadd crimes: Crimes specifically defined in the Quran: unlawful sexual intercourse outside of marriage and including homosexuality; false accusations of unlawful sexual intercourse; banditry; theft; apostasy.

Hadith: Compilations of the reported views and sayings of the Prophet.

Hajj: A pilgrimage by Muslims to Mecca once in their lifetime, mandated by the Quran.

Haqqani: A school or seminary for ultra conservative religionists.

Haram: Forbidden

Al Hijrah: The migration of the Prophet from Mecca to Hathreb (later Medina), in 622.

Hojjatieh: A secretive, ultra conservative group in Iran who believe in the return of the Twelfth Imam, accompanied by a form of Armageddon.

Ijtihad: The process of developing laws.

Islam: Surrender to the will of God.

Al-Jazeera: (The peninsula) The Middle East's most popular independent media organization and satellite network.

Jihad; its several meanings: The struggle to lead a good and devout life; efforts to defend/protect the Muslim community; efforts to actively promote the Faith; positive efforts to expand the Muslim community and its influence, often by aggressive and authoritarian means; efforts to force Islam on others; Holy War.

Kifaya: Meaning "enough" as a movement protest against intolerable conditions, and tyrannical regimes.

Mahram: Male guardian or sponsor

Muhammad Ali: The founder of an Egyptian dynasty which was founded in 1801 and lasted until 1956 when King Farouk was forced from office.

MENA: The Middle East and North Africa. MENA region includes Algeria, Bahrain, Djibouti, Egypt, Iran, Iraq, Jordan, Kuwait, Lebanon, Libya, Malta, Morocco, Oman, Qatar, Saudi Arabia, Syria, Tunisia, United Arab Emirates, the West Bank and Gaza, and Yemen.

Mukhabarat: The State Security Police in Jordan.

Mulahid: A Muslim holy warrior.

Muslim: One who has surrendered to the will of God.

Muslim Brotherhood: A political and civic organization founded in Egypt in 1928 by Hassan al Banna.

Nahda: An Islamic political party inTunesia

Omayyad: A Sunni ruling dynasty extending from 661 to 750.

Salafyah: A form of Islamic renewal based on a return to Muslim "roots" and their presumed "purity".

Six Day War: A war fought between Israel and several Muslim nations in 1967.

Sunnah: The Path as defined by the words and acts of the Prophet.

Sunni Schools of legal thought: There are four distinct schools of interpretation of the Sharia law: the Hanifi, the Hanbali, the Maliki and the Shafi. In addition, there are Shia schools as well: Zaydis, Ismaili, Ithna and Ashari.

Takfir: The accusation of apostasy.

Ulama: Religious scholars and teachers

Waqf: Private trusts, usually associated with Muslim religious organizations, and usually devoted to the provision of social service.

Wahhabis: A very conservative form of Islamic religious observance. The movement was founded by Muhammad ibn Abd al-Wahhab in the 18th century.

END NOTES

Chapter I: Background And Demographics

1. Kennedy, Hugh, "The Great Arab Conquests", De Capo Press, 2007.
2. Esposito, John L., and Mogahad, Dalia, "Who Speaks for Islam", New York, Gallop Press, 2007.
3. World Development Indicators, Washington, D. C., World Bank 2012.
4. Kepel, Gilles, "Jihad: The Trial of Political Islam", Cambridge, Mass., The Belnap Press, 2002.
5. The Economist, July 25, 2009
6. The Arab Human Development Report, "Job Creation in Arab Economies: Navigating Through Difficult Waters, UNP, 2010. Also, see UN Population Development, "Youth Population and Employment in the Middle East and North Africa: Opportunity or Challenge?". Also, World Bank, "Middle East and North Africa Region Economic Developments and Prospects", 2011. Also, IMF Group of Eight, "Economic Transformation in MENA: Delivering on the Promise of Shared Prosperity", 2011
7. Global Integrity Report, 2008.
8. Feldman, Noah, "The Fall and Rise of the Islamic State", Princeton U. Press, 2008.
9. Fuller, Graham E., "The Future of Political Islam", New York, Palgrave Macmillan, 2003.
10. Smith, Lee, "The Strong Horse", New York, Anchor Books, 2010.
11. Wright, Robin, "Rock the Casbah", New York, Simon and Schuster, 2011.

Chapter II : Economic Development

1. Economic chart: "World Development Indicators Issue Paper #3", Washington, D. C., World Bank, 2001.
2. Kuran, Timur, "The Long Convergence", Princeton U. Press, 2011.
3. See World Economic Forum, "Global Competitiveness Report, 2010-2011", World Bank Development Indicators, 2010; IMF Economic Outlook: "Recovery, Risk and Rebalancing", IMF World Economic and Financial Surveys, "Regional Outlook: Middle East and Central Asia, 2010.
4. Bingman, Charles F., "Why Governments Go Wrong", p. 197-206 New York, iUniverse Press, 2006.
5. Waterbury, John, "Exposed to Innumerable Delusions: Public Enterprise and State Power", Cambridge U. Press, 1995.
6. Sumvasan, Thisumalai G., "Afghanistan Economic Update", World Bank, Human Development Group, Middle East and North Africa, 2010.
7. Salchi-Isfahani, Dhavad, "Revolution and Redistribition in Iran: Poverty and Inequality", Virginia Tech U., 2006.
8. Nihou, Semira N., "Iran: The Subsidies Conundrum", United States Institute of Peace, 2010.
9. Javedanfar, Meir, "The Worsening Housing Crisis in Iran", The Center for Iranians Studies, January, 2007.
10. Numbeo Quality of Life Index, 2012.
11. Global Integrity Report, 2011.
12. Middle East Quarterly, "The Collapsing Syrian Economy", September, 1999.
13. Schlefir, Yigal, "Turkey Revives Stalled $32 billion GAP Dam and Irrigation Project", Christian Science Monitor, May 28, 2008.

Chapter III: Sharia Law

1. These countries, ranked by population, are: Indonesia (213 million); Pakistan (162 million); Bangladesh (130 million);

Egypt (71 million); Iran (67 million); Morocco (52 million); Afghanistan (30 million); Saudi Arabia (26 million); Sudan (26 million); Iraq (25 million); Yemen (21 million); Syria (16 million); Tunisia (10 million); Tunisia (10 million); Libya (6 million); Jordan (5 million). In addition, there are countries with less than 5 million population, including Bahrain, Brunai, Djibouti, Kuwait, Oman, Qutar, and the United Arab Republics.

2. These countries are India (134 million); Nigeria (55 million); Algeria (32 million); Russia (21 million); and China (20 million).

3. Beltrametti, Sihua, "The Legality of Intellectual Property Rights Under Islamic Law", DigitalIslam, February, 2012.

4. Pakistan Penal Code/Act XLV of 1860. See Siasat.pk, January 12, 2011. See also Dawn.com "Blasphemy Law, August 23, 2012; Human Rights Watch Weekly, "Pakistan Repeal of Blasphemy Law", November 23, 2010.

5. European Court of Human Rights.

6. Zeldin, Wendy, "Criticism of Anti-terrorism Laws, Turkey", Library of Congress, November, 2012.

7. European Court of Human Rights: "Turkey is by far the worst violator of human rights among the 47 signatory states of the European Consortium on Human Rights", January 27, 2011.

Chapter IV: Education

1. The British Council, "Education in Iran: Overview", EFA 2000 Assessment: Country Reports, 2001.

2. Turkish Ministry of Education, "Basic Education in Turkey: Background Report", Ministry of Education, June, 2008.

3. StateUniversity.com, "Egypt—Educational System Overview", 2012.

4. Khalaj, Monavar, "Critics Give Iranian Education Low Marks", Financial Times, July 11, 2011.

5. The Guardian, "World Educational Rankings: Which Country Does Best at Reading, Maths, Science?", Datablog,

The Guardian, 2010. See also Wikipedia, "Programme for International Student Assessment", November, 2012.

6. New York Times, "Education in Morocco: An Analysis of Morocco Educational Sector", March, 2011.

7. Landzettel, Marianne, "Pakistan Faces Educational Emergency Says Government", BBC News, South Asia, March, 2011.

8. Bajoria, Jayshree, "Pakistan's Education System and Links to Extremism", Council on Foreign Relations, October, 2009.

9. Wikipedia, "Education in Pakistan", June, 2011.

10. Turkey: Ministry of Education, "Basic Education in Turkey: Background Report", June, 2008.

11. Vorkink, Andrew, "Education Reform in Turkey", Conference at Hacetkepe University, December 22, 2005.

Chapter V: Health Care

1. World Health Organization (WHO), "Health Performance Rank by Country", 2011.

2. Independent Lens, "Afghan Reproductive Health", 2011. Also, U. S. Library of Congress, "Afghan Health", 1997.

3. Marie Stopes Clinics, Bangladesh, 2012.

4. Arfaoui, Jamel, "Libyan Critics Dispute Health Care Quality Reports", Magharibia, April, 2010.

5. USAID, "Front Lines: First Agency Task Force Visits Libya as Sanctions Fall", May, 2004.

Chapter VI: The Environment

1. Rivlin, Paul "Arab Economies in the Twenty-First Century", Cambridge U. Press, 2009. Also, Noland, Marcus, and Pack, Howard, "Arab Economies at a Tipping Point", 2008.

2. Berman, Llan, and Wihbey, Paul Michael, "The New Water Politics in the Middle East", Institute for Strategic and Advanced Policy Studies, Tel Aviv and Washington, D. C., 1999.

3. National Geographic Magazine, "Bringing Water and Life to the Nuba Mountains of Sudan", July, 24, 2010.
4. Caritas Internatialis, "Climate Change in Algeria, July, 2011.
5. Sudan Tribune, "Jonglei Canal Project Needs to be Revisited, South Sudan Says", August 8, 2009.
6. Hadadin, Nidal A., and Tarawneh, Zeyad S., "Environmental Issues in Jordan, Solutions and Recommendations", American Journal of Environmental Sciences, 2007.
7. Weidnitzer, Eva, "Environmental Policy in Morocco: Institutional Problems and the Role of Non-Governmental Organizations", German Development Institute, Berlin, February, 2002.
8. Morocco Business News, "Pollution Threatens Casablanca", April, 2010.
9. Khan, Mohammad Hussain, "Dilapidated Irrigation Network In Sindh", Dawn.Com, May, 2012.
10. Pearce, Fred, "When the Rivers Run Dry", p. 61, Boston, Beacon Press, 2006
11. Dahlberg, Emelie, and Slunge, Daniel, "Sudan Environmental Policy Brief", Goteborg, Sweden, Goteborg University, December, 2007.
12. Pearce, Fred, "When the Rivers Run Dry", p. 253, Boston, Beacon Press, 2006.
13. Allan, Tony, "The Middle East Water Question: Hydroponics and the Global Economy", New York, St. Martins Press, 2001. Also, an interview with Dr. Allan at Kings College, London, "The tension between sustainability and intensification", May 23, 2011.

Chapter VII: Social Services

1. Arab Human Development Reports, UNDP, 2009.
2. World Bank definitions of "abject poverty" and "poverty".
3. UNDP report: Human Development Index, 2008.
4. UNDP report: Human Development Index, 2010.

5. World Economic Forum: The Global Competitiveness Report, Middle East and North Africa 2010-2011.
6. World Bank Country Report: Iran, 2007.
7. Nissaramanesh, Bijan, Trace, Mike, and Roberts, Marcus, "The Rise of Harm Reduction in the Islamic Republic of Iran", The Beckley Foundation, July, 2005.
8. Entelis, John P. "Morocco's 'New' Political Face", Project on Middle East Democracy, December, 2011.
9. World Bank Report: "Managing Household Risks and Vulnerability", Washington, D. C., 2011.

Publication Statement

Never in modern times has there been a greater need for understanding the Muslim world. Nothing in that world is more important than the relationship between Muslims and their faith, yet now that faith has become far more confusing and challenging. The emergence of religious fundamentalism, often linked to terrorism seems wholly inconsistent with the teaching of the Quran and the other holy documents of the faith, which is a religion of peace and forgiveness. Muslims everywhere have found themselves facing two dilemmas: first, a failure of the governments that demand to rule them; and then a major concern over what kind of Faith true Muslims should believe in. But while religion tends to control people's lives, it is not the primary source of conflict in the Muslim world. That source is the yearning for power which has produced an unwillingness of leadership to negotiate or compromise, along with the sins of personal greed and a culture of corruption.

What do most Muslims really want? To live in peace, to live a devout life, and to achieve a successful life for themselves and their children. "Governments in the Muslim World" describes in many ways how far they are from these desires.

ABOUT THE AUTHOR

Charles F. Bingman had a thirty-year career as a U. S. Federal government manager and executive with service in the Atomic Energy Commission, the National Aeronautics and Space Administration, the Department of Transportation, and the Office of Management and Budget in the Executive Office of the President.

After retirement, he began a second career of teaching and consulting. He taught public management at the George Washington University in Washington, D. C., and as a Fellow of the Center for the Study of American Government at the Johns Hopkins University Washington Center. He has published reports on the history of management responsibilities in the U. S. Office of Management and Budget, and written numerous articles in professional journals.

Bingman has done consulting assignments with various organizations in the Muslim countries of Saudi Arabia, Jordan, Egypt, and the Palestinian Authority in Gaza. He has also consulted in China, Japan, the Russian Federation, Kazakhstan, Romania, Estonia, Botswana, and other countries. He is the author of: "Japanese Government Leadership and Management"(1989); "Why Governments Go Wrong" (2006); "Reforming China's Government"(2010); and "Changing Governments in India and China"(2011). Bingman is an elected Fellow of the National Academy of Public Administration, and of the Cosmos Club in Washington D. C.

INDEX

Muslim Brotherhood, 7, 28, 49-51,
82, 99, 146
Muslim conflicts, 15-29, 162
Muslim economies, 60
Muslim future, 7, 8, 47-50
Muslim governments, 5, 7, 62,
92, 107
Muslim public opinion, 6, 48, 118,
263, 294
Muslim victimhood, 5, 6, 94

N

NAHDA, 51
Narcotics traffic, 77
Nasser, Abdel, 122, 198
Nat. Council of Religious
Scholars, 126
National Iranian Oil Co., 84
National Iranian Gas Co., 84
National Iranian Petrochemical
Co. 84
National Political Front, 51
Niger, 12
Nigeria, 11, 12, 15, 25
Nile River Basin, 241
Nubian Aquifer, 265
Numeiri, Gaafar, 145

O

OECD, 42
Oil production, 79,94
Ottoman Empire, 5, 113, 119,
149, 161
Oman, 11, 251

P

Pakistan, 11, 15, 25, 36, 89, 132,
175, 213, 253, 282, 288
Palestinian Authority, 25
Pearce, Fred, 265
Philippines, 26
PLO, 7, 25
Polygamy laws, 128, 132
Poverty, 60, 73, 81, 83, 89, 197,
271, 273
Public attitudes, 40, 48, 94, 294, 297
Public sanitation, 205, 208, 211,
217, 222

Q

Qaeda al, 32, 148
Qatar, 12, 13, 14
Quality of Life Index, 88
Quran, 48, 52, 54, 114, 115, 116,
120, 121, 126, 129, 140, 155,
157, 161

R

Radical Islam, 5, 40
Reform proposals, 46-48, 53, 186,
263, 293
Regulation, 58, 62
Russian Federation, 26

S

Sadat, Anwar, 122
Saudi Arabia, 10, 26, 63, 89, 178,
215, 254, 291
Secular law, 111, 115, 117, 149